CLASSROOM MANAGEMENT
and
EFFECTIVE STRATEGIES TO MOTIVATE STUDENTS

GLORIA KIRKLAND-HOLMES

Kendall Hunt
publishing company

Cover image © Shutterstock.com

Kendall Hunt
publishing company

www.kendallhunt.com
Send all inquiries to:
4050 Westmark Drive
Dubuque, IA 52004-1840

Copyright © 2017 by Kendall Hunt Publishing Company

ISBN: 978-1-5249-2405-8

All rights reserved. No part of this publication may be reproduced, stored in a retrieval system, or transmitted, in any form or by any means, electronic, mechanical, photocopying, recording, or otherwise, without the prior written permission of the copyright owner.

Published in the United States of America

Contents

Chapter 1	Racial Perceptions of Children in School Settings	1
Chapter 2	The Classroom Management Stories	7
Chapter 3	No One Ever Told Me Discipline Was Going to Be Like This	13
Chapter 4	It All Starts with Preschool!	21
Chapter 5	Are Preschools Fading Out or Are We the Faders? The Real Issues	25
Chapter 6	So What Has Happened to the Good Kindergarten Programs?	33
Chapter 7	Home Visits	39
Chapter 8	Parent Conferences, Outdated or Time for a Change?	49
Chapter 9	The Loosening of School Lunch Nutrition Standards: Helpful or Hindrance?	65
Chapter 10	So What Is Going on with Recess Time?	69
Chapter 11	Do School Uniforms Make a Difference?	73
Chapter 12	Achievement Gaps: What Role Does Absenteeism Play?	81
Chapter 13	Invented Spelling Can Improve Reading Skills	85
Chapter 14	The Effects of Low Teacher Expectations on Students of Color	91
Chapter 15	It's Not Just Preschool, But Are Black Children Being Dehumanized?	97
Chapter 16	Tantrums: Growth and Development for Young Children	103
Chapter 17	Black Lives Really Do Matter	111
Chapter 18	Placing Educational and Cultural Values on the Lives of Blacks, Latinos and All Children	115
Chapter 19	Placing Educational and Cultural Value on Latino and African-American Students Part 2	123
Chapter 20	The Legacy of My Own Second Language: Gullah	131
Chapter 21	The Realities about Unequal Education	137

Chapter 22	Real Teacher Shocking Experiences Part 1	143
Chapter 23	More Real Shocking Experiences Part 2	151
Chapter 24	More Real Shocking Experiences 3	157
Chapter 25	Hip Hop-Rap That Teaches	163
Appendix-A	Motivation to Share	187
Appendix-B	Anti-Discrimination Position Statement	243

Racial Perceptions of Children in School Settings

Teacher, Teacher, Why Are You So Brown?

Being a preschool-kindergarten teacher gives one many opportunities to experience firsthand children's perceptions on race. So a 4-year-old little girl kept coming up to me and appeared to be staring at me for long periods of time, until I began to wonder myself about what was on her mind. So I decided not to say anything but continue to observe why she kept coming up to me, looking at me in a very curious manner, but not saying a word. She went off to play for a few minutes, but came back again and looked in my face. But the fourth time, she came closer to me. This time she came up to me as I was sitting down and began touching my face. Again, she did not say a word, but kept touching my face. Then the magic thoughts came to words.

"Teacher, why is your face so brown?" Well I wasn't quite prepared for the question, so it took me a minute to think of the answer to this question. I said, 'this is the color of my skin—my skin is brown and when I was a baby my skin was brown. When I was a little girl, my skin was brown and now my skin is brown. My skin is brown like toast. My skin is brown like the color of chocolate milk. My skin is also brown like some animals. She looked at me and said, "your skin is brown just like Jared's" (Jared is a 4-year-old in our class). This was a wonderful observation as well as a thoughtful analysis by this 4-year-old.

Teacher, Teacher, Did Someone Bake You In the Oven?

I am so appreciative of the fact that throughout my teaching career, I was always open minded and understanding of the innocence and honest questions and responses that young children have about race. I was always happy to share with young children in their questions about race with them. I have to admit that when I started teaching, I realized that I was one of the few African American teachers in the entire school. So I quickly became Aware of the fact that they may have many questions and lots of stares. Not only would they notice race, but they would also notice ethnicity/culture because I wore braids that took a long time at the braiding salon.

So I was passing through the hallways and working diligently to set up some paint for the children before their arrival. When all of a sudden I heard a student say to me, Ms. K., "did someone bake you in the oven?" Interestingly that was the first time I had been asked that

1

question outright, but it certainly was not a surprise to me. The small percentage of Blacks in my new employment town would prepare one for the wonders of the majority of White children as well as students. I know that some of the parents were afraid of what their children might ask or say to me. I could read the nervousness on their faces as fear crossed many, hoping that their child would not say or ask me anything that might offend me. But more so, they were nervous about their child's comments being a possible reflection of what they heard at home or didn't hear at home. But trying to shhhhhhh the child is not the answer because then the child begins to wonder why they can't ask a curious racial question. So the answer to "did someone bake you in the oven?" can be answered very simply because sometimes the child still has another part to the question or comment. And sure enough this child did. The child proceeded to ask, "did they put you in the oven to bake like chocolate chip cookies?" Wow, another great analysis and expression of relationships between two things—chocolate chip cookies come out of the oven looking brown, pretty and yummy. The child's analysis of my shade of brown was also beautiful and beauty for the eyes to behold. My answer, "No, no one put me in the oven to brown. But I was born with brown skin. Let's see what skin you have and that you were born with? Let's look at Jamika's skin and see what color her skin is that she was born with? Each of us have a skin color that we have not because we were put in an oven. Thank you for asking a great question." This lets the child know that it is okay to be curious about race just like curiosity about other things in life and education.

I Don't Like Monika, She Is Too Tan/Black

It is amazing to hear young children determine who their friends are or not by the color of their skin. How is it a child so young begins to internalize or socialize in the context that certain shades of skin, certain races, and/or ethnicities exist? So how is it that a child so young is able to tell another child, "I don't want to play with you because I don't like you." The child who is hurt and suffering from the comments may wonder why. Then the child expresses further views by saying, "You're too Black or too tan." So what does this mean? What is the child implying? Does the child mean that certain people with certain skin colors should not be accepted or treated the same? We must be clear that children are not isolated from their environment, family, and friends and the world around them. The media certainly, over periods of time, have displayed some negative information about what appears to be certain groups of people. Why is it that the only stories shown of certain groups of people are often crimes or some negative activities? This is where little subtle forms of racism are introduced, often with no one pointing out anything in particular. Or there may be the exclusion of Blacks for example in books and magazines. Again efforts are being made to ask teachers to make sure they have multicultural resources everywhere in their classrooms so that children can become familiar with and used to.

Please Don't Make Me Play with That Ugly Doll

A story on the Internet went viral simply by a parent not knowing how to handle a situation when two White female sisters received a gift from their White mother. The gifts just so happened to be two Black dolls. So when the girls first took a look at the dolls, both of them started screaming, "get this ugly thing away from me." So by that time the second child exhibited the same behavior, saying to please take those ugly dolls away and that they didn't want them. So the mother took the dolls from the girls and said, "that's o.k. You don't have to play with them. I will get you another doll." Somehow, whether it was implied or stated, it meant White doll. So there are people who put the actions of the mother into several categories and what she could have done differently or what could have been considered to be more appropriate:

Group 1 The mother could have spent more time with the girls prior to presenting them with the gift of these cultural dolls.

Group 2 The mother should not have taken the dolls back or away, but instead read several books with the girls about how people are different and unique, including skin color.

Group 3 The mother should have spent time asking the girls what was it about the dolls that made them think that they were ugly or unattractive. The mother should listen for special clues to see if the girls mention race or other ethnically related descriptions. Thus this would let the mother know what the girls are thinking and perhaps what next steps should be.

4) The mother should begin helping the girls understand the concept of doll collections and begin sharing that the other dolls that they had were White and now that she was helping them expand their collection by adding the Black dolls this time. Then she could suggest the next culture or sex of the dolls or have them make their own suggestions.

5) Add some new Black dolls to the collection after introducing some other cultures so that they can also see that all Black, White, or other dolls, even though they may be of the same race, do not look the same.

Student Assignment: Add your own suggestions for how you think the mother could have handled this situation with her daughters rejecting the Black dolls given to them.

My Mama Says I Can't Play with You

These are the words that devastate a teacher and anyone who has to bear hearing this sad news when a child says this. As a teacher, I could remember the grief I felt when I first heard one of my young students say this. Somehow, I had a few sufferings when deciding how to deal with this. First of all, I was feeling so upbeat about all of the parents of the students in my class because they had been so respectful to me. They were all so supportive of our program and made every effort to make sure that their children were able to successfully participate in all of our planned activities

The teacher feels the hurt, pain, and suffrage deep down inside because of the fact that it appears that all was well with the parents and students as well. So it is a little surprising when the comment is revealed still that there are some parents who don't want their children playing with certain children. So as the teacher thinks about how best to deal with such a request effectively, some questions come forth when I realized that I did not know the answer. Not knowing the answer, I still had to think about how, when, and whether I should deal with the issue since the parent did not bring the matter to me. So in thinking about some ways to deal with the situation, I pondered:

1. Was the request based on race? Let's hope not?
2. Was the request based on a matter related to the child's alleged behaviors?
3. Was the request based on hearsay from the child or someone else?
4. Was the request based on some outside matter that I am not aware of?
5. Was the request based on speculative matters?

Regardless of the basis for the request, it was not brought to me but relayed by the child. As the teacher, even if I do not address this issue directly, I will certainly be very observant to make sure that this message is not carried out in my class with the intention of possibly tainting the peaceful environment. Also, it is not fair to the child who brings the request nor the child who is being requested ineligible to play with this child. In any case, I decided not to direct this matter with the parent, but instead attempt to deal with it as a whole class social-emotional issue.

So I found a couple of great books in the library about being left out, no one wanting to play with certain children and how that could make the child feel. I must admit it looked to me like they all became closer than ever before as good comrades/friends.

If You Don't Mind, I Don't Want My Daughter Playing with the Black Boys

What does the parent mean by saying, "If you don't mind?" Well I do mind, so why are you even asking me to do this? So this request is similar to the aforementioned one, except there were two differences.

1. The parent brought the matter directly to me in an informal manner early in the morning before classes started.
2. The parent mentioned race of these students directly. Although I only had four Black boys in my class, she did not single out any particular one; instead, she included all of them.

While I had this request directly from this particular parent, I just wondered what did she really think my answer would be? I wasn't sure what she thought my answer would be or how many other teachers or adults had she had similar conversations with on such a matter. Well none of those thoughts really mattered, because we had an issue right before us that had to be dealt with.

In my years of research, I had come across some information where Black boys as young as kindergartners were often feared by White female teachers. While some of the reasons may be difficult to understand, it often comes back to the concept of negative and biased perceptions of Black males. So as one thinks about the concept of being fearful of Black adult males, it does make it a little difficult to imagine that these same types of feelings exist among and add about the youngest Black male students. Wow, were there feelings that these students would hurt/harm the teacher or others in the school environment? Certainly, there are no data to support such actions. It has not been found that Black male students have gone into schools to harm certain teachers or students.

So I immediately began to think whether this parent was exhibiting signs of these same types of fears. Or was there something that she could find that would make the interactions of her child devastating or negative by playing with Black boys in the classroom in particular?

What I did do is not allow the parent to explain to me why she did not want her daughter to play with the Black boys in the class. The reason I made this decision is that typically these boys were not around her daughter at school anyhow because most of their interests were very different. Another reason that this decision was made was because if there truly was something that happened with Black boys outside of the classroom, it was not fair to generalize to all Black boys, including the ones in my classroom.

So I decided to make the response very easy and simple by saying, "I am so sorry that you don't want your daughter playing with the African American boys in my class, but as the teacher I can not support your request. I work so hard every day encouraging the students to share, work, play, and share together. So if I agree to your not allowing your daughter and any of the students to not play together, then I would be going against what I have tried to instill in the students.

Student Assignment: How do you think you would have dealt with this situation if you were the teacher?

So Why Did the Doctors Have to Be Two White Male Students?

Wow, there were about 150 first graders in the room and I was singing some chants, songs, and games with themes. So we all had partners and sang Miss Mary Mack, Mack, all dressed in Black, black, black, with silver buttons down her back, back, back. She jumped so high, high, high, she touched the sky, sky, sky and never came back, back, back, till the fourth of July, ly, ly, ly.

Then we did five little monkeys jumping on the bed, one fell off and bumped his head, mama called the doctor and the doctor said, "No more monkeys jumping on the bed."

Select from among the students, five little monkeys (pretending to be jumping on the bed). Choose a mama and a daddy, who will have a telephone and pretends to call the doctor. Choose two doctors to give more students a chance to participate.

Now making these assignments were the teachers of these 100+ students and it was just so obvious that each time, the choices were made for the different roles, the doctors just happened to always be White.

Student Assignment

Do you think that there was an unconscious effort on the part of these White female teachers to always choose Black students for the monkey roles and White boys for the doctor roles? Or do you think this is an example of a coincidence?

Chapter 2

The Classroom Management Stories

Talking with a childcare provider on some information regarding other sites and places for her childcare program captured my attention right away. Unfortunately, the information that she decided to share with me was not shocking, alarming, or new. Now when I reflect on her statements as well as my attitude of "I have heard or seen this management behavior over and over again across ages and stages of development. So she decided to share about a 2-year-old and the challenges for her as a provider.

All across America on a daily basis we hear stories of the "terrible twos," the "terrific twos" as well as too many adults' misunderstandings of their need to become independent as a part of their growth and development. Yes there are many stories about the 2–year-old's demonstration of expressive behaviors by their physical actions, especially when they do not yet have the developed expressive language. One of my sons decided that he would fall out on the floor when he was 2 years old. I never really called it a tantrum, if there were to be such. He fell out on the floor as a way of expressing his displeasure with what was going on. I always made it a point to see how, when, and why 2-year-olds decided to have a tantrum or other expressions of displeasure. So what made me decide that I was not going to accept his actions as a tantrum was when I began to observe closely what and how he did what he did. First his approaches were well planned and implemented—hmmmm, so were they typical of what we consider to be tantrums? I myself was not convinced in any way that he was having a tantrum. So he would carefully fall down on the floor, not abruptly like many of the 2-year-olds. He would visually study the area around him, as to the designated falling area, then take a careful look as to where his head is usually supposed to land. So, ready-set-go—legs, feet, hands, and upper body gently land on the floor and lastly, all-wonder head! Okay, now the head never touches the floor's surface, it is held away from its potential landing.

Without drawing his attention to my observation of his "so-called tantrum, I say (if and when it was the best approach)" you need to get up off of the floor, please? What is that resultant action all about? He got up—looked around. My intent was to get him to attempt to verbalize a part of what was disturbing him. He was the one of my children who had certain expectations that the adult had to try to figure out what his needs really were.

So I could tell many 2-year-old stories with my own children and children with whom I have worked over the years. So back to this childcare provider's story, which was not new, but concerning. Our conversation focused on his inappropriate behaviors and actions. Questions arose about how did he learn the types of inappropriate behaviors at such a young age. This question is often the center of attention on many matters related to young children, especially in cases of unexpected behaviors that do not correlate with their ages nor stages of development. Teachers, childcare providers, and educators are often faced with the dooming tasks of either having to share with or relay information that is urgent for the child's parent to know. The decision to tell or not tell is usually at the discretion of the person responsible for or working with the child. Some educators hesitate about telling if they think the report may be damaging enough that a parent may hurt or harm a child as a result of the information. Some adults feel that some of the challenging behaviors are to be expected and that we should be prepared to meet the individual needs of each child. Yet some adults respond so negatively that it can be very discouraging to the person caring for the child. Or both sides, the parents and/or the educators either perceive and/or give the impression that the implications are that the child learned the inappropriate behaviors from home. So the defensiveness of the adults in the home can cause conflict between the providers and the parents. Sometimes it seems like there are no neutral grounds. Sometimes it is the end of a relationship or specific program for that child. Removing the child from the site by the provider or the parent most often does not seem to be the wisest choice in regard to the child.

Educators often wonder what happens to the child after they leave their site. It is usually the hope that the child will be in a positive environment and that the experiences do not worsen as a result of the information provided to the family about the child's inappropriate actions.

There is always the decision to be made, especially in regard to child/sexual abuse and/or neglect cases, whether it is appropriate to make contact with the new place where the child will be attending. Some believe because of confidentiality reasons, one provider should not share information with another, but I do believe that most experts will agree that professionally handled sharing of information is appropriate, especially in critical situations.

Even with children who are not toddlers, one finds that the sharing among educators in regard to professionally dealing with private and confidential information can prove to be so valuable for saving the lives of so many children. With many of the school age students, if unacceptable behaviors or treatment of children that may be detrimental to their welfare is unfolded, situations can and may become tense, threatening, and negative. So educators have to be strong, stand their ground, and remember the welfare of the child is the center of the focus. In a case of a school age student, the teacher was able to unfold systemic information that the child had already attended and transferred from five different schools in the district and it was still not the end of the school year. So it was determined that the abusing parent would be the leader in having the child transferred from the school where questions arose about the abuse of the child. That type of voluntary transfer is seen especially among school age family members. But with younger children, it seems to be the opposite, where often the educator/provider ends up asking the parent not to bring the child back for fear of the overall impact on their program as well as the other children. Devastating, yes, especially because of the high rate of expulsions and suspensions of young African America children. (Articles are included on this page in this submission)

So now, I am finally sharing with you about the 2-year-old that I started out this chapter about. For confidentiality, we will call the child Sylvester, who is 2 years old. The childcare provider was disturbed enough that she had just spoken with the mother most recently. She had spoken with the parent on this occasion and the child's dad previously. 1) The child hid behind boldness without the provider hearing at first, but in the presence of the children telling them "kiss my as------------!" By this time, all of the other children were yelling, "He said a bad word—no, no, no." To begin with, having a talk, straight talk with child and parents was at the critical stage.

So the childcare provider continued by saying that the child was calling other children the b-i-t- --.

When I asked how did she handle it, she responded by asking him to stop. She had several conversations, first with the mom who admitted that her boyfriend called her the "b" word and the child has heard it many times. Later the provider spoke with the boyfriend who denied everything and said the child had learned how to be aggressive from the childcare setting. So defending her program, she told him that she promotes harmony in her day care and not violence. But later after conversing with both adults, the mom approached the childcare provider telling her that whatever they discussed stayed there and nowhere else. She was referencing the fact that when the childcare provider spoke with the dad, she mentioned the conversation about his calling the mother a "b."

What About Those Children Who Seem to Not Differentiate between the Roles of a Child and Adult

1. This little girl is interesting in that I only know her from the afterschool program, which is held once a week. At first glance, one might think of how smart the girl seems by her actions, questions, and comments. But the closer I observed her, I began to sense other issues that were not always so positive. I kept thinking about what a teacher should do with a child such as her to help develop her maximum potential? Here are some initial observations:
   1. Student loves to read
   2. Seems to retrieve back to reading if something doesn't go her way
   3. Any attention given to other children causes her to come and demand those roles for self
   4. Tries to stay two steps ahead of adults and teacher in the environment
   5. Will immediately go to an adult for extra/special privileges if she can get away with it
   6. Will ask for permission from the adult that she assumes is not the one in authority
   7. Will use a helpful, inquisitive approach to take on the leadership role that may not call for a student leader
   8. Consistently seeks attention no matter what is going on in the class
   9. Has figured out who is the less aggressive, or children who are followers and attempts to put them in positions to assist her in carrying out her plans
   10. Boldly stands in front of adults to inquire about her next actions or to see if they recognize that she is standing there and to find out if they will have the audacity to ask her to please go sit down and join in what other children are doing
   11. Will pick up materials or items not made available to students to determine if she will be asked to put them back or would she be the only student with the materials that none of the other children have been bold enough to obtain.
2. This little girl, 8 years old, is really a challenge for the teacher who would like to bring out her leadership skills but realizes that she seems to be so far out of control with her advanced manipulative tactics, that there should be a limitation on what she is allowed to do. The approaches seem to not stop if she is not stopped. It appears that she will seek and demand all that she can get despite what the other children may be doing or no matter what they are supposed to be doing.
3. She is consistently focused on what other children are doing, what the teacher has planned for next, and if she cannot visually figure out, will ask the teacher what they are going to do next. If she discovers or finds out what is to happen next, she will kindly ask the teacher if he/she wants her to tell the other children what to do. For example, it may be 30–45 minutes before it is time to eat snack or a meal, and she will come up to the teacher and ask if he/she wants her to tell the children to wash their hands? The teacher's response, "No thank you, it is not time yet." She waits a few more minutes and comes back up, asking the same question about the situation/condition.
4. Mrs. J. selected Amilayah to be the teacher-leader of an art activity with the younger students. This seems to have disturbed this student, so she immediately stood up and decided to make herself the teacher-leader or one of the teacher-leaders for that particular activity. Since she was reminded that another child was the teacher, she continued to look for the opportunities where she would still become the teacher. So when a new group of students arrived back to the classroom, she immediately went over to them to show them the bookmark activity that they needed to do. She didn't show them how to do it, instead she was doing it for them. The teacher reminded her to show them how to do it and not do it for them.
5. Just as Mr. J was putting out some materials that all of the children would receive as gifts to take home, she came over to the table and asked the teacher, "did he want her to pass the items out to the children as they were preparing to line up to go catch their respective buses. Instead, the teacher asked one of the adults to help with passing out the items since there were different ones for different children. She went and joined the children in the line.

6. So as the children were leaving to catch the bus, a younger child who was in front of the line was told by this student to move back because she was too young to be in front of the line. The child complied but not without telling the teacher that the student told her she was too young to be in front of the line. The teacher informed the young student that it was okay for her to be in front of the line.
7. All of the students were working diligently on a teddy bear traveling project when the teacher asked the three girls to type on the computer given to them about their respective bears in order to make the project a go. This student said, she didn't want to. So she decided to use the strategy of checking her elementary school systemic e-mail. She asked the student next to her if she checks her mail from school and the other students who were younger than she continued typing the information given to them about their project. Both girls are now done typing and asked the teacher if she had some more that they could type. The teacher happily gave them some more and told them how proud she was of their hard work on the typing task. The student who still has not started typing at this point and in a few minutes everyone would be getting ready to go to the university's dining center, and look around. She waited and after still not attempting to type the assignment, she tried distracting the girls who were on their second typing document and seemed to be loving it. But they just kept on working so hard. Finally the boom for not doing her work came to the forefront after the teacher and the other adults in the classroom decided to ignore her not attempting the assignment. She asked could she go and wash her hands in preparation for the meal, although the teacher had not excused anyone else to go wash their hands. The teacher responded, "No you may not because you did not do/complete what I asked you to do. I think I will talk to your mother about this." She immediately grabbed up the information that needed typing, began typing, and did an excellent job. After she completed it, she decided to come up and show the teacher her completed work and said, "Do you have anything else for me to type, that was fun." Wow.

Student Assignment

Choose one of the scenarios above (1–7) and tell how you as a teacher would have dealt with the aforesaid student. Tell:

1. Your initial approach
2. Your summary of the student's behaviors
3. Your perceptions as to some of the reasons for the student's behaviors
4. Are there any ways to take this student's behaviors and help her turn them around to benefit school performance?
5. What would be your final recommendation to the teacher?
6. What would be your final recommendation to the parent?

Resources for Preschool Suspensions Expulsions

Cassandra Johnson, Hope Center, BCDI-Denver, "Taking Action to Purge the Pipeline in Colorado"
https://www.nbcdi.org/taking-action-purge-pipeline-colorado

David Johns, White House Initiative on Educational Excellence on African Americans
https://www.nbcdi.org/removing-barriers-opportunity-eliminating-preschool-suspensions

Harold Jordan, American Civil Liberties Union of Pennsylvania, Dignity in Schools
https://www.nbcdi.org/whats-wrong-criminalizing-our-early-learners

NBCDI Parent Power Bootcamp Call to Action Toolkit
https://www.nbcdi.org/nbcdi-parent-power-bootcamp-call-action-toolkit

Firstschool
https://www.nbcdi.org/point-of-proof/firstschool

Girl Power, World Literacy Crusade of Florida
https://www.nbcdi.org/point-of-proof/girl-power-world-literacy-crusade-florida

Border Crossers
https://www.nbcdi.org/point-of-proof/border-crossers

Public Policy Initiative: Equity in Early Childhood Education
https://www.nbcdi.org/node/793

Flamboyan Foundation Family Engagement Partnership
https://www.nbcdi.org/point-of-proof/flamboyan-foundation-family-engagement-partnership

Rasheed Malik. " 4 Disturbing Facts About Preschool Suspension, March 30, 2017.
https://www.americanprogress.org/issues/early-childhood/news/2017/03/30/429552/4-disturbing-facts-preschool-suspension/

Joe Davidson. Preschool Suspensions are made worse by racial disparities
https://www.washingtonpost.com/politics/preschool-suspensions-are

Corey Turner, All Things Considered (audio) Why Preschool Suspensions Still Happen, June 20, 2016
http://www.npr.org/sections/ed/2016/06/20/482472535/why-preschool-suspensions-still-happen-and-how-to-stop-the

NAEYC (National Association for the Education of Young Children) Standing Together Against Suspension and Expulsion in Early Childhood Education
http://www.naeyc.org/suspension-expulsion

Office of Special Education and Rehabilitative Services Blog, U.S. Department of Education, Preschool Suspensions: Addressing Disproportionate Discipline
https://sites.ed.gov/osers/2016/08/preschool-suspensions-addressing-disproportional-discipline-practices/

US Department of Health and Human Services, U.S. Department of Education. Policy Statement on Expulsion and Suspension Policies in Early Childhood Settings
https://www2.ed.gov/policy/gen/guid/school-discipline/policy-statement-ece-expulsions-suspensions.pdf

Melinda D. Anderson. "Why Are So Many Preschoolers Getting Suspended? December 7, 2015.
https://www.theatlantic.com/education/archive/2015/12/why-are-so-many-preschoolers-getting-suspended/418932/

Walter S. Gilliam and Golan Shohar. Preschool and Child Care Expulsion and Suspension.
http://ziglercenter.yale.edu/publications/Gilliam%20and%20Shahar%20-%202006%20Preschool%20and%20Child%20Ca

Joy Resmovits. Black preschool kids get suspended much more frequently than white preschool kids, U.S. survey says, June 6, 2016
http://www.latimes.com/local/education/la-na-suspension-rates-preschool-crdc-20160606-snap-story.html

Reducing preschool suspensions, expulsions goal of new state guidance, September 22, 2016
http://www.mlive.com/news/index.ssf/2016/09/reducing_suspensions_expulsion.html

No One Ever Told Me Discipline Was Going to Be Like This

With so many years of teaching and having dealt with discipline of students, it has never seemed so far as it is now from reaching out and doing the right thing for each child. One message that we all should receive is that there cannot be a one method fits all. We realize the need for individualizing discipline because of how each method varies for each child.

Student Assignment 1

Write a paragraph about why the same method of discipline cannot and should not be used for every child.

Are Children Today Really Different from Children of the Past?

Some say that children who come to us are so different from those of the past. I am not sure if that is really true in the sense of differences. One might ponder whether students are coming to us having been reared and disciplined or not disciplined so differently that it has made the teacher's job extra challenging. So what has made it so difficult? There is no one answer and certainly no one right answer.

1. Are teacher training institutions not preparing our teachers for so many different discipline challenges?
   As teachers are leaving educational institutions, many cite the fact that they usually might have taken a course—one that is on discipline. Yet they wonder why there is only one course when this is such a major part of a teacher's job. So how are teachers expected to learn about so many discipline strategies for so many different needs in the classroom?
2. Are children really behaving that differently in the classroom that teachers are scratching their heads about what and how to deal with them?
   This has become a major head-scratcher for too many teachers as they strive to find answers to what seems like major changes in student behaviors especially in comparison to when teachers themselves were students in school. There are many insinuations in that some feel that the home environments of students are so different today. There are issues such as the number of female-single headed families/households as one of the key differences. Others feel that the

incarceration rates of one or both parents make it such that many children are being raised by grandparents and many non-blood friends and others. Then there seems to be differences in diet, what children eat, and less physical activities.

3. What impact does the rigid school curricula have on children's behaviors?

   Teachers as well as families often share that the emphasis on reading has surpassed the word "bad" when it comes to school curricula. Reading scores on standardized tests are among nightmares for many. In order to look like the students in a teacher's class is achieving, more, teachers find themselves trying to teach to the test as much as possible. There have also been a few caught cheating in various ways. Some teachers focus the curricula 4 majority of time in efforts of having students be better prepared when taking the tests. A few have been caught marking the correct answers for their students, so that teachers can be looked upon more favorably.

4. Do we have sufficient physical activities and movement integrated into the curricula as to effectively deal with students' need to participate in movement?

   In early childhood education, we have been taught to make sure that we provide transitions knowing that we should be getting students up and moving as often as possible. The movement is believed to stimulate the brain and thought processes so that the student can be more attentive and successful in completing assigned tasks.

5. What about recess? Is taking away a child's recess a form of punishment, cruel punishment when all of the research is showing that every child should have the right to outdoor play as the weather permits?

   Research is showing that we have gotten this one wrong for a long time. Too often, too many teachers decide to take away recess as the first source of punishment or taking away of privileges during the school day. While many agree that recess is the favorite time of day for students, this time should not be taken away from students regardless of what may have happened at school that day. Denying the child the right to recess causes major problems in other areas of the child's school day. Deleting or decreasing outside physical play is a problem in that every child should have the privilege of outside physical recess without disruptions, especially because of cited behavioral changes.

6. What about corporal punishment? Some are surprised to learn that there are states where this is deemed legal for designated school officials to impose?

   More and more school districts are using corporal punishment in their efforts to decrease misbehaviors and behavioral challenges. A map of the number of states enforcing corporal punishment tells the story. Some say it is a matter of bringing back the old school ways of disciplining students in schools. They believe that the older practices worked and that they did not have all of the challenges that they have in schools today.

7. Does race, ethnicity, and cultural background make a difference in how children are disciplined or not disciplined in educational environments?

   According to current data, there are significant differences among students of color and other students in regard to the inequities within discipline among students in schools. Many rationales are given for why they do what they do, but the data support the fact that we need to take a closer look at why students are being treated differently based on race/ethnicity.

8. Do male teachers discipline differently from female teachers?

   While I did not research the area, this is a topic that many like to reference based on perceptions and their viewpoints on the differences in perceptions and expectations of the general public of male teachers, especially male elementary teachers. It appears that student responses to elementary school male teachers are more positive, accepting, and willing to cooperate. There are other issues that may come into the forefront in that there are so few male elementary teachers that students look upon it as a privilege to have a male teacher versus a female one.

9. Are Black girls disciplined disproportionately in comparison to students of other races and ethnicities?

   Yes, Black girls are disciplined differently from other students. Black girls seem to pose a threatening area for educators when it comes to discipline. They seem to be the most misunderstood by their actions, comments, and behaviors. Their mannerisms are unique as well as their nonverbal communication, thus posing problems for teachers who do not seem to understand them. Research shows that a Black girl and another girl of a different race or ethnicity could be seen doing the same thing or exhibiting the same behaviors, yet the decisions regarding discipline or disciplinary actions vary widely.

10. Is there a divide about discipline of students of color?

    Yes, there is a divide that seems to correspond with some of the racial and cultural inequities as in other areas of life for people of color. There are societal inequities and disparities in ways in which people of color are treated quite harshly compared to others.

11. Is there a divide about discipline of students of color with special needs?

    Yes, just as students of color are treated despairingly in many ways, adding the special education component exacerbates the problem, thus increasing the chances for suspensions and expulsions while other students remain in school when exhibiting the same behaviors.

12. Is there a divide about discipline of students with disabilities/special needs?

    Yes, data show that students with various identifiable disabilities are treated differently by those who work with them or who are responsible for making decisions about their educational opportunities. Thus students with mental challenges, disabilities are looked upon as having more serious disabilities than those with learning disabilities. Thus those with learning disabilities should be disciplined more mildly than those with other more serious disabilities as perceived by some.

Student Assignment

Choose two of the 12 conditions aforementioned in regard to disparities and inequities among students of color and others and elaborate upon them. You may need to do further research on the topic to be able to write a one-page opinion/reflection about each of the selected ones.

Kindergartner Arrested At School

I am still appalled when I see so many cases on the Internet, YouTube, and in the media about the youngest students overpowering the teachers with noncompliance. I was very surprised when I watched the video and read the story about a kindergartner being arrested. So in viewing the video, the child refused to comply and come down off of something in the classroom that she had climbed upon. Although all the details of the situation are not known, it appeared that the administration could not handle her either. So the next step was to call the police. I wasn't sure what the rationale was behind school officials' decisions/actions. In the video one can visibly see the young child being handcuffed. Back in the day, I do NOT ever recall anyone calling the police on so young of children. So have times changed or are schools changing their rules and policies?

How Dare You Take My Hard-Earned Halloween Candy?

Another situation that seems to have gotten out of hand was when an elementary school teacher took the student's Halloween candy that she received while trick-or-treating. The student became very upset and began fighting back to get her candy. The student was suspended and charged. Was there a different way to deal with the candy issue? Was there an alternative practice that could be put in place?

School Safety Patrol Officer Drags Female Student

The high school Black female student in South Carolina made national news as she was observed being dragged from her desk by a school safety officer. The situation was frightening for those in the classroom, in the community, and throughout the United States. Again could this situation have been handled differently? The question still remains for many, who is responsible?

Disrespectful Students Take Over the Classroom!

A high school in Chicago was beyond disturbing as I observed students taunting a substitute teacher on a video on the internet. The entire class was out of control and the total disrespect for what seemed like a helpless teacher was painful to watch. The students, who appeared as bullies, took candy from her desk, challenged her, and made the scene very frightening for everyone. It was obvious that there were no fears of anyone coming into the classroom to stop them. There was no one who was coming to rescue this substitute teacher from this hostile classroom environment. I could not watch this video without saying where in the world did schools go wrong? Are these students being held accountable for their actions? What are teachers expected to do in these types of situations? Is it realistic to expect teachers or substitute teachers to be successful in such pre-established hostile classroom environments?

Third-Grade Girl Whips Her Teacher!

I couldn't believe my ears when the students told me that a little girl in third grade had whipped the teacher. I wasn't sure of what they meant by whipped but it became increasingly sad to me as I listened further into the story and what really happened. They continued on by saying she had physically attacked this teacher. I was not able to get the facts/details behind what really transpired to cause the student's actions. I was not able to find out what the teacher had done that prompted the child's inappropriate actions. But they did say the student was suspended and was back in school by the time I heard about it. One child went a step further by saying, "she's just like her mama, they fight all the time." What are legal rights of students as well as teachers in physical confrontations?

So Are We Allowed to Touch Students or Not?

Do we touch students or not? Schools seem to have differing viewpoints on whether teachers should or could put their hands on or near students or not. Some districts say keep your hands fully off of students because of some students' sensitivity to touch. Others say that touching students can be misconstrued by some in demeaning ways, so it is best not to touch. Other schools say it is okay to touch students in ways of providing support and encouragement for and to them. So one of the cooks recently told me about a male student in second grade, who is usually passive and cooperative, often allowing what it seems like other students running all over him. So for some reason the teacher was standing there poking this child in the sides. As the cook observed, she did not understand the teacher's actions with this seemingly quiet and overly compliant student. So somehow the teacher's actions brought out the worst in this student. So this student decided to fight back. The teacher became very irate when the principal would not or did not suspend this student. So when one of the other staff asked this same teacher if she wanted her to ask the students to please settle down and get ready to return back to class, the teacher responded, "I don't care if they kill each other, no one around here cares what happens anyway." She was very upset because the principal did not handle the situation the way that she wanted her to—so her attitude certainly was not one representative of a positive, supportive teacher.

Being Treated As a Criminal in School

This young kindergarten student brought mom's boyfriend's loaded gun to school. Luckily another child noticed it and told the teacher. The teacher quickly took the weapon away from the child. The teacher immediately contacted the principal who in turn contacted law enforcement, who immediately went to the child's home. It was found out right away that it was mom's boyfriend's loaded gun that he hid in the child's backpack and forgot to take it back out and so the child unknowingly took it to school. So in order to not suspend or expel this young student, there were some policies put in place that would allow the school to check for the safety of everyone in the school.

1. The child had to have a clear, see through backpack every day.
2. The child and the backpack would be searched upon entrance into the building.
3. The child and the backpack would be searched upon entering the classroom in the morning.
4. The child and the backpack would be re-searched after recess or any other reentry into the building.
5. While this may seem inhumane to some, this was the safety policy the school came up with as an alternative to suspending or expelling the child.

Special Note: The parent and boyfriend were dealt with in the local law enforcement system. So how are children dealt with when parents are inconsiderate or irresponsible? What happens when children are innocent victims?

Passing Out Crack Cocaine to My Elementary Friends

The student who had rocks of crack on the school bus and had started distributing them to elementary students after getting off the bus. So this kindergarten student gets off the school bus and starts passing out what parents who were witnesses thought were drugs outside of the school shared with the media. The parents shared the frightening fears about what could have happened with the children had a parent not seen it and immediately questioned it with staff who were greeting students. For sure the school officials did not respond publicly to the media, but the parents did. Because this story made the local news and law enforcement had to be called in on the case it became a legal matter. It was discovered that mom's boyfriend had his backpack full of the drugs for distribution and the child picked up the wrong backpack and took it to school. Exactly what packaged crack cocaine looks like to a young child is frightening that he thought it was something to pass out and share with friends.

Teacher: How Are You Going to Make a Judgment Call?

The students who say that the teacher made them mad is trying to share experiences that schools should be attentive to. Others share that the teacher falsely accused them of something that wasn't true. So where does a teacher get his/her facts if something happened that he/she did not witness? How is it that a teacher makes a decision about situations and conditions, especially based on what other children perceive or observe? Are there any record keeping or documents of children's actions/behaviors that will assist the teacher in making wise decisions about proper discipline?

So What's The Big Deal If You Are Called the "N" Word?

Teachers must be aware that some discipline is forced beyond the classroom. A teacher who chooses to ignore the "N" word or other racially biased names may find that is not a good strategy to follow. Once a child makes it home and is able to tell family members what happened, the story may expand beyond where the teacher may have desired for it to go. So as much as we may not want to deal with some issues, it has proven over and over again that efforts to deal with racial issues at school work out so much better rather than allowing them to spill over at home.

Snitches Wear/Get Stitches

So many children say this as a rhyme and chant, "Snitches wear stitches" or "Snitches get stitches." So one must only ask any student at any grade level and they will quickly tell you what it means. They describe that if one talks and tell on others that you are considered to be a snitch and if you are a snitch you can get hurt by the ones who do not like snitches. The question is whether the concept of snitching in school is the same or similar to snitching in the street?

As educators, we would tend to think that there is a difference between the two. But the truth of the matter is that one of the experiences of a teacher showed that while educators may look at it one way, some families perceive it a different way.

So the teacher was having a challenge with the students in her class taking pencils and school supplies that belonged to another student. She worked hard to stop the problem and began having daily discussions with the class about how pencils in particular were coming up missing on a daily basis. So to her amazement, one of the male students came forward after school and told her that he knew who was taking the pencils. He thought that his actions would help solve the problem in their class.

The teacher thanked him personally for being brave, bold, honest, and coming forth to help solve the problem. So what happened next posed a problem for the teacher when she thought that she was doing the right thing or an encouraging thing when she decided to call the boy's grandmother. She called the grandmother to tell how proud she was of her grandson for coming forth and helping her with who was taking the students' pencils and school supplies. But to her amazement, the grandmother became irate and very upset with the teacher's call and with her decision to call her rewarding her grandson for what she perceived to be a snitch. She told the teacher to never call her again like what her grandson did was something positive about his being a snitch. She told the teacher that she teaches all of her children and grandchildren not to go around snitching on others because it is dangerous. The teacher felt hurt because she thought that she was doing something positive and to give the student a reward with the call, not knowing that it would turn into a negative. So the message is understand what could be perceived by some families as snitching and use a different approach. Or teachers need to be prepared for a shocking, disturbing discovery that something that he/she thought would be positive may be assessed as negative by some parents.

Inappropriate Use of Time-out

Lots of questions and concerns today are about the inappropriate use of time-out. Some say time-out is an outdated method of discipline that does not work.

1. It doesn't work sometimes because of how it is used.
2. It doesn't work sometimes because the child does not know why he/she is in time-out.
3. It doesn't work sometimes because the child is placed in an isolated area for too long a period of time.
4. It doesn't work sometimes because the children who need to be in the group are being sent out of the group.
5. It doesn't work sometimes because other more positive approaches are recommended and more acceptable.

So why would a teacher decide to have a student stay in a time-out area for 2–3 hours with no work, assignments or communication? So the teacher's attitude was one of "he/she doesn't want to learn so I am not going to waste any time on him/her. So I just let him sit there."

I Hit the Teacher with a Chair

When I asked the student why was she suspended, she hesitatingly said, "because I hit a teacher with a chair." I remember saying to her so why did you hit her with a chair? She responded by saying, "she made me angry." So I spent a substantial amount of time with her talking about alternatives as well as ways of avoiding some of the behaviors exhibited by hitting the teacher? I asked her who were some school officials that she could find to talk to next time? I also shared with her that we would work on some ways to decrease anger and frustration as we worked through some of the situations and conditions.

Student Assignment

If you were working with this student, what are some recommendations that you would make for a student aforementioned who hit the teacher? Please list them and tell why.

It All Starts with Preschool!

School districts all over the United States are pondering ways of developing comprehensive educational plans starting as early as preschool that would lead to long-term success.

With the long-term success thoughts, they are now beginning to realize the importance of a very positive and developmentally appropriate preschool for all children.

We are now seriously looking closer at America's schools and what entails higher graduation rates and better overall academic performance of all students. Questions continue to arise about what needs to happen so that America's schools continue to be among educational leaders of the world. So as plans related to school success are developed, evidence points to the fact that America's youngest children are often excluded from the plans. One such example is cited in Cleveland Metropolitan School District, Ohio where it was relayed that more than half of the children who entered kindergarten had very little opportunities to be a part of high-quality preschools.

With such devastating results, Cleveland set out to do something about it. They developed a plan to provide high-quality preschool for all children in the Cleveland area. This came about as a result of a private–public partnership citing some of the major challenges as to why so many children were not a part of high-quality preschools.

The rationale for the need to focus on preschool education is because of the substantial amount of research showing that the ages from birth to age 5 are critical in that this is a key time for providing the framework for a successful and accomplished life.

The U.S. Department of Education reports that a child's brain is developed by the time a child turns 5.

1. A study in 2014 that was released by the White House cited projects that offered early childhood programs for low-income children revealed that low-income children who had attended high-quality preschools were four times more likely to graduate from college by age 30 more so than those who did not attend.
2. These findings reveal significant results that starting children in kindergarten is not good enough or early enough. So instead of introducing children to school through kindergarten, school districts realize the seriousness of bringing them to school earlier so that their first years are not spent on remediation or struggling to overcome some of the barriers they face by not attending a high-quality preschool.
3. What is not being said is the failure to acknowledge and speak out about the fact that there are not enough high-quality preschools for all of the children who are eligible to attend/participate.

4. High-quality preschools are not free for all children. Thus affordability can become an issue.
5. Being able to get the child to the program can be another major issue if transportation is not a part of the services offered, especially to low-income families.
6. Educating parents to the values of high-quality preschool programs is another barrier faced by some school districts. This can range from the disbelief that the earlier children enter educational/early childhood programs they could be beneficial. Others believe that children should stay at home until they "become of age."

So What Do We Do to Enhance High-Quality Preschool Programs?

1. Research-based curricula: Schools must plan, develop, and implement high-quality and effective curricula that provides for successful learning experiences for all students enrolled.
2. Teachers and staff who are working with these students must be trained and have high expectations and developmentally appropriate knowledge of what children need to learn.
3. Regardless of what other grade levels are cutting out of the curricula, those working with preschool children realize the importance of keeping imaginative play as a key factor in the classroom and in educational programming.
4. There should be ongoing assessments and alignments with goals on whether a child is on track for successful kindergarten readiness.
5. There should be a planning process with all concerned parties at the table—teachers, staff, principals, preschool administrators, parents, local businesses, and community partners.
6. A part of the inclusion meetings should include data representative of the population of families to be served. This information would serve as the focus for meeting individual family needs. These inclusive strategies should build a format/platform for engaging families.

Using What Is Working to Make More Successful Early Childhood Education Programs

1. There is no need to build something new when it comes to high-quality programming for young children.
2. Use and study good existing models to build a great, highly successful early childhood program.
3. Most states do not require children to attend pre-kindergarten programs or before their sixth birthday.
4. With states not requiring children to attend school before kindergarten, many parents find the search for good and appropriate early childhood programs as a big challenge for them.
5. There are questions posed by some that children who have at least one parent at home should be at home with them rather than enrolling them in a preschool program.
6. While more free early childhood programs are being offered, some parents find that preschool programs are sometimes connected to childcare programs that are not free.
7. More parents are choosing childcare programs that offer or say they offer a preschool program and then the parent is able to get the child in one stable place for the day.
8. Because of the beliefs of educators and researchers, more transitional kindergartens are on the rise. These programs are designed to help young children make a smooth transition between preschool and kindergarten.
9. Transitional kindergarten programs are for 4 years-old and those who will turn 5 during the year prior to kindergarten.

10. There must be considerations for what might be best for specific children such as whether a school year (all-year-round), calendar-year, full-time or part-time preschool program.
11. Some researchers share that preschoolers who attended high-quality preschools tend to score better on achievement tests and in the long term, earn higher salaries once they are adults.

Who Is Holding the String for Financing High-Quality Preschool Programs?

1. It is important that we do more to educate those who hold the purse for the funding of preschool programming. In some areas of the United States, some have chosen to raise public and private philanthropic funds. This is needed in some areas where it appears that the dollars are either missing or so low that it truly impacts the quality of programming.
2. Some believe that it is a must for the existence of seed funding in order to strengthen the opportunities or expansion of enrollment diversity and for additional research based on information on families and the need for long-term funding for preschools.
3. While we know the need for high-quality preschools, we must realize that it is not the answer to all of the issues focused around the needs of young children and families. There are still many questions about the team that needs to be in place for the development of genuine models so that children are able to perform to their maximum potential.
4. The messages seem to be consistent that there is definitely the need to be able to make a smooth transition for the transferal of children's performance from one grade level to the next. The critical stage is being able to successfully transfer performance data from preschool-kindergarten and then on through third grade.
5. While the focus seems to be on the child, it is recognized that it is important to develop an outreach family plan. There must be plans in place, especially for those families who have children enrolled in preschool programs that may not measure up to the high-quality standards.

So How Are Parents/Families to Know How to Choose Quality Preschools?

It has been acknowledged that while we talk much about high-quality preschool programming, we also realize that there is a big gap in our mission. The mission should be to make parents/families more aware of what to look for in finding a high-quality program for their child. It would be unfair to assume that parents automatically know what to look for when choosing a program.

Often we realize that quality may not be the first or main priority of parents when choosing an early childhood program. Unfortunately, convenience, proximity from home, familiarity of teachers, or the program may take precedence over quality.

We should help parents through various types of informational approaches with the selection of quality preschools. There are several recommended approaches such as:

1. Going to each child's home, doing door-to-door neighborhood visits, dispersing information, and having conversations.
2. Promotion of listing of openings in different programs and their availability to families in designated neighborhoods.
3. Making individual and informational phone calls, e-mails, texts to parents about high-quality preschool programming.
4. Help programs that may be in need of assistance in a variety of ways such as financial support, curricula, and up-to-date classroom materials.

5. Making sure that teachers and staff receive the necessary training and support to be effective in high-quality preschool programs.
6. One recommended model of support for preschool programming is that of developing a community-based supportive model. This would include bringing people from the school district, the community, churches, as well as early childhood educators together.
7. Every preschool program must be knowledgeable of the benchmarks related to enrollment, recordkeeping of each student's growth, and development with the collection of data showing how the program impacts each child.

So What Should Children Learn in Preschool?

First of all, high-quality preschool programs must include most importantly the domains of social-emotional development, language and literacy, expansion of English language knowledge/vocabulary, mathematical computations/concepts.

It should also include perceptual and motor development, ages and stages of development of young children and cognitive development. Most importantly, the curricula must adhere to preschool more so than kindergarten so that it is not a watered-down kindergarten program.

The good thing is that the quality of the program is centered around play, thus their models of learning are child centered and creative. With language and literacy, teachers include experiences of listening as well as concept development. Authentic objects and materials are used to motivate the children to learn.

Fine motor skill development is introduced allowing children to work on skills like drawing, painting, using keyboards and other technology measures.

Gross motor skills are emphasized through use of spatial awareness and awareness, body awareness, working with large motor objects/materials, cooperating and sharing of personal space with others.

With many of the creative, child-centered experiences, children learn to write their names or part of it, some letters of the alphabet, learning sight vocabulary that is meaningful to them.

So expanded transitional kindergarten begins with high-quality programming that should adhere to the proper early childhood curricula and standards that are developmentally appropriate and using best practices. Expanded kindergarten programs last a full day, while other types of programs do not.

Many of the transitional programs align with Common Core standards and many others do not. These programs are usually free. Thus the issue becomes whether the child will attend a state-run/operated program and not so private.

Some are automatically enrolled in Head Start programs, which are federally funded and enrollees must be below the federal poverty income guideline.

In some states there are school readiness language development programs. These types of programs do not have any income nor language developmental requirements. However, these schools in many states have been taken over by the transitional programs.

Student Assignment

List at least three recommendations you might make to parents to assist them in locating high quality preschool programs.

Are Preschools Fading Out or Are We the Faders? The Real Issues

Many have been shouting about how preschool education can and will make a difference in the lives of children. But today, with so many challenges, questions, and concerns, some are wondering if this is still a true reality. For many, the questions continue to rise about the real effects on young children who have been actively enrolled.

There are some studies that are longitudinal and others short term, but they still are causing nationalists to scratch their heads. The findings from some of the research are short lived. Some findings show that all of these great benefits occur during the early years, but by third grade many of the gains move in the losses categories. Thus many of what were considered gains showed up in the losses column.

Well, some felt that the answers would be in universal preschools in that any child who wanted to could attend preschool free of charge. Thus attempts to decrease the achievement gaps between the haves and the have nots. So where does the concept of the fade-out of preschool come from? They come from the fact that earlier studies revealed that there were major differences in success and progress by those who attended.

Those decision makers who are responsible for foreseeing the funding noted their disappointment in the fact that though the funds were placed there, they were not able to view evidence of what was hoped for and that was that they would be able to see the growth and development over a longer period of time. This is critical especially for some who doubted whether early childhood education is really the answer to some of the problems, situations, and conditions involving the youngest students.

They are now stating that there is no sufficient evidence of social and economic benefits to society. Still, at the center of attention is the fact of whether providing preschool education to low-income children would demonstrate long-term achievement effects.

So one theory of thought focuses on the fact that if indeed there is going to be proven evidence in regard to being able to maintain the real and successful effects of preschool education, educators must look at what happens AFTER children actually matriculate in school as demonstrated by the graph by Getty.

While there may be disagreements, it is believed that a good and appropriate curriculum that works specifically builds upon what the child already knows. The recommended model demonstrates the importance of continuing to add to the knowledge base of the child.

26 Classroom Management and Effective Strategies to Motivate Students

So what then are we or should we really be looking at in order to provide the needed evidence and support for early childhood education success?

1. The high quality of elementary school years of educational programming is the key to what matters!
2. Are we looking closely at the quality of teachers who are hired to teach in elementary schools after children have had successful years of early childhood education?
3. So who is really minding the children? Who is really monitoring the success, progress, and advancement during the early years?
4. So who is really screening the quality of programming being provided to children after the preschool years?
5. So do we automatically expect that once young children are exposed to a quality education during their most formidable years that they will remember everything that they learned?
6. How many educators are truly aware of the fact that poor teaching can undo all of the great efforts and effects of high-quality preschool experiences?

One of the issues that is not usually being dealt with but is highly recommended is that there be a strong and often uniformed curriculum across grade levels. This would put some consistency in the expectations of what children should begin to know in order to be successful during the elementary school years. A word of caution: While a systemic, consistent educational model for learning is highly recommended, there is no guarantee that children would transition across various grade levels and programs during the elementary years with ease.

Bringing Forth Information about the Child's Preschool Years

One of the desired actions, for sure, will be a simple one that should have been happening all along. So why is it that teachers in the elementary grades do not receive the needed information from the child's preschool educators so that teachers can be real builders to strengthen each child's educational base?

1. One of the effective approaches to dealing with deficits is to successfully implement what is needed to help young children close in on the achievement gap.
2. In order to prove that the appropriate program to help young children develop cognitively requires a continuation of high-quality teaching that is beyond good, and focuses on very good!

3. Good instruction in the early elementary grades needs to be aligned with the high-quality curricula taught during the preschool years.
4. Research by early educators in mathematics shows that teachers helped the learning process of children by taking what they knew prior to entering preschool, building upon it, and incorporating repetition on a continuous basis.
5. Continuous repetition really helps those children who did not attend preschool because it allows them the opportunity to try to catch up on information that they had not yet learned.
6. There is that gap that may not allow the children who did not attend preschool to fulfill the same requirements as those who did.
7. While there is directed specific curriculum for children without preschool experiences, the implication is that these children do not gain the same results as those who attended, which implies the investments are not made as desired.
8. The roles of kindergarten teachers are critical in regard to preschool investments. Thus they MUST know well the skills that children enter their classrooms with.
9. Kindergarten teachers must be flexible in the provision of a positive, child-centered curriculum as well as an individualized teaching-learning plan that helps each child move up the ladder of maximum success.
10. Initial school assessments of each child's individual skills in the beginning of the school year can make a big difference. Again these assessments are to be used to build upon what children already know, but does not guarantee that each child will experience continued success that extends their learning in addition to what was previously learned.

"Bad instruction can undo the effects of high-quality preschool experiences."

Making Learning Connections Can Make a Major Difference

Children's learning can be expanded with the provision of opportunities to apply their acquired knowledge with new ideas, topics, and constructs.

Teachers need to know what children learned the previous year and in what context they did so. Again this opens the door for substantial cognitive growth when appropriate.

It is so important that children's social and emotional development are a part of the learning strategies used with them. There cannot and should not be any separation from the cognitive. The absence of connectedness definitely contributes to "preschool fade-out."

Why? Why is no attention given to children's social and emotional development beyond preschool? Because of so much pressure on kindergarten and elementary grades, teachers have expressed the lack of time and concern for the child's social and emotional development.

In most states, accountability programs for curricula development do not include any social-emotional developmental experiences. There are no known strategies and approaches that are typically used beyond preschool encouraging children's social and emotional development.

1. One of the known determinants is that many elementary school teachers do not continue the strong social-emotional development.
2. The critical point is that somehow we have got to find ways of advocating on behalf of young children and requiring that teachers provide supportive experiences for young students that are inclusive of their gains from high-quality preschool programs.
3. The reason that the roles that elementary teachers play are so critical is because most of the social-emotional experiences of preschoolers are highly connected and correlated with their successful academic experiences.

4. Too many educators fail to recognize the facts related to a child's social-emotional development, such as self-esteem, self-confidence, self-control and independence are skills that can maximize children's learning in their early years of schooling.
5. Another critical component to closing the achievement gap and providing positive learning opportunities for young children is related to parental engagement/involvement.
6. Some nationally recognized early childhood programs—Perry Preschool Project, Child-Parent Centers—have demonstrated the important roles that parents and families play in the successful development of cognitive skills of young children. These programs have become models because they are supportive and encourage parents to be involved in their child's education.

How Do We Move Toward the Process of Long-Term Benefits of Enhancing the Learning of Children's Preschool Experiences?

1. There needs to be an alignment of the curricula as well as assessments in order to provide for long-term research-based evidence of preschool benefits.
2. There should be an alignment of preschool learning experiences and progress of children that will allow for tracking their success across grade levels.
3. Teachers need to be provided time and support so that they can learn the content of the grade level before and after the one that they are currently teaching. This will allow them the needed knowledge on expectations for the children they are currently teaching.

Are Our Teachers Prepared to Teach Students across Levels and with Varying Skills?

While it sounds good, when we say we expect teachers to provide for the individual needs of students, do we really mean this? Do we really feel that we have allowed the time and preparation for teachers to get to know the students and their needs and varying levels of performance? So when we learned of "No child left behind," there were many rumblings of whether this was the proper program and whether it really could be successfully done. But what is being uncovered with the mysteries of why some feel that preschool programs are fading. The issue behind this is that teachers need to be trained and have the time to study and learn how to help each child in their classroom successfully achieve so that they can go on to the next level.

So What Are Some of the Ways That Are Recommended for Helping to Maintain the Positive Effects of Preschool Education?

1. There are many suggestions to help schools maintain what children successfully learn in preschool.
2. There are many ways that schools should be able to provide supportive programming that meets the needs of children and their families.
3. The key goal for success here is to make sure that everyone works together for the betterment of the child's success and achievement that can be long-lasting. There should be many efforts to help the child perform well in school over the years.
4. If preschool gains are to pay off and be well worth all of the efforts, everyone must pay close attention to what needs to happen after preschool.
5. We need to make sure that what happens after preschool will be all-inclusive in that there are numerous solid opportunities to take advantage of the gains that have been achieved.
6. Some share their opinions that among the biggest detriments to successful school sequencing for young learners is the fact that kindergarten expectations have changed drastically all over

the United States. Among these changes are the removal of toys and centers such as art, music, blockbuilding, woodworking, housekeeping, etc. Many believe that kindergarten should be about the children getting down to very serious work.

7. Others feel that we rush and push young children entirely too much, taking away the time and opportunities for them to grow and develop at their own rates.
8. Kindergarten and early elementary grades that teach to the test are also believed to be those of setting young children up for failure.
9. Educators can also stop not recognizing the fact that the youngest students realize when there are gaps between their learning and that of others.
10. Until schools realize that providing a curriculum that is not "a one-size fits all" curriculum will not work, especially for children from diverse and low-income backgrounds.
11. The most important message out of the whole discussion on this matter is that the more disadvantages and limitations of children show that the more delays, the further behind these children will fall.

Resources

https://www.education.com/activity/preschool/
http://handsonaswegrow.com/activities/preschool-activities/
http://www.first-school.ws
https://www.familyeducation.com/school-learning/activities-preschoolers
http://www.enchantedlearning.com/categories/preschool.shtml
http://kidsactivitiesblog.com/26338/preschool-activities
http://pineswestacademy.com/preschool-activities
http://sunshinepreschool.net/about/faqs/89-activities-and-daily-interactions
https://www.himama.com/preschool-activities-for-learning-your-name
http://thestay-at-home-momsurvivalguide.com/preschool-activities
http://www.jumpstart.com/parents/activities/grade-based-activities/preschool-activities
http://www.parents.com/fun/entertainment/gadgets/best-apps-for-preschoolers/
http://www.preschoolrainbow.org/preschoolers.htm
http://www.pocketofpreschool.com/2015/06/letter-books.html
http://structuredplay.blogspot.com/2012/08/play-to-write-week-3.html
http://iheartcraftythings.com/apple-tree-abc-match-preschool-printable.html
http://mominspiredlife.com/science-activities-preschoolers/
http://livingwellmom.com/2015/08/scissors-cutting-practice-preschoolers/
http://b-inspiredmama.com/numbers-game-car-parking/
http://busytoddler.com/2016/08/sponge-painting-process-art/
http://www.schooltimesnippets.com/2016/04/fine-motor-letter-matching-preschool.html
http://www.icanteachmychild.com/printable-cereal-sorting-mat/
http://rainbowswithinreach.blogspot.com/2013/04/springtime-science-with-seeds.html?_szp=447639
http://curry.virginia.edu/readingprojects/projects/pll/images/pdf/justice.teambasedaction.pdf

This is a PDF for teachers with information about a team-based plan for creating language-rich preschool classroom environments.

https://www2.ed.gov/documents/early-learning/talk-read-sing/preschool-en.pdf

This site gives some "tips that you can use to help bridge the word gap by enriching the language environment of all young children in your care, including children who do not speak yet, children with disabilities or delays, and children who are learning more than one language.

https://www.babycenter.com/0_how-to-prepare-your-child-for-preschool_64536.bc

These ideas, from preschool teachers and the U.S. Department of Education's Learning Partners Program, will help prepare your child to listen, follow directions, and get along in a group—three important goals of any preschool program.

http://www.huffingtonpost.ca/2015/08/06/preschool-activities-kindergarten-prep_n_7948920.html
http://www.kidsacademy.mobi/free-preschool-kindergarten- worksheets/?aw=PKworksheets&gclid=CKGpur-GmNMCFQcLaQodKqkKDg

This is a collection of free kindergarten and preschool worksheets on every subject from alphabet and reading to math, writing, and spelling.

http://hodgepodgecraft.com/crafts-to-prepare-kids-for-pre-school/
https://www.ocps.net/lc/southeast/ewn/parents/documents/bridge_to_kindergarten_packet_2013.pdf
https://www.parentmap.com/article/25-indoor-play-activities-from-a-preschool-teacher
http://www.learning4kids.net/3-year-4-years/
http://www.kidspot.com.au/things-to-do/collection/games-crafts-and-activities-for-3-4-year-olds

Paint with cotton balls: http://www.sheknows.com/parenting/articles/1085738/activities-that-keep-toddlers-engaged?utm_source=AMPH&utm_medium=SI&utm_campaign=6073361

Ceral Sorting Map: http://www.icanteachmychild.com/printable-cereal-sorting-mat/
Painting on Foil: http://www.messylittlemonster.com/2016/05/painting-foil-kids-art-ideas-van-gogh.html
Shaving Cream Hide and Seek Letters: http://littlebinsforlittlehands.com/alphabet-sensory-play/?utm_content=buffer787f0&utm_medium=social&utm_source=pinterest.com&utm_campaign=buffer
Nature Scavenger Hunt: http://www.lifewithmylittles.com/2016/06/nature-scavenger-hunt-toddlers/
Play Dough and Alphabet Beads Activity: http://mominspiredlife.com/play-dough-and-alphabet-beads-activity/
Rainbow Model: http://b-inspiredmama.com/rainbow-mobile-craft-kids/#_a5y_p=5088067
Cutting Busy Box: http://www.acraftyliving.com/cutting-busy-box/
Surprise Color Fizz: http://www.powerfulmothering.com/preschool-science-experiment-surprise-color-fizz/?utm_content=buffer3fbe2&utm_medium=social&utm_source=pinterest.com&utm_campaign=buffer
Number Dab It: https://www.teacherspayteachers.com/Product/Apple-Numbers-0-25-Dab-It-2707811?pp=0
Shape Hunt: http://frugalfun4boys.com/2015/10/01/preschool-shape-scavenger-hunt/
Counting Caterpillar: http://www.123teachwithme.com/2012/12/letter-c-activities.html
Farm Animal Washing (sensory table): http://www.coffeecupsandcrayons.com/washing-farm-animal-sensory-bin/
Beanbag Matchup: http://princesspinkygirl.com/easy-indoor-activities/
Do-A-Dot Letters: http://totschool.shannons.org/do-a-dot-letters/
Snack Math: http://fun-a-day.com/snack-math-for-preschoolers-with-box-tops-for-education/
Colored Pompoms: http://raisinglittlesuperheroes.com/colors-and-patterns-busy-bag/
Ice Cream Math: http://fun-a-day.com/summer-math-preschool-ice-cream-theme/
Photo Name Puzzle: http://www.totschooling.net/2015/02/photo-name-puzzle.html
http://living.thebump.com/child-should-before-starting-kindergarten-10181.html
http://www.education.com/activity/article/Make_Four_Season_Trees/
http://www.education.com/activity/article/Fishing_for_Numbers_Game/
http://www.education.com/activity/article/fingerprint-fall-trees/
http://www.education.com/activity/article/paint-with-ice/
http://www.education.com/activity/article/South_American_Rainsticks/
http://www.education.com/activity/article/alphabet-trees/

http://www.education.com/activity/article/musicalmotor_preschool/
http://www.education.com/activity/article/Blow_Painting/

The Giant Encyclopedia of Preschool Activities for Three-Year-Olds

- This is an actual book that can provide several activity ideas for three-year-olds.
- The activities could be useful for children close to this age as well.
- http://www.clcd.com.proxy.lib.uni.edu/#/bookdetail/1/4/ojKKhjknhpIlmLkj/bdrtop

101 Rhythm Instrument Activities for Young Children

- This is an actual book that provides 101 different activities to teach children about rhythm.
- http://www.clcd.com.proxy.lib.uni.edu/#/display/1

Mother Goose's Playhouse: Toddler Tales and Nursery Rhymes, With Patterns for Puppets and Feltboards

- This book provides nursery rhymes, song, simple stories, and patterns for felt figures and stick puppets.
- It also provides instructions for how to make the felt figures and stick puppets.
- http://www.clcd.com.proxy.lib.uni.edu/#/display/1
- http://www.education.com/activity/article/Paper_Plate_Tambourines/
- http://www.education.com/activity/article/Color_Collage_Kindergarten/
- http://handsonaswegrow.com/blowing-balloon-baking-soda-vinegar/
- http://www.familyeducation.com/fun/activities-preschoolers/animal-charades
- http://www.education.com/activity/article/underwater-spy-alphabet-bottle/
- http://www.education.com/activity/article/Tin_Can_Phone/
- http://www.education.com/activity/article/ball-toss-game/

Letter Books
These are books the students make for each of the different letters as they learn them. The student then puts the books together so they can remember the letters and work on them.
http://www.pocketofpreschool.com/2015/06/letter-books.html

Writing Name
This is an activity to scaffold the toddler. It gives them the opportunity to see their name, then write parts of their name, and then write their entire name. It starts with no responsibility and ends with all responsibility.
http://structuredplay.blogspot.com/2012/08/play-to-write-week-3.html

Word Building Kit
This activity is one that allows you to give the child a word and they can see the word and then they can build the word. It shows them how they do it and allows them to do it. It is super fun for the student and lets them interact with the materials.
http://iheartcraftythings.com/word-building-activity-travel-kit.html

Alphabet Bingo
This Bingo game has all alphabet letters on it. When the teacher calls the letter, the student finds the letter on their own without help from a teacher. It gives them the opportunity to practice hearing the letter, then finding the letter. It takes it from audible to visual.
http://frugalfun4boys.com/2016/06/28/learn-the-alphabet-bingo-game/

Science Activities
This is a website of many different science activities to use in the preschool classroom. The reason this is important is because there is so much that preschool students are curious about and want to learn about

and there are so many opportunities for this in science. Doing these hands-on activities helps to keep the focus of the students and develops those early molds and perceptions.
http://mominspiredlife.com/science-activities-preschoolers/

Practicing Cutting
This is an activity used in a classroom to practice cutting. There are a variety of lines to cut; squiggly, straight, slanted, etc. Cutting is a hard task and those fine motor skills need to be developed, which is why I chose this activity.
http://livingwellmom.com/2015/08/scissors-cutting-practice-preschoolers/

Letter Recognition Activity
This is another letter recognition activity. You give the children a piece of paper that has all the letters on it. Then the students get a bag with letters in it and they choose a letter. Every time they choose a letter, they color it on the sheet.
http://thelettersofliteracy.com/letter-recognition-grab-bag/

Busy Bags
These bags can be used in the classroom to keep students busy when they finish something early. They can also be used when there are just a few extra minutes during the day that need to be filled. The bags help to continue to develop fine motor skills.
http://mrswillskindergarten.com/tips-for-best-kindergarten-round-up/?utm_source=feedburner&utm_medium=feed&utm_campaign=Feed:+MrsWillsKindergarten+(Mrs.+Wills+Kindergarten)

Color Hunt
This fun activity sends preschool students on a scavenger hunt to find different colored objects. It allows the children to see that there are multiple colors in their daily lives and lets them recognize them.
http://www.thepoefam.com/2013/03/goin-on-color-hunt.html

Ring Toss Game
This ring toss game is great when the students are inside during the winter and are antsy. This game gives the students a chance to get up and move around and allows them to work on their coordination.
http://fromabcstoacts.com/ring-toss-circus-game

Chapter 6

So What Has Happened to the Good Kindergarten Programs?

For years now, I have been communicating with kindergarten teachers in particular about their changing roles and the ever too many changes for children in the respective school districts.

So being a member of a university's early childhood faculty, we talked about some of our concerns and that's what they were truly concerns. But in regard to taking action and knowing exactly what to do remains a puzzle. So there were some indirect strategies used to begin to educate the public more about good early childhood programs in general.

So a group of faculty decided to get together and write a letter to the editor of the local and state newspapers in hopes of reaching out to others sharing the importance of having strong early childhood programs for young children. I heard a few of the responses but not many and am not sure if those who penned the letter had received much feedback. But nevertheless, this was a great first step.

I know that years ago, some of the others had recommended not placing any of our potential early childhood teachers in local kindergarten programs, citing not so positive program models. Not much had been stated, but with some of our master's level students being out as practicing teachers, one could get a clearer picture of some of the frustrations of those teachers.

What Has Happened That Brought about Drastic Changes in Kindergarten Program

To be honest, I am not sure of all of the stories nor the accuracy of too many stories afloat about the ineffectiveness of today's kindergarten programs in meeting the needs of our students.

Kindergarten Teachers

It has been the dreams of many kindergarten teachers, just like it was for me and that is to provide a good, positive program for those students who just left the preschool level (or are of the age of having attended) or those who are about to venture into the world of becoming a first grader.

Some kindergarten teachers find themselves in positions of too many inappropriate changes in their expectations in regard to their relationships with their students and families. Many have been forced to change kindergarten into primary grade classrooms with high expectations and often that results in failure for all involved—the children, the teachers, the administrators, family support workers, administrators, and all involved in the demand for change that has proven to be ineffective.

So Who's Going to Speak Out, Speak Up on the Matter?

When this question came to mind, as I could not help but think back over my years as a preschool-kindergarten teacher in a multiage classroom. I can vividly remember that we two teachers were somehow required to administer the Metropolitan Readiness Test, the red book or the green one. One was for our 4-year-old preschoolers and one was for our kindergarteners. As I said previously, I do not recall from whom the orders/request came from? Nor can I say how long they had been administering these tests prior to my arrival.

It was so interesting observing the actions of the preschoolers as well as the kindergartners who were enrolled in my classroom. The tests were to be administered in the cafeteria area of the building. Now when I look back I am truly grateful that we did not have to give them in our classrooms.

So another unfortunate fact is that the cafeteria with its poor lighting seemed to be rather cold and callous to me. The real impact on that atmosphere should be considered by all when planning to approach young children with this task.

Luckily the space did not look the same as when we went to the area for lunch time. Certainly would not have been too cool to have children dislike coming to the area where lunches are served daily because of the negative connotations of taking these inappropriate tests.

So notes were sent home to parents informing them that their child would be taking the standardized test during the next week. That was all of the information that we as the teachers provided at the request of the administration. The only request that we received from the parents was that they be informed of the results as they related to their child. So I don't think the administration wanted the results released to parents or others since this was like a pilot testing. They were also very careful about releasing any standardized scores to parents at all other grade levels in the school entirely. I think that it was very clear that the administration realized the anxiety that can be experienced by parents with all of the uncertainties of administering these types of tests to their children. Overall, I think everyone is usually nervous about how the results would be used. Where would these results go? Where would these results be stored? Who has access to these results? What are the purposes for the call for administering these tests anyhow? Surely, the validity and reliability of these tests were open to doubt. Certainly, these tests would not be used to assess and evaluate teacher effectiveness as it relates to student performance.

The Results and Actions Taken As a Result of the Implementation of Testing

Being the protective, caring, considerate, concerned teacher that I am, I was very sensitive about how these tests would impact the lives of the children, their families, and my relationships with them. Although it did not concern me, I could see the results down the road in regard to the potential for something not too positive happening. Again, I was hopeful that I was not overanxious about the whole matter and process myself.

So the day before we were actually administering the first part of the test, I made a brief statement to the children that the next day, we would be going downstairs to take a test. What I as the kindergarten teacher experienced next seemed so devastating to me. All ages of my students began to show what I thought was to be considered—"test anxiety." I must admit this was rather shocking for me, because of my naivety that they would more than likely not know much about a test and would not take it too seriously and go in and just try to find the right answers the best way they could like many of us as high schoolers and post-secondary students do. These students began asking me questions such as "Suppose I fail?" "What about if I don't do well?" "What will my mom and dad say if I don't do well?" I tried to answer the questions as best I could without appearing to be hypocritical. So I as the teacher did the best that I could trying to squelch some of the anxieties.

Now the Tests—Days of the Testing

So now it's time for us to go downstairs for the actual testing—day 1 has now arrived, it's official and here we go. The only thing that I could say is that it was now in my hands. I had the test booklets and in the environment's presence—just me and the students. So some of the typical things that teachers and schools must consider about the fact of the students being properly spaced so that they could not copy or help each other really was not necessary. The important point was dealing with these young children's early knowledge of test anxiety. I had to quickly realize that the children's exposures to others all around them had made them aware of the importance of passing a test and how their connections realized that supposedly there was value in doing well.

So I began by passing out the red booklets to the preschoolers and the green booklets to the kindergartners. Difficult challenge #1: I was required to administer both tests and was doing at the same time. So figured out space wise as well as allowing for "freedom gaps of devaluing the anxiety time between each question."

So as I began with question #1 for the preschoolers, I realized right way that I had a big problem that was bigger than the actual test. Difficult challenge #2: "Put your finger on the cup" which was to be the student's marker of beginning and then what they were to do on that row's instruction would follow. I realized right away that these young children had no concept of the simplest step in taking the test and that was to put their finger on the cup which was at the beginning of the first row where they were going to touch the answer to the first question on the test. So as I walked around helping these children put their finger on the cup, I realized that there were some basic instructions and concepts that we had not covered in class like, "row." The child had to understand and know that they needed to stay on the row where the answer was straight across from that cup that they had put their finger on. Difficult challenge #3: they were all over the page, way over the page, in the middle, at the bottom when they should have been at the top on one row. So I knew from this behavior alone that there was no way that they could possibly get the answers correct. These actions of the children preschoolers and kindergartners disturbed me greatly causing me a sleepless night after test day 1.

Someone, Please Come See What My Children Are Doing on This Test

So when I went to school the next day, I decided that it was time that I let my kindergartner teacher voice be heard on behalf of the students and families that we serve. Our school was one of excellence and believed in developmentally appropriate practice. This was one of the only schools that did not require grade level texts in reading and math; instead, we were granted the freedom of using the language experience approach in helping children learn through their child-centered language acquisition/development approach. We teachers were proud to stand up and tell the world that the approaches that we were using worked; we knew it and guaranteed that our students would be able to stand out among any of their peers from school districts that used textbooks as well as teacher-directed curricula and teachings. Our students learned through experiences that were meaningful to them, thus they were intrinsically motivated to learn. Add on top of all of that parents who were concerned about the welfare of their children and who were very involved and active in their education. Our home–school connections were among some of the best that I have seen throughout my many years of teaching.

So my question is "with all of this great-teaching-learning, what are we doing in this cafeteria administering a standardized test and our children are in no way used to any of this style of learning? Is this fair to them? Is this fair to these innovative and creative teachers who provide some of the most stimulating learning experiences in the United States?

So early that morning after day 1 and a sleepless night for me as the teacher, I needed to go ask for help on behalf of my students, who looked so teary-eyed, knowing that we were supposed to go back downstairs in that dreadful cafeteria to take day 2's part of the test. So I asked the teacher associate to stay in the room with the students as they arrived, while I hurriedly went upstairs to talk with the principal about this fiasco. So I decided to invite him down to the area as I was administering day 2 of the test. I pointed out to him how devastating this was for me as the teacher to see the painful actions of the children. I also pointed out that I wanted him to observe with his own eyes the fact there was no way that they could mark the correct answer when they had no knowledge how to stay on the row where they needed to mark the correct answer.

The Principal Sees the Kindergarten Fiasco Himself

So as I returned to my classroom, I felt somewhat better that I was relieved of the fact that I was bold enough to go and approach my boss, the principal, about an administrative decision that he had made for whatever reason. So I felt like the only hope that I had was if I could convince this non-early childhood person to use the naked eyes to see the effects of this inappropriate test on these students. I did not point out about whether he was prepared to share with parents of these gifted, talented, and eager-to-learn students that their child did not do so well on an inappropriate standardized test that the National Association for the Education of Young Children (NAEYC) decried and opposed? But I knew this would be the next part of him taking an in-depth well rounded decision about this test. He typically had the support of these parents and I knew he wanted to keep it that way.

So now that he had arrived, I began administering the test just I had done the day before. I spent most of the time on question 1, part 2 a second day because they could not stay on the row, therefore they could not find the right answer, they were going crisscross the page, from top to bottom. It was like a miracle after the principal observed a few minutes of the test and told me to stop. He said to me, "Stop the test right now." I knew that he had seen enough to convince him of how inappropriate this was.

But he explained that pressures began to rise on schools that did not necessarily have written data to support the documentation of their students' performance. But he knew that we had data, especially observation recordings, document boards and books, and many video and audio recordings. So thank goodness, I was able to stand up and address this issue without fear of loss of my job. More of us educators need to stand up with so many inappropriate issues that are facing our children today.

People in High Places Making Inappropriate Kindergarten Decisions

It is still amazing to me that there are people in high administrative positions who are making so many of the inappropriate decisions about curricula, school attendance patterns, teacher qualifications, school schedule patterns, etc. who need to come down and out of these positions.

So What Has Happened to Our Good Best Practices Early Childhood Classrooms?

I am not really sure, but many claim that the reasons for so many inappropriate and disastrous changes in early childhood programs are the results of "No Child Left Behind." Do you agree or disagree with this? So teachers are forced to have additional and more instruction time? Is that accurate? So let's see what is really going on in so many schools where early childhood students are suffering. Is anyone looking and listening to the cries of children?

Recently, I spent the entire day in a kindergarten classroom. I was asked to go in to see if I could help, because there are some challenging children in this particular classroom.

1. So upon my early arrival the classroom teacher had to leave because the well-known, well-respected former principal had died. But before I could get to the classroom where I was assigned, a teacher-staff person from the school was standing in the hallway with a Black male student, whom I just guessed was in first grade, but wasn't sure. But this staff person, who also was Black, wanted me to know that they were standing in the hallway waiting for mom to come get him because he did not want to be at school. Okay there were so many questions that went through my mind that I decided not to say anything since I had just arrived, had no background information on this situation, and so silence was my best bet at this time. I had to remember that I was asked to please come and help in the kindergarten classroom.
2. But I am free to share my initial thoughts on seeing the teacher-staff saying that this child was waiting for mom to come back and pick him up to take him back home. But I can share my thoughts with just this initial experience, right?
   a. School had only started 30 minutes earlier. So what was the main point; what had happened with this child in the past 30 minutes prior to my arrival?
   b. Is this an everyday happening? Is this child allowed to go back home at his request?
   c. This child is a Black male student and sorry but most of them need to be in school every possible minute to be assured that they have a fair and equal opportunity for learning and advancement.

And Now I Am in This Kindergarten Classroom

I was going to give my opinions on the classroom, but I knew that the teacher was considered as one of the best and she has been identified for a while as genuinely caring for her students despite their backgrounds.

1. The teacher's approach to discipline was tied into her teaching style and expectations of her students. She wanted to make sure they understood that while she was away for the day that the rules and expectations are the same as if she were still there.
2. As soon as she left, they immediately decided to test the water by beginning to quietly misbehave, but I was able to help them to stop right away.
3. The morning seemed rather challenging for the substitute teacher and the other adult who was assisting.

IMPORTANT! PLEASE SEE THE NEXT CHAPTER ON WHAT IS HAPPENING IN OUR KINDERGARTEN CLASSROOMS—THE SCHEDULE, CURRICULA, TEACHER, KNOWLEDGE EXPECTATIONS, EXPERIENCES, STUDENT INTERACTIONS, PARENTAL RESPONSES, INQUIRIES, ETC.

Chapter 7

Home Visits

All over the United States, school districts are continuing to explore and establish teacher–family home visiting programs.

There are many reasons for why school districts have decided to make home visits a part of their family engagement models. These visitations allow for parents to become actively involved in their child's education. Some say there are messages portrayed to children and parents about how much the teacher cares.

Principal Charlie Denis, Saddle Ranch Elementary School, Highlands Ranch, Colorado, shares about a pilot visitation program conducted by his school, "Parents, teachers, and students were very positive in their response." Parent–teacher communication has been a beacon light in the school. This relationship really developed into an even more supportive and stronger one after teachers participated in a 1-year home visitation program.

Thus some administrators share and express their feelings about home visitation programs as direct evidence of how they can make a difference in the learning experiences of children.

Home visit programs that provide the appropriate resources for teachers to visit students and their parents have shown many successes such as:

1. The teacher can learn more about the students.
2. The teacher can get the parents more involved in their child's learning.
3. The teacher can help bridge cultural/ethnic gaps that may occur between the teacher and parents.
4. Teachers can help bring about a lasting effect on child, parent, and parent–teacher communication.

Home Visits Are Not New

It is a well-known fact that Head Start programs have had home visits as an integral part of their model for many years.

Fact: Head Start teachers are required to make a minimum of two home visits for each student during the school year.

Fact: Required home visits are in addition to regularly scheduled parent-family conferences.

Fact: Many kindergarten programs in the United States also require home visits by teachers before school starts. These have various purposes besides the teacher getting to meet the families. This is also a great time to make sure all of those needed forms and required paperwork are completed and submitted. Also, this is a time to help if there are parents with English as a second language or families with minimal education that may have limited or hindering experiences causing them to not complete some of the needed information.

Cross Grade-Age Level Home Visits

It has been a pleasure for advocates of home visits to recognize that home visits are now across grade and age levels. They are also being more accepted around the world.

Fact: It has been noted that schools in Japan, Australia, England, as well as the United States report that home visits have all been successful.

Fact: School age and programs in the United States as well as in other countries require that teachers visit student's homes at least once a year.

Fact: When teachers visit students' homes, there are many formats that are used.

Fact: Each visit takes on variant approaches with them being different by school as well as each teacher.

Fact: While there is not always much information on the funding of home visits, it definitely impacts the nature of the required visits.

Fact: While the approach is highly recommended for teachers to travel in pairs, it is also the preferred format for them.

Fact: Teachers who travel in pairs report feeling more comfortable and safer.

Fact: Teachers who travel in pairs may also benefit from having an interpreter/translator as a part of the travel team.

Fact: Other teachers still visits one-on-one with the parent rather than in pairs.

Fact: With many of the one-on-one visits in particular, teachers often take learning activities/experiences to share with the parent and child.

Fact: Home visits vary from 30 to 90 minutes depending on need, the teacher, and the planned activities/experiences.

Fact: Because of the variant forms of communication, many of the teachers at Saddle Ranch Elementary School personally scheduled their home visits by telephone.

Fact: Some ask what are some of the purposes of home visits and they vary. They are to learn about 1) student needs, 2) student interests, 3) student concerns, and 4) establishment of rapport with family.

Fact: Schools and teachers must be prepared for the various scheduling because family schedules can be very different.

Fact: Finding a mutually agreeable time for teachers and parents to meet can be difficult.

Fact: At another school in North Carolina, some of the teachers reportedly go to the workplace of the parents to do the home visit. These are called site visits.

Fact: At another school district in South Carolina, a home visit program was started and implemented with three teachers whose sole responsibilities were to make home visits.

Fact: One report shared that these three teachers made about 719 home visits with parents.

Fact: The South Carolina school district has grown from three teachers to 22 parent educators. These educators conduct monthly home visits.

Fact: In addition to the parent educators, the teachers conduct three home visits annually in addition to the parent educators' visits.

Fact: Some school districts especially require home visits for 4-year-olds. This is to help prepare them to be successful in first grade.

Fact: In districts where some teachers were given the option of home visits or not, those who did not want to do them the first year participated by the next year because of the enthusiasm seen from the home visits in teachers and families.

Fact: Those school districts that have home visits as a required part of employment make sure that they inform the teachers before hiring them. They want them to know of the importance of their beliefs in home visits.

Funding Sources of Home visits

Fact: Funding for home visits come from a variety of sources.

Fact: Some home visit funding comes from state funds for school districts.

Fact: In one school district, a local Rotary Club gave the school district funds for teacher home visits.

Fact: Some home visits are funded by the federal government's Title I program.

Fact: One school district received grant funding from a local university for home visits.

Fact: Another school district received donations from charitable and humanitarian organizations for home visits.

Fact: Some schools incorporate home visits into teacher contact/contract days, just as if they were teaching.

So Where Do We Stand?

As expected, some teachers do not feel comfortable going on home visits at first. The idea of visiting their students' home was a little frightening for some. Many shared that once the visits actually begin those fears disappeared.

In some districts, if a parent is uncomfortable with the teacher coming to their homes, they were invited to meet with the teacher at school.

The Truth from Parents and Teachers

School districts seem to truly believe that encouraging parents to become more engaged in their child's education by allowing for home visits has been positive for parents and teachers.

It is truly believed that as we delve in the future job descriptions for teachers, there will be more districts requiring home visits as a part of the teacher's jobs.

Online Links to Resources on Home Visits
A Guide to Home Visits

The Michigan Department of Education's Division of Early Childhood Programs produced this thorough guide. Sample forms included.

A Guide to Team Home Visits

This guide from the San Francisco Unified School District provides rationale, preparation tips, protocols, timelines, and other suggestions.

Recruiting for Opening Day

Explains how one district uses home visits to ensure that all students attend class on the first day of school.

Strategies to Serve and Involve Families

This paper discusses seven schools' parent involvement programs; six of the schools employ homevisitors as part of their programs.

Excellence in Education through Innovative Alternatives

You can read the testimony several educators gave before a Senate subcommittee on education. Some testimony related to home visit programs in Greenville, South Carolina.

Parents Grateful That Teachers Make House Calls

This CNN article discusses a home visitation program in Sacramento from the parents' point of view.

Bill Calls for Parent-Teacher Home Visitations

This article talks about the California Legislation that created funding for teacher home visits.

Source: *Amy Schulting from the Center for Child and Family Policy at Duke, The Kindergarten Home Visit Project*

It becomes more and more amazing how homevisits can be the turning point for successful strategies in early childhood education.

The recommendations are that homevisits should between infancy and 4 years old. For some they feel that waiting until kindergarten is late for some children. The transition to a positive kindergarten program is critical for meaningful academic performance and social/emotional development.

They are also looking for answers to ways of engaging parents in the educational process before children's first day of school. Thus, meaningful collaboration and communication are very important between schools and families prior to a child's transition to kindergarten and beyond. One answer that schools are looking at closely is the process of home visits.

Many early childhood educators do home visits in hopes of informing parents of child development as well as effective parenting strategies.

Amy Schulting, being a prior teacher, decided to use a different approach to home visits when she developed the Kindergarten Home Visit Project. In the research of this project included 44 teachers from 19 elementary schools and 928 families.

In this Kindergarten Home Visit Project, they did a reversal of the roles of parents and teachers as far as expectations.

So Ms. Schulting decided that the goals of this project were not to change families, but to listen to them and better understand them.

Thus, teachers who participated in this project spent time to learn about each child and their family. Interestingly, the parent would be the expert. This was the opposite of what typically happened in the home visits. Usually the teacher provided information to the parent about the child's performance and areas that could be improved upon. There are usually activities that could be shared at home.

Very seldom are there opportunities for parents to share their areas of expertise regarding their own children.

This type of home visit allowed for the parents to share about their own children in their homes. Parents shared that they felt so much better because of the value of being heard by their child's teacher.

1. The project was evaluated using a randomized study.
2. The study revealed positive outcomes for families and teachers.
3. Teachers reported that there were improved relationships with the families.
4. Teachers reported that this allowed them to reach out to non-English-speaking parents also.
5. Non-English-speaking parents reported that there were fewer barriers to the development of their relationships with their children's school.
6. Teachers and parents shared how much they enjoyed these home visits.
7. Teachers and parents found that home visits were the connective forms of communication needed for the success of the children.

Source: Home Visiting Program Supports Early Childhood Education *Authored by Heidi S. Roibal* Aug. 25, 2014

Children are our state's most precious resource. Kids Count ranked New Mexico lowest in children's well-being of all the 50 states. Although we have many unique challenges, we also have unique resources in New Mexico such as home visiting and other prevention services that can help address this issue.

Home Visiting Program in New Mexico

Home visiting has strong backgrounds in New Mexico. They are recognized as national leaders in this area. Their home visiting began around a basis of welcoming new parents. They are among one of the only where the development of universal voluntary home visiting serves families from pregnancy up to age 5.

New Mexico is also one of the first states to implement a standards-based program as well as merge evidence-based federally funded home visiting programs together to create a common system of infrastructure, with a vision, goals, and quality components that support short-term and long-term outcomes. In the model, there is a framework to promote the child's well-being and to prevent adverse childhood experiences. So Mexico's families are supported through the home visiting program. There are some long-term goals:

1. That babies are born healthy
2. That children are nurtured by parents and those who care for them

The New Mexico Home Visiting Program Can Benefit from Our Help

The program appreciates partners and collaborators to enhance the home visiting program. They are looking for supporters in the following areas to enhance collaborative opportunities for children and their families:

1. Early interventionists/specialists
2. Child care personnel
3. Pre-K program directors/staff
4. Family childcare providers/sponsors/staff
5. Head Start Program Directors/Leaders

6. Kindergarten teachers/administrators
7. Prenatal program specialists
8. Visit http://cyfd.org/homevisiting to help or inquire

Many school districts have established successful teacher home visit programs. Home visitations by teachers get parents involved in their child's education, and they let parents and children know how much teachers care.

Also, programs that provide time and funding for teachers to visit students and parents on their own turf are a way for teachers to learn more about their students, get the parents more involved in their child's education, and bridge cultural gaps that might occur between student and teacher. Most teachers report their home visits have a lasting effect on the child, the parent, and parent–teacher communication.

Home visits by teachers aren't a new idea. The Head Start program has used them for many years. Head Start teachers are required to make at least two home visits for each student during each school year, in addition to regular parent–teacher conferences at school. Many U.S. kindergartens also require home visits by teachers before school starts.

Teachers' visits to students' homes can take many forms. The visitation approach might vary from school to school and usually depends on the funding source. In some schools, teachers prefer to travel in pairs to their visits. They feel more comfortable that way and sometimes need a translator in order to communicate with a child's parents. Other teachers visit one-on-one with the parent. Some interact with the child and the parent. Many teachers may bring along learning activities for the child that also involve a parent's participation. Normally, visits can last anywhere from 30 to 90 minutes, depending on the teacher and the activities.

When teachers get to know their students and their families, the parents become powerful advocates in their children's education. Home visits can give teachers the insight they need to help all students succeed.

Summary

- There are six benefits of home visiting programs
    1. Home visits provide organized visits by professionals and paraprofessionals and provide support to/for families.
    2. Moms and babies are healthier because of visits before and after birth of the child.
    3. Children are better prepared for school because home visiting helps with age-appropriate books, engagement in organized learning, and safe play environments, thus providing positive long-term effects.
    4. Children are safer. Home visiting programs are associated with reduced child abuse and injuries.
    5. Families are more self-sufficient—Participating in heisting programs lead the parents to increased rates of enrollment in educational/training programs, thus allows for improved and increased hours during employment adding to their income level.
    6. Home visiting programs save money—the short-term and long-term benefits of home visit programs outweigh the cost for implementation. Research shows returns of $5.70 return for every dollar spent.

Family Resources for Home Visits

Books to Read: http://growingbookbybook.com/101-books-read-kids-kindergarten/

What To Do: http://www.pre-kpages.com/home-visits/

Activities to Do: https://www.teacherspayteachers.com/Product/Summer-Color-Activities-for-Generalization-Autism-Early-Childhood-1863163

Goals of Home Visits: http://mchb.hrsa.gov/maternal-child-health-initiatives/home-visiting-overview

Results of Home Visits: http://www.pthvp.org/

Home Works: http://www.teacherhomevisit.org/about-home-works/program-models/school-wide-model/

There's No Place Like Home Visits: http://www.nea.org/home/34090.htm

First Home Visit: http://www.colorincolorado.org/article/making-your-first-ell-home-visit-guide-classroom-teachers

Positive Effects: http://www.projectappleseed.org/teacher-home-visits

The Power of Home Visits

- Home visits are a new and upcoming thing in our nation's school system. Due to the newness of this, one can imagine many parents/guardians struggling with the concept of an educator entering their homes. This source explains the many benefits of home visits, which may potentially help parents/guardians understand why we are pursuing to do this.
- Source: http://www.npr.org/sections/ed/2015/08/26/434358793/knock-knock-teachers-here-the-power-of-home-visits?utm_source=facebook.com&utm_medium=social&utm_campaign=npr&utm_term=nprnews&utm_content=20150826

What You Can Do As a Parent/Guardian(s)

- Since this is such a new concept, many parents/guardians are not quite sure what to expect. This source provides its readers with an overview of what they can do prior, during, and following the home visit.
- Source: http://www.nea.org/home/34090.htm

Building Relationships

- Connecting and building a strong relationship with their students is a huge goal of the average educator. By arranging a home visit, the relationship can really begin to grow. This source explains how this partnership truly can be built through this visit.
- Source: https://www.edutopia.org/blog/home-visits-reaching-beyond-classroom-jill-thomas
  Due to the fact that this concept is such a new and coming thing, there are many parents/guardians who have questions. This site answers some of those questions and some others they may be curious about.
- Source: http://www.teacherhomevisit.org/about-home-works/frequently-asked-questions-faq/

Letter to the Parents

- Since this visit will take place in the child's home, it is important that a time is arranged that fits into a parent/guardian's hectic schedule. This source provides a letter, in both English and Spanish, about the visit and arranging a time.
- Source: https://www.teacherspayteachers.com/Product/Home-Visit-Letter-To-Parents-English-and-Spanish-1663444

Ideas

- Home visits can be used for numerous things, for example, tutoring, activities, relationship building, etc. This source displays ideas of various activities that could be done and are presented by everyday ordinary people; this helps the reader better grasp what may be done in their upcoming home visit, or could potentially help an educator plan their next one.
- Source: http://www.perpetualpreschool.com/homevisitideas.html

Home Visitation Forms
- Due to the fact that the educators will be entering many different homes, it is important that proper documentation is kept and taken to ensure a safe and beneficial visit. This site provides its readers with a few different visitation forms that could be used to document the visit.
- Connecting and building a strong relationship with their students is a huge goal of the average educator. By arranging a home visit, the relationship can really begin to grow. This source explains how this partnership truly can be built through this visit.
- Source: https://www.edutopia.org/blog/home-visits-reaching-beyond-classroom-jill-thomas
- Due to the fact that this concept is such a new and coming concept, there are many parents/guardians who have questions. This site answers some of those questions and some others they may be curious about.
- Source: http://www.teacherhomevisit.org/about-home-works/frequently-asked-questions-faq/

From a Parent's Perspective
- Parents/guardians may understand why a home visit is being implemented these days, but they still may be hesitant on the matter. This source provides nervous parents/guardians with a parent's perspective on the matter and what they got out of their experience.
- Source: http://neatoday.org/2014/10/28/all-in-the-family-how-teacher-home-visits-can-lead-to-school-transformation/
- This source provides its readers with just about everything a parent/guardian could want to know regarding a home visit. It is a created handbook about the matter. From FAQ's to community engagements, this source provides a great resource.
- Source: https://eclkc.ohs.acf.hhs.gov/hslc/hs/resources/ECLKC_Bookstore/PDFs/05F613A8CC15D89DAFE1D1568DB0719A.pdf
- If a parent/guardian remains to be hesitant on the matter, even after reviewing these sources, I would recommend them looking into purchasing this packet that includes forms, profile forms, activities, etc., that could help them feel more prepared.
- Source: http://www.pre-kpages.com/home-visits/

Relationship Building
- Connecting and building a strong relationship with their students is a huge goal of the average educator. By arranging a home visit, the relationship can really begin to grow. This source explains how this partnership truly can be built through this visit.
- Source: https://www.edutopia.org/blog/home-visits-reaching-beyond-classroom-jill-thomas
- Due to the fact that this concept is such a new and coming thing, there are many parents/guardians who have questions. This site answers some of those questions and some others they may be curious about.
- Source: http://www.teacherhomevisit.org/about-home-works/frequently-asked-questions-faq/

Overview
- This source provides its readers with just about everything a parent/guardian could want to know regarding a home visit. It is a created handbook about the matter. From FAQ's to community engagements, this source provides a great resource.
- Source: https://eclkc.ohs.acf.hhs.gov/hslc/hs/resources/ECLKC_Bookstore/PDFs/05F613A8CC15D89DAFE1D1568DB0719A.pdf

Above and beyond
- If a parent/guardian remains to be hesitant on the matter, even after reviewing these sources, I would recommend them looking into purchasing this packet that includes forms, profile forms, activities, etc., that could help them feel more prepared.
- Source: http://www.pre-kpages.com/home-visits/

Parent Teacher Conference Packet: https://www.teacherspayteachers.com/Product/Free-Parent-Teacher-Conferences-Packet-for-3rd-6th-Grade-1461164
This electronic packet will be very good for the first couple of parent–teacher conferences that a new teacher has. It is important to use these documents so the new teacher knows they are on the right track. Once they understand what they are going to do at the conferences, then they can make their own documents. This is a good website to use for both the parents and the new teacher to get off to a good start.

Surveys for Parents: http://primarychalkboard.blogspot.com/2014/08/back-to-school-getting-to-know-your.html
This is a great blog that will help teachers prepare to talk to parents about what their students need. This website is great to get to know what other teachers have had success with. It also gives the do's and don'ts on what teachers need to do in during a meeting. Surveys are also good for one of the first times parents are meeting teachers. This survey would work great to get to know the parents of the students.

Parent Volunteers

50 Ideas For Parent Volunteers: http://daughtersandkindergarten.blogspot.com/2016/03/50-ideas-for-parent-volunteers.html

- This is a great website for teachers to get an idea about what parent volunteers can do with their time as a volunteer. Sometimes it is hard for teachers to come up with productive ways to use parent's help in the classroom, but this website helps find some ways of doing that. This was also made based upon other teachers' ideas from the past. That makes it easier for other teachers to use since it was already proven to work in the past. Teachers will have jobs for every parent from this list.

Chapter 8

Parent Conferences, Outdated or Time for a Change?

In the September 2016 issue of *Education Update* from the Association for Supervision and Curriculum Development (ASCD), the article Parent–Teacher Conferences: Outdated or Underutilized? considers how school administrators and teachers can improve upon the traditional parent–teacher conference. Harvard Family Research Project's M. Elena Lopez and Margaret Caspe recommend the following strategies for strengthening interactions between families and educators:

In the article about parent–teacher conferences, the questions are definitely relevant to what is going on in schools today. Parent–teacher conferences have been around for many years and is still typically traditional in every way except for a few exceptions.

Schools spend a substantial amount of time working on strategies and approaches to get parents to schools during scheduled parent–teacher conference times. Attitudes of those in educational arenas all over the United States have not changed in regard to parents who do not or cannot attend their child's parent–teacher conferences. Being an experienced teacher, I still recall how we preschool kindergarten teachers took the lead in asking the administration to listen to our pleas for some of the changes that were needed in conferences.

First of all the entire school conferences were for 2 days, 8:00 am to 5:00 pm. We began to ask questions about those parents whose schedules would not allow them to be available during those hours. For most of our parents who worked full time, this time frame would not work for them. Although some had found squeezing times such as their lunch hours or some could take time off of their jobs to attend conferences because they meant that much to them. However, we noticed that some of our parents worked in jobs where their schedules changed weekly. For example, one of my parents who was a nurse, worked days 1 week, evenings another week, and nights the third week. Some of them would not receive their work schedules until that week, which made planning ahead even more difficult for them. Also, some of the parents who worked in some of the food establishments found that they did not really have any time off and that they could lose their jobs if they just took the time off. A few were able to get someone else to cover for them while they take an hour or so off for conferences. However, if they had more than one child in the school, they needed additional time. Tough planning just to get the conference on their schedules.

Another need that we noticed was that it made it easier for many of the families if they could bring their child(ren) with them to the conference. Finding childcare for 1–2 hours is not appealing to many who are in the business. It is also not easy to get a babysitter for those limited hours, especially if and when they are paid by the hour. So we suggested that we have an area set up in our classroom for the child to play while we met with the parent(s). Of course this would work for some children and for others not.

We also tried having some university students to volunteer a few hours in our classroom or another designated area in our school to provide for the children while we met with the families.

Then we realized that school was not always a welcoming environment for some of our families. Low-income, minority and English as a second language parents seem to be the most hesitant about coming to parent conferences. Parents of those children with behavioral challenges, special needs, and those children who were not faring well in our schools, tended to be the parents who felt somewhat uncomfortable or were hesitant about coming to parent conferences at school. Parents who were receiving negative reports weekly on their children also reported that they didn't feel like they had anything to look forward to.

Also, it was obvious that many teachers need help, teaching, and training on what conferences are, their purposes, and the do's and don'ts for teachers when conducting them.

I can still recall any conference for any of my four children such that when I left I felt worse than when I came in. So I will take a few minutes to highlight those conferences. It is my hope that this chapter will cause all of us to take a closer look at parent–teacher conferences, what needs to be changed, eliminated, and what could be alternatives to the traditional parent conference.

Conference Travesty 1—The Teacher of A Bully

My son, I will call him Miguel (not his real name) was in middle school and his class went on a field trip where they were told to play race to be the first to get to a destination. So when he won and passed all of the children, I receive a note saying that my son was a bully and that they wanted to visit with me during parent conferences further since he was such a strong-built child.

Wow, there were a lot of problems with holding a conference on topics of my child winning the game, but yet he was being labeled as a bully. Sounds pretty nasty to me, when the rules were preestablished and he followed them to be the first. Should he be judged differently or fairly on his size? Did they really know what bullying is? Well they should have asked some of the bullies what it is. There were no complaints from the students, only the teacher who was the lead and observer.

"Let's cut to the chase," I said more than once. "How can we help him at home?"

The assertiveness paid off, at least in part. We left with good suggestions for how we can help our son get the most from his time in school, including a list of useful websites and ideas for out-of-class enrichment. I still thought the schedule was too frantic, but looked at the meetings as the start of a conversation, not the final word.

The conferences were a little more satisfying, but not entirely. That might be as good as it gets.

Conference Travesty 2—Angry Hostile Teacher

I had three out of four conferences to go to back to back. So the first two that I had attended were all positive and I had their portfolio samples with me. As I moved to the third conference, I was in an upbeat mood until I got in the room of Mrs. B. I really did not have much contact with this teacher, but did learn that my son Miguel was the only African American child in her room. So I was very interested in finding out how he was doing. All four of my children always loved school irrespective of what some of the circumstances or conditions might have been. So none of my children were at conferences with me and thank God my son was not at his. As I entered the classroom and was sort of waiting for the teacher to say hello and at least ask me to have a seat, she never did. So after a while I decided to sit down at what looked like it was the table where other parents had sat for their children's conference. So she went into a little office and came back out shortly afterward. What she did next, shocked me so bad that I could feel the tears begin to well up in my eyes.

She slammed and threw some papers down on the desk where I was sitting. Stunned, I was not used to seeing this type of behavior from no teacher, my children's or not. My son had won an award, but the way she presented it, you would have thought that he had committed a crime. She was hitting the table with his certificate as she meanly said he won an award on his leadership skills. She said it like she was angry that he had received the award, so I picked it up off the table. So then she proceeded to go to his classroom work, and she didn't know how to start with the positives, so she continued. He needs to improve on this, yet he was in the 90th percentile, so now I am totally confused. She proceeded and everything that she said was negative but did not correspond with how he really was doing. So she hurried through the conference as if she could not wait for me to get out of the conference and I couldn't wait to get out of her room. So I quickly gathered up my son's work, trying not to break down crying in her presence. I certainly did not want to give her the satisfaction of seeing me boo-hoo. So as I left out of the building, I thought what am I going to do? I certainly did not feel good about my son being in the same classroom with her. How did she treat him when I wasn't there and all of these thoughts went through my mind. When I got home, I told my husband about the travesty and he encouraged me to visit with the principal. I did the next day, and then she started writing my son letters of apology. But about a week later she was gone.

Next thing I knew they said she had gone back out west where she came from. Even after she got back out there she was still writing him these letters of apology until I had enough and stopped her. I do hope that no other teachers are conducting such conferences for if they are, they will probably be gone also.

Parents should come away from the meetings with a sense of their child's strengths as well as weaknesses, and a good idea of what they can do at home to help.

"You want to get information about your child's performance, you want to understand it, and you want to know what the school is going to do and what you can do to improve it," Weiss said.

Conference Travesty 3—The Standardized Test Teacher

Well this parent conference sort of went over the top of my head and I never tried to get it to come back to earth. When I got to this conference, the teacher decided that his role was to go over the Iowa Test of Basic Skills, which my children's school never focused on it a lot because these students ranked among the highest nationally in every other aspect of education attainment. He was trying to explain the scores to me and he really did not know what they meant and so he kept getting worse and worse with one mistake after another on his interpretation. So I thanked him and asked for a copy for my own perusal. He obliged me, I thanked him, and that was the end of that conference travesty. He had nothing else to show me about my child's overall performance in his class—wow, what a real failure as a teacher–meaningless parent conference.

"Do I think (standardized test scores) are important? No," said Chaya Rubenstein, a retired special education teacher from Cook County School District 130 in Blue Island. "You should be more interested in the classroom, how kids are doing in the subject areas, how they're doing socially and emotionally and what you can do for them (at home). The teachers will tell you all of those things."

How to Get the Most Out of Parent Conferences

Usually when there is a comment about what can be done to make parent conferences more effective and meaningful, it is important to consider the roles of the parents so that there would be collaborative input.

1. Begin by showing empathy toward each other.
2. Teachers should develop an ongoing understanding, especially before conferences.

3. When appropriate, make sure that teachers present data in an appropriate manner understood by families.
4. Use meaningful action steps that allow families to assist with and support their child's education while at home.
5. Districts can improve their school's data systems so that they are more family-friendly.
6. Be in touch with parents on an ongoing basis throughout the year, keeping channels of communication open.

As we continue providing information that we hope will be helpful to the readers, the issue of increasing parental/family attendance at parent conferences continues to be at the forefront. Also, we will include ideas from schools all across the United States that are thinking of innovative and creative ways to provide more meaningful family engagement experiences and finding alternatives to the traditional parent conferences.

Being a parent of four children, there were always various types of emotions that occurred before the time to attend parent conferences. Not sure if there was nervousness about what the teachers may say or questions they may ask. I was always hopeful that if any of my children were having any difficulties that their teachers would let me know before arriving at the conferences. I always thought that it seemed rather insensitive to wait until parent conferences if we had some very important information that parents needed to know.

Being a teacher who conducted parent conferences always made it even more interesting when it was time for me to go to my own children's parent conference. The overwhelming number of conferences that we originally had to do in 2 days really got to us prior to stepping forward to let the administration know that we had double the number of students compared to other teachers at various grade levels. We were doing 40–30 minute conferences in 2 days while other teachers were doing 20 in 2 days. Unless you were in our shoes, I do not believe that people really even realized what we had to do. Take a look at this schedule:

Conference Day One
8:00–8:30: Parents 1
8:30–9:00: Parents 2
9:00–9:30: Parents 3
9:30–10:00: Parents 4
10:00–10:30: Parents 5
10:30–11:00: Parents 6
11:00–11:30: Parents 7
11:30–12:00: Lunch break
12:00–12:30: Parents 8
12:30–1:00: Parents 9
1:00–1:30: Parents 10
1:30–2:00: Parents 11
2:00–2:30: Parents 12
2:30–3:00: Parents 13
3:00–3:30: Parents 14
3:30–4:00: Parents 15
4:00–4:30: Parents 16
4:30–5:00: Parents 17
5:00–5:30: Parents 18
5:30–6:00: Parents 19
6:00–6:30: Parents 20

Conference Day Two
8:00–8:30: Parents 1
8:30–9:00: Parents 2
9:00–9:30: Parents 3
9:30–10:00: Parents 4
10:00–10:30: Parents 5
10:30–11:00: Parents 6
11:00–11:30: Parents 7
11:30–12:00: Lunch break
12:00–12:30: Parents 8
12:30–1:00: Parents 9
1:00–1:30: Parents 10
1:30–2:00: Parents 11
2:00–2:30: Parents 12
2:30–3:00: Parents 13
3:00–3:30: Parents 14
3:30–4:00: Parents 15
4:00–4:30: Parents 16
4:30–5:00: Parents 17
5:00–5:30: Parents 18
5:30–6:00: Parents 19
6:00–6:30: Parents 20

We had two groups of students, half in the am class and the other half in the pm class. When we switched to alternate full days the numbers remained the same.

We decided to go to the administration and ask for a third day of conferences and that did lighten up our schedule some. So we decided to do either 12+12+12=36

Then we were able to have four other conferences after school or during the lunch period if needed. The schedule of 12 conferences per day was much lighter than 20 per day for 2 days.

Some schools have only 15 minute conferences which have caused many parents to say they felt rushed and when they left they really wondered how could they help their children at home. So there are many who do not feel 15 minutes is sufficient to give the needed information on their children.

Advanced Preparation and Planning Can Help

The issue of sufficient time for conferences is still a question today. Harvard Family Research Project's Director Heather B. Weiss shared that those teachers who plan in advance can make an important difference in making conferences more meaningful as well as informative.

She shares that when parents know what type of information they would like to learn about their children's performance and any answers to questions they may have certainly adds to making the meetings more positive, productive, and satisfying.

One very important addition that I came up with prior to my parent conferences really seems to make a difference for my families during parent–teacher conferences. I sent home a list of questions that I will be responding to during conference and if I didn't cover them, encouraged the parents to ask about it. Also I encouraged parents to bring this parent bring-with-you sheet to the conference and have their own questions for me jotted down on the form. Wow, did this make conferences go smoother. Parents seem to have felt so much more empowered. They would walk into the conference with their conference-bring-along sheet and felt like they knew what was going to happen during conferences.

So I had the questions divided under four categories which would be similar to the written conference reports that they would get to take home with them.

Parent Conferences-Bring-along-Questions
Social-Emotional Development
1. Does my child interact with other children?
2. Does my child participate in group discussions/language experiences
3. Does my child listen and/or is attentive during group activities?
4. Does my child seem to have a positive attitude about school/learning?

Work/Play Habits/Interests
1. Does my child seem to enjoy a variety of activities, materials, experiences?
2. Does my child choose the same activities most of the time or do they show different interests at different times?
3. Is my child able to complete assigned tasks?
4. Is my child able to complete assigned tasks or work independently?

Cognitive/Academic Learning—Math/Literacy
1. Is my child showing an interest in books?
2. Is my child showing an interest in learning letters, numbers, and shapes?
3. Is my child able to recognize his/her name and other significant environmental words?
4. Does my child show an interest in writing words, names, or drawing objects?

Fine Motor/Gross Motor Development
1. Is my child able to dress/undress independently during swimming and outside play?
2. Is my child able to climb on the outside apparatus or show an interest in using the equipment?
3. Is my child able to walk on a balance beam, catch a ball, hop, and gallop?
4. Is my child able to cut with scissors?
5. Is my child able to trace letters, numbers, and shapes?

Other Questions—Jot Down Your Own to Bring with You!
So as this article focused on ways that teachers can help focus on how children are performing in the classroom, especially with some of the cognitive areas, I highly recommend the original idea that I used and saw work.

Alternatives to Parent Conferences
1. Eliminating parent–teacher conferences is not the answer.
2. Five minutes is definitely not enough time for a parent conference, some say this short time makes it feel like speed dating.
3. There are some creative ideas that can be implemented while still maintaining parent–teacher conferences.
4. Allow parents to participate in student presentations as well as parent conferences. Parents would reserve a time to be in the presentations room to see their child's presentation. Teacher facilitators would be in the room to make sure there is smooth sailing. Parent–teacher conferences are still held during this same time.

a. Have parent–teacher conferences in fall and student-led conferences in spring.
b. Provide parents with the option of attending a student-led conference or the traditional parent–teacher conferences.
c. Those who choose the student-led conferences can observe their child's presentation at school. Those who choose the traditional conferences will view their child's presentation at home.
d. Hold traditional parent conferences in the fall and then BRAG Night in the spring which allows students to give an annual reflection of their work, share their portfolios while a teacher is in the room facilitating if necessary.
e. Allow for the same option as in d, except for the traditional conference selectors, the student would share their portfolio progress reports nightly at home for a week.

The idea of allowing students to feel/experience ownership over their achievements and honoring/respecting the roles that parents and teachers play in helping students meet their goals are key.

Those who advocate that our traditional parent conferences are outdated, state how and why there needs to be some adaptations, adjustments, eliminations of some parts, etc.

Here are some additional alternatives and innovative ideas for replacing parts of outdated conferences:

1. **Group Conference:** This is where teachers and parents meet as a group three times a year. Each parent learns about benchmarks, assessment data, and setting academic goals for their child. Then the parent also has one individual conference during the school year.
2. **Student Showcase:** This should be an annual event where family members as well as community members are invited to come be a part of the student highlighting his/her work which would include 21st-century skills.
3. **Grade-Level Dialogues:** These are conversations that are organized around students' academic success and are held between parents and teachers. Teachers will host an across grade levels meeting, exchanging information and encouraging parents to find ways to support each other.
4. **Student-Led Conference:** Students help document their school work and are taught how to prepare and share this information during conferences.
5. **Off-Campus Conference:** Stop complaining about those parents who never show up. Some can't take time off from work, others are not so comfortable with the school environment. So why not take the conference where there is a mutual agreement on a place or even a telephone call or video conference may have to suffice.

Erin Anderson
Middle School Tests: A Flexible Schedule to Personalize Learning
Ankeny Looks for Alternatives to Parent Conferences

A school district in Iowa found out that in Spring, 2015, only 33 percent of the parents attended conferences at the high school level. Knowing that percentage was very low to say that the conferences were effective was not true. So the school district began to look for alternative ways to communicate with parents.

1. They began to look at the possibilities of email or video conferencing to keep parents updated on their child's academic progress.
2. The district noticed that by eighth and ninth grades and then in high school, parental attendance at conferences began to decrease.

3. It is recognized that there are challenges to the traditional conference format because the differences in elementary and middle high school conferencing. In the elementary grades, children mostly have one teacher, but in the upper grades they have several teachers. Thus parents complain of the difficulties in tracking down all of their child's teachers during conferences, especially if there are no limits placed on some parents.
4. It was also found that schools are not as considerate as they should be when it comes to parents' work schedules and those who rely on public transportation. In one survey, parents noted that they had long wait times and still missed opportunities to meet with their child's teachers. One parent complained of being in the area for 3 hours trying to meet with teachers.
5. New options the district is looking into include video conferencing, telephone calls, emails and special software that can allow teachers to send video messages online. They are also looking how to have more frequent interactions with parents throughout the year, rather than twice a year
6. Trent Grundmeyer, a Drake professor suggested looking into virtual parent–teacher conferences through use of a Flip Grid, which is a video collaboration tool that allows teachers to send 3-minute videos to parents. Thus, this helps with the complaint of not hearing from all of their child's teachers. The parent can hear from each teacher on their own time such as hearing from six teachers in a row.
7. Teachers felt that they could reach out more to parents who typically do not come to conferences.
8. Another school district with low parental attendance tried having teachers schedule one-on-one classroom appointments with parents of at-risk children, but still scheduled time for all parents during regularly scheduled conference days.
9. It is very critical at the high school level for parents and teachers to find positive ways of communicating because this is the time when students begin to really focus on college readiness.

Reflecting Back Over Whether We Need Conferences or Not?

1. Parents are now able to view student grades online on a consistent/regular basis.
2. Many teachers and counselors make it a part of their responsibilities to regularly communicate with families. In so doing, they share positive information on student progress and challenges.
3. Those students who are struggling or at-risk are parents are met with frequent phone calls trying to collaborate on some ways to help the students. All of this takes place prior to parent–teacher conferences.
4. Some say that by the time students reach high school that parents have heard the same information for most students over the years.
5. The real idea behind parent conferences is supposed to be to support student success while engaging parents, but if the parents are not coming to the conferences, there must be alternatives for more creative family-friendly ways to share and support student learning.

So what if, instead of parent–teacher conferences, we used the allotted and required parent–teacher conference days to plan for and conduct student showcases?

Research suggests that having student showcases should be part of the solution to this ongoing important problem.

Student showcases are typically annual events where others are invited to share with the student authentic work showing their valuable skills that can connect them to the community and may lead to future opportunities.

In closing, here are a few suggestions for some student showcase ideas:

1. Culinary-cooking demonstrations.
2. Mini-choir, orchestra and band concerts, including solo presentations.
3. Students in fashion, floral design, and other artistic skills present.

4. Presenting new knowledge of foreign language, making speeches, or special research projects.
5. Science or lab experiment presentations.
6. Health/PE students sharing games or other physical skill building activities.
7. Students in photography, technology, or computer programming share either newly learned skills or newly created ones.

Source: How to Get the Most Out of Parent–Teacher Conferences (Chicago Tribune, Oct. 6, 2016)

Parent–Teacher Conferences Resources

http://families.naeyc.org/learning-and-development/child-development/parent-teacher-conferences
https://www.nhsa.org/event/2015-parent-and-family-engagement-conference
http://www.hfrp.org/var/hfrp/storage/fckeditor/File/Parent-Teacher-ConferenceTipSheet-100610.pdf
http://www.colorincolorado.org/article/tips-successful-parent-teacher-conferences-bilingual-families
http://eclkc.ohs.acf.hhs.gov/hslc/tta-system/family
http://kindergartensquared.blospot.com/2013/10/conference-tips-and-ideas.html
http://www.parenting.com/article/5-smart-ways-to-handle-teacher-troubles
http://www.scholastic.com/teachers/top-teaching/2013/10/tips-setting-parent-teacher-conferences
https://www.teacherspayteachers.com/Product/Student-Led-Conferences-877626
http://www.educationworld.com/a_admin/admin/admin112.shtml
https://s-media-cache-ak0.pinimg.com/564x/7c/ae/c8/7caec86b67e64442d47771c820362a70.jpg
https://s-media-cache-ak0.pinimg.com/236x/ac/f8/73/acf873cb4261c520d2725295b9fbba34.jpg
https://s-media-cache-ak0.pinimg.com/236x/fe/60/e9/fe60e93ae9d8119a16c1cfc013d49b79.jpg
https://s-media-cache-ak0.pinimg.com/564x/44/1d/5c/441d5cf2a327a32ac61a1e45fbb43bcd.jpg
https://s-media-cache-ak0.pinimg.com/236x/c7/a8/e0/c7a8e0e645afbcc6603c502c414baed8.jpg
https://s-media-cache-ak0.pinimg.com/236x/8f/c5/5b/8fc55b865884b9230cd7cbef0688c4d1.jpg
https://s-media-cache-ak0.pinimg.com/236x/ae/1c/4b/ae1c4b28f864c42f7424f267b4c9376c.jpg
https://s-media-cache-ak0.pinimg.com/236x/d3/f1/45/d3f1453f5f7fe4f386b36c5a47e53006.jpg
https://s-media-cache-ak0.pinimg.com/564x/09/45/62/0945624997d90295dfb9821b9c6753bc.jpg
https://s-media-cache-ak0.pinimg.com/564x/fa/7a/6d/fa7a6d8115227f6e1df44594c625490a.jpg

1. Parent/Family Conferences (Articles and or sample conference forms, assessments)
    a. Teacher-Led Conferences
    b. Student-Led Conferences
    c. Running Records/Anecdotal Notes
    d. Assessments Completed/Standards & Benchmarks
    e. Conference Reminder Slips http://www.livinglaughingandloving.com/2013/01/parent-teacher-conference-forms-free-printables.html
    f. Pre-Conference notes from the student http://www.myprimaryparadise.com/tag/conferences/
    g. Student self-evaluation form http://www.weareteachers.com/free-printable-of-the-week-self-evaluation-sheet-for-parent-teacher-conferences/
    h. Teacher Documentation Form, to be filled out before conferences https://drive.google.com/file/d/0BzsMGA2JXT0wekpRT2xfU3dlaXM/view
    i. Behavior Chart, if a child needs an extra reminder on behavior standards https://www.template.net/business/charts/behavior-chart-template/
    j. An article for parents and teachers on tips for a smooth conference http://www.ascd.org/ascd-express/vol6/612-wilson.aspx
2. Child Assessments/Evaluations (samples of appropriate assessments to use with young children)
    a. GOLD standards/benchmarks http://teachingstrategies.com/content/pageDocs/IA-GOLD-Alignment-PS-2010.pdf

    b. Iowa Early Learning Standards (IELS) http://www.state.ia.us/earlychildhood/files/early_learning_standarda/IELS_2013.pdf
    c. Running Records (Clay/Shea)
    d. Anecdotal Notes
    e. Student Observations
    f. Formative Assessments
    g. Summative Assessments
    h. Diagnostic Assessments
    i. Rubrics/Checklists
    j. Identifying a child's strengths and weaknesses. http://ectacenter.org/topics/earlyid/screeneval.asp
       Parent to Parent USA http://www.p2pusa.org/p2pusa/sitepages/p2p-home.aspx
       M.O.R.G.A.N. Project http://themorganproject.org/
       Federation for Children with Special Needs http://fcsn.org/
       Center for Parent Information and Resources http://www.parentcenterhub.org/nichcy-gone/
       Family Voices http://www.familyvoices.org/
       Council for Exceptional Children http://www.cec.sped.org/

Parent/Family Conferences
Teacher-led conferences: teacher discusses student's work and progress with parents
Council for Exceptional Children http://www.cec.sped.org/
Conferences: include information about timing, goals of conferences, as well as alternative scheduling options
Review student work: go over data, assignments, and assessments
Create an agenda or list of key issues to discuss about each student's progress and growth
Send reminders to parents
Focuses on student learning, and what the child can do even better
Opportunities and challenges are discussed during conferences
Parents' thoughts and feelings about their child should be discussed if desired
How parents can support learning at home should also be included in parent–teacher conferences

Nighttime: https://www.teacherspayteachers.com/Product/Meet-the-Teacher-Newsletter-EDITABLE-Bright-Stripes-2626358

1. **"I Can" Statements:** http://www.thecurriculumcorner.com/thekindercorner/2013/11/18/early-learning-i-can-statements/
2. **My Daily Schedule:** http://gglearningzone.blogspot.com.au/p/daycare.html
3. **What to Share with Parents:** http://www.rtinetwork.org/essential/family/engagingfamilies
4. **What to Discuss:** https://www.care.com/c/stories/3265/6-things-to-discuss-during-a-parent-teacher-c/

What the Parents Need to Talk About: http://kidshealth.org/en/parents/talk-to-preschool-teacher.html#
Teaching Our Youngest: http://www2.ed.gov/teachers/how/early/teachingouryoungest/page_pg11.html
Parent Teacher Conference Packet: https://www.teacherspayteachers.com/Product/Free-Parent-Teacher-Conferences-Packet-for-3rd-6th-Grade-1461164
Surveys for Parents: http://primarychalkboard.blogspot.com/2014/08/back-to-school-getting-to-know-your.html
Conference Reminders: http://www.thehappyteacher.co/2015/09/parent-teacher-conferences-8-more-tips.html
Writing Conferences: http://whattheteacherwants.blogspot.com/2013/04/writing-conferences.html?m=1
Portfolios: http://www.justaprimarygirl.com/2016/01/data-tracking-for-running-records-and.html
Things to Review: https://www.bloglovin.com/blogs/a-teeny-tiny-teacher-4572363/parent-conference-notes-2015-4596442909
Conferences and Educational Relationships: https://teaching-family.org/conferences/
Summary for Parents: http://teachingstrategies.com/content/pageDocs/IT2R-Family-Conference-Form.pdf

Gold: http://tnl.esd113.org/cms/lib3/WA01001093/Centricity/Domain/290/WaKIDSFamilyConferenceForm.pdf
Resources: https://www.teachervision.com/teacher-parent-conferences/resource/3713.html
Harvard Study: http://www.hfrp.org/var/hfrp/storage/fckeditor/File/Parent-Teacher-ConferenceTipSheet-100610.pdf
Pinterest Accounts can be used to share: https://www.pinterest.com/explore/parent-teacher-conference-forms/
Home Visit Conference: https://www.hsolc.org/policies/education/education-home-visit-parent-teacher-conference

Tips and Tricks
- Conferences may seem to be easy for teachers, but a lot of thought and preparation actually goes into executing them. This article provides its readers with a few tips and tricks for a positive conference, beyond that it even contains a few forms that could be used as well.
- Source: http://luckylittlelearners.com/2015/11/conferences.html

Reflection Forms for Conferences
- Parents/guardians enjoy viewing their child's work. This source provides the viewer with a form that could be filled out by the children prior to the conference, and then given to the parents by the teacher during their meeting. It has the children list what they enjoy about school, what they need to work on, and what they are proud of.
- Source: https://www.teacherspayteachers.com/Product/Student-Reflections-Page-Great-for-Report-Card-time-1460065?utm_campaign=TransactionalEmails&utm_source=sendgrid&utm_medium=email

Reminders to Parents/Families about Conferences
- Parents/guardians have busy schedules, and sending them a reminder is something that teachers can easily do to help them remember their conference date and time. This source provides the viewer with a printable form that could be sent home with the students that could then be pasted along to the parents/guardians.
- Source: http://www.thehappyteacher.co/2015/09/parent-teacher-conferences-8-more-tips.html

Rubric Can Help Simplify the Conference discussion
- During the duration conference the teacher has a good deal of information to get through. One way this can easily be organized is by them creating and/or using a rubric. The rubric, like the ones provided on this source, displays/breaks down a variety of topics in a clean and organized way.
- Source: http://www.onceuponalearningadventure.com/2015/10/how-to-approach-parent-teacher.html

Questions That Might
- This source provides parents with examples of questions that they could potentially ask during their conference with their child's teacher. The questions target many different topics and could really give the parents a better idea of where their child stands.
- Source: https://www.care.com/c/stories/3264/20-questions-to-ask-during-a-parent-teacher-c/

Video
- There is a teaching channel that has put together a great video regarding the preparation, delivery, and following days of a conference. From tips to ideas, the video covers it all.
- Source: https://www.teachingchannel.org/videos/parent-teacher-conference-tips

Before, During, and after Conferences
- Conferences can be a bit intimating for some parents who haven't gone to them before. Those parents may enjoy reading an article, like this one, to get an idea of what happens before, during, and after the conference.
- Source: https://www.teachervision.com/new-teacher/teaching-methods/48464.html

60 Classroom Management and Effective Strategies to Motivate Students

Guide
- This source provides its reader with numerous different articles to aid both a parent/guardian and a teacher in their execution of a conference. They discuss discussion points, keeping records, and the power of parent/guardian involvement.
- Source: http://www.scholastic.com/teachers/collection/guide-parent-teacher-conferences

Self-Evaluation
- Beyond the topic of their academics, teachers also like to speak with the parents/guardians about their child's behavior. This is done through a self-evaluation and can be done by using a form like the one on this site.
- Source: https://www.teacherspayteachers.com/Product/Parent-Teacher-Conferences-Self-Evaluation-473303

Timeline
- Teachers tend to have an ideal timeline of how the conference will play out. This source provides such a timeline and could inform and/or give parents/guardians an idea of what to expect going into the conference.
- Source: http://www.ascd.org/ascd-express/vol6/612-wilson.aspx**Mini Report Card**
- The assessments found on this page are basic, clean-cut assessments of shapes, letters, colors, scissor skills, etc. It is assessing the child's knowledge of each and if they are able to successfully complete and or recall what each of the concepts is. The assessment is one that could quickly and easily be done by a teacher and/or helper in the classroom.
- Source: http://meandmarielearning.blogspot.com/2011/01/preschool-assessments.html?m=1
  - **Parent–Teacher Conference Packets:** https://www.teacherspayteachers.com/Product/Free-Parent-Teacher-Conferences-Packet-for-3rd-6th-Grade-1461164
    - This electronic packet will be very good for the first couple of parent–teacher conferences that a new teacher has. It is important to use these documents so the new teacher knows they are on the right track. Once they understand what they are going to do at the conferences, then they can make their own documents. This is a good website to use for both the parents and the new teacher to get off to a good start.
  - **Surveys for Parents:** http://primarychalkboard.blogspot.com/2014/08/back-to-school-getting-to-know-your.html
    - This is a great blog that will help teachers prepare to talk to parents about what their students need. This website is great to get to know what other teachers have had success with. It also gives the do's and don'ts on what teachers need to do in during a meeting. Surveys are also good for one of the first times parents are meeting teachers. This survey would work great to get to know the parents of the students.

Parent Informational Meetings

https://www.nationsclassroomtours.com/blog/save-time-other-benefits-of-a-parent-meeting-before-your-school-trip

http://www.lcfs.org/events/categories/foster-care-informational-meetings/

http://www.familiesandschools.org/our-organization/contact-us/?gclid=CISG8o3pvdMCFQItaQod2DsO3w

http://americanspcc.org/parenting/positive-parenting/

http://www.sfx-school.org/sfx-newsblast/parent-informational-meetings/

http://www.smartkidswithld.org/getting-help/the-abcs-of-ieps/iep-meeting-6-tips-parents/

https://www.povertyactionlab.org/sites/default/files/resources/Guide1_GettingParentsInvolved_France.pdf

https://katyisd.instructure.com/courses/82971
http://www.colorincolorado.org/article/tips-successful-parent-teacher-conferences-your-childs-school
http://www.educationworld.com/a_curr/curr291.shtml
http://www.parentcenterhub.org/repository/iep-meeting-checklist-for-parents/
https://www.understood.org/en/school-learning/special-services/ieps/checklist-what-to-bring-to-the-iep-meeting?utm_source=pinterest&utm_medium=social&utm_campaign=understoodorg
https://www.edutopia.org/blog/parent-teacher-conference-resources-matt-davis
https://www.care.com/c/stories/3264/20-questions-to-ask-during-a-parent-teacher-c/
http://kidshealth.org/en/parents/parent-teacher-conferences.html
https://www.teachingchannel.org/videos/parent-teacher-conference-tips
https://www.scholastic.com/teachers/collections/teaching-content/guide-parent-teacher-conferences/
http://www.educationworld.com/a_curr/curr291.shtml
http://www.babycenter.com/404_what-happens-at-parent-teacher-conferences_70472.bc
http://www.icanteachmychild.com/seven-things-you-should-be-doing-as-youre-reading-to-your-child/
https://s-media-cache-ak0.pinimg.com/564x/72/af/c2/72afc2247f93e2b72db96c53391a3b4c.jpg
http://www.thehealingpathwithchildren.com/2016/08/22/worry-bag-growth-mindset-children/
http://www.fortheteachers.org/friday-five-ways-parents-can-help-with-math/
https://s-media-cache-ak0.pinimg.com/564x/0b/c8/60/0bc860c23bc1a6a1d9138377cd5ef06c.jpg
https://s-media-cache-ak0.pinimg.com/236x/78/d5/b9/78d5b9358da60da10f6df8b98e149c58.jpg
https://s-media-cache-ak0.pinimg.com/236x/4c/34/23/4c342315f92c3f04f74d3173f52a6651.jpg
https://s-media-cache-ak0.pinimg.com/236x/c2/4d/d5/c24dd59ffcf3bf05c3a0d013517327fd.jpg
https://s-media-cache-ak0.pinimg.com/564x/b8/72/11/b87211f6ee56eaf378486eb80c148f26.jpg
https://s-media-cache-ak0.pinimg.com/236x/6e/c2/da/6ec2dac15fa5c9685555de251c753b67.jpg
https://s-media-cache-ak0.pinimg.com/236x/bd/f1/3d/bdf13de62192f11b326c02f40ff23fe7.jpg
https://s-media-cache-ak0.pinimg.com/236x/77/41/76/77417637615006f95e9a3767a18c9487.jpg http://2.bp.blogspot.com/-WSzhsjCQgMI/Vm47fa1PvzI/AAAAAAAAAo/YzDLleNXqOU/s320/DSC_1895.jpg
http://1.bp.blogspot.com/-ljgpJICAmTE/UiFuAScw1mI/AAAAAAAAHWo/ClffKyNb2nU/s640/Fullscreen+capture+8302013+91528+PM.jpg
https://s-media-cache-ak0.pinimg.com/564x/c8/d4/09/c8d409dd912b3dcc1cffcc03841daa5c.jpg
http://www.efoza.com/postpic/2014/10/positive-behavior-charts_619333.jpg
https://s-media-cache-ak0.pinimg.com/736x/0e/ea/94/0eea94eda555ca52ba039dffa6ef3d8e--sweet-notes-encouragement-ideas.jpg

1. **What to Cover in an Informational Meeting:** http://www.thehappyteacher.co/2015/09/parent-teacher-conferences-8-more-tips.html
2. **Meet the Teacher Night:** https://www.teacherspayteachers.com/Product/Meet-the-Teacher-Newsletter-EDITABLE-Bright-Stripes-2626358
3. **"I Can" Statements:** http://www.thecurriculumcorner.com/thekindercorner/2013/11/18/early-learning-i-can-statements/
4. **My Daily Schedule:** http://gglearningzone.blogspot.com.au/p/daycare.html
5. **What to Share with Parents:** http://www.rtinetwork.org/essential/family/engagingfamilies
6. **What to Discuss:** https://www.care.com/c/stories/3265/6-things-to-discuss-during-a-parent-teacher-c/
7. **What the Parents Need to Talk About:** http://kidshealth.org/en/parents/talk-to-preschool-teacher.html#
8. **Teaching Our Youngest:** http://www2.ed.gov/teachers/how/early/teachingouryoungest/page_pg11.html
9. **Parent–Teacher Conference Packet:** https://www.teacherspayteachers.com/Product/Free-Parent-Teacher-Conferences-Packet-for-3rd-6th-Grade-1461164
10. **Surveys for Parents:** http://primarychalkboard.blogspot.com/2014/08/back-to-school-getting-to-know-your.html

1. **Importance of Bringing and/or Supplying Your Child an Extra Pair of Clothing**
   - This source supplies its readers with a handout that may be administered to parents/guardians regarding the importance of supplying your child's teacher with a spare set of clothes. Children have accidents, and even if it is not common with your child, it is still a topic that needs to be discussed, especially if spare clothes are not an option due to financial reasons.
   - Source: http://freebie-licious.blogspot.com/2014/08/free-parent-letter-for-change-of.html?utm_source=feedburner&utm_medium=email&utm_campaign=Feed:+blogspot/CgoIa+(Freebielicious)

2. **Guest Police Officer and Importance of Car Safety**
   - This source is a guest forum where an individual listed the idea/experience of having a police officer come in and speak during a meeting to the families about car/car seat safety. This is a topic that is important for families to understand and I believe it would be best delivered by a police officer.
   - Source: http://forums.atozteacherstuff.com/index.php?threads/parent-meeting-need-ideas.104204/

3. **Bully Awareness**
   - This site lists Bully Awareness as a possible topic for parent meetings and I could not agree with its importance anymore. All parent/guardian(s) want their children to be in an anti-bully environment, and if all parents/guardians are on board and are educated on the various red flags to look for, then I believe it may be achieved.
   - Source: http://www.kingsvilleisd.com/apps/pages/index.jsp?uREC_ID=460484&type=u&pREC_ID=664903

4. **Making the Transition from Preschool to Kindergarten (Special Education)**
   - This site provides the reader with quite detailed information regarding how parents/guardians can help transition their special needs child from preschool to kindergarten classroom. It targets what to do during their preschool years as well as what to do during the summer before their kindergarten year. This would be a great resource to use for parents/guardians and its content could be discussed both at the beginning of the year as well at the end of the year.
   - Source: http://www.pacer.org/parent/php/PHP-c196.pdf

5. **Introductions**
   - This source explains how a school may organize a parent meeting that occurs prior to the beginning date of the school year. This meeting allows the teachers to meet the parents/guardians firsthand and learn a little bit about the routine their child will be having, the school's layout, and what they can do as an involved parent/guardian.
   - Source: http://www.pjcc.org/preschool/preschool-parents.html

6. **Sleep Schedules**
   - Transitioning into a routine school day is rough for young kiddos, particularly due to the fact that they have to stay awake and alert during the day without taking naps whenever they choose. A possible topic that could be discussed at a parent meeting would be the topic of sleep schedules, how much sleep is necessary, and what time is appropriate for the children to head to bed.
   - Source: https://www.angieslist.com/articles/bedtime-how-much-sleep-should-your-child-be-getting.htm?CID=Social09202012BedtimeGraphic

7. **How to Help Children Succeed**
   - Every parent/guardian wants their children to succeed, and what they may not know is they themselves are a large component of that. A topic that could be discussed at a meeting would be what they can do as role models to aid and/or guide their children to succeed in their learning.
   - Source: http://funinfirst.com/tips-for-parentshow-to-help-my-child/

8. **Importance of Reading at Home**
    - A large concept that young children struggle to conquer is reading. It is tricky, and although educators are working with the children on it each and everyday, parents/guardians can also aid them in their learning/understanding of reading. This source displays a handout that discusses what parents/guardians can do at home to help and/or aid their child's reading ability.
    - Source: http://www.allstudentscanshine.com/2014/04/reading-at-home-tips-for-parents.html

9. **Volunteering**
    - Teachers are always looking for parents/guardians who are willing to lend some of their time and come in to prep, help our, or chaperone for their child's classroom. At this meeting the information could be addressed, and an interested parent/guardian could then also communicate with the teachers regarding what they would be willing to do.
    - Source: http://www.scholastic.com/teachers/top-teaching/2014/09/tips-easy-and-almost-paper-free-curriculum-night

10. **Joining PTA**
    - Although parents/guardians are busy with their own lives, work, and taking care of their children, schools are always looking for parent/guardian(s) who are willing to join PTA. What is PTA, some may ask, this meeting would discuss just that. It would be an informative meeting of what PTA is and what it has to offer the children and/or the children's parents/guardians; this source displays a clear and informative chart that breaks down just that.

Sources

1. Parent–Teacher Conferences: Outdated or Underutilized? (Education Update, Association for Supervision and Curriculum Development (ASCD), September 2016)

2. 21st Century Parent–Teacher Conferences: 5 Alternatives to the Traditional Conference (California Casualty) Feb. 2, 2017

Chapter 9

The Loosening of School Lunch Nutrition Standards: Helpful or Hindrance?

Recently, U.S. Agriculture Secretary Sonny Perdue announced that there would be an interim ruling that would provide more flexibility in meeting school meal nutritional standards that were put in place by the Obama Administration.

So what does this mean? It means exactly what it says in that the recommendations that became a part of former first lady Michelle's hope for improving health and nutrition of students in America's schools. She had pushed for decreasing salt and fat serving more whole grains, fresh fruits and vegetables. Sounds good, well many are in agreement, while others are not.

The standards that were connected to these nutritional standards are under the jurisdiction of the Healthy, Hunger-Free Kids Act of 2010.

So who were some of the supporters of this initiative?

1. These changes were very well accepted by organizations and agencies who were concerned about the growing number of America's children who are considered to be victims of childhood obesity.
2. These changes were greatly appreciated by some parents and educators who were grateful to see school lunches looking closer at how to successfully provide healthy meals for students.
3. Those who supported the school meal programs as they were share their disappointment in Perdue's implementation of these changes so rapidly with such a short tenure in office.
4. Along with this disappointment is the lack of knowledge about the quality of meals and how so much sodium is impacting the lives of America's children.

Those who opposed the initiative seemed to scream louder:

1. Education and industry groups complained about the costliness of trying to implement such a plan and the difficulties for many school districts/schools.
2. Still these changes did not meet the interests of some of the conservative members of congress.
3. The School Nutrition Association expressed its appreciation and support for the changes that have been made in the school meal programs. They too believe that these changes will make the food more appealing to the children.

Recent changes that are coming forth:

1. States can grant exemptions during 2017–2018 from meeting the requirement that schools serve whole grain if the schools are experiencing difficulties in meeting this.
2. The federal agency stated that it would take the necessary regulation procedures to begin to look more so for a long-term solution on whole grains.
3. This regulation on sodium will be recognized as in compliance if it meets the "target one" required. This made food seem less desirable for students.
4. Schools will be able to serve 1 percent flavored milk.
5. Perdue announced that the requirements that were in place previously cost school districts and states a whopping addition of $1.22 billion in the year 2015.

So how were some of these immediate changes made and why?

1. There has been years of collecting data and feedback from school food service personnel and experts, students, and schools.
2. Reports of, and complaints about, some of the difficulties that they experienced in meeting the regulations for school meals were among the final deciding factors about the need for changes.
3. According to Perdue, if the students aren't eating the food and it is being thrown in the trash, then the students aren't receiving any nutrition. So it is best for them to receive some nutrition rather than no nutrition. If this is the case, then the entire lunch program is being undermined.

The facts if indeed they matter:

1. According to Margo G. Wootan, nutrition policy director at the Center for Science in the Public Interest, 90 percent of American children eat too much sodium daily.
2. She further stated that the school meals program was moving in the right direction by providing a more quality nutritional program for students and it is ashamed to see it be stopped while allowing dangerous and high levels of sodium in school lunch programs.

Other Issues Facing School Lunch Programs

Salt Lake City was the focus of national attention in 2014 when one of the cafeteria workers took away lunches from 32 students whose lunches were not paid for or bill was not paid in full. The lunches were taken away and thrown in the trash.

This brought about national outrage and media attention. However, school nutrition leaders defended the matter of unpaid lunch bills, being able to manage budgetary matters for the operation of school lunch programs. However, everyone was in agreement that being sensitive to the student needs is a key factor.

Thus the U.S. Department of Agriculture (USAD) stated that it believed this to be an isolated incident, but would bring it for the group to discuss and implement some best practice policies for dealing with unpaid student meals. The School Nutrition Association also called upon the USDA to give clear guidelines on how to professionally and compassionately deal with unpaid student meal bills.

So how devastating are some of the current practices for students having unpaid bills?

1. Some school districts do not allow students with negative meal balances to eat.
2. Some school districts provide alternate meals for the students such as peanut butter sandwiches. This is for students with deficit balances as well as those who cannot pay for meals at all.
3. Some schools send home notes, sticky notes, as well as online communication about school meal deficits in hopes of keeping students out of this so that they can continue to concentrate on their learning and not on adult financial matters.

So what was really wrong about the way that Salt Lake City Utah handled the school lunch situation with the 32 students with deficit meal bills?

1. Is it appropriate for any employee to take freshly made lunches out of the hands of students, throw them away in the trash? Even more so, how about doing this within the visible eyes of other students watching?
2. The students were then given replacement meals of milk and fruit. Is that really a nutritional meal even if it is a replacement one?
3. So what about the children whose parents were not notified that there was a negative balance or if and when they were made aware of this, did not provide enough time for them to rectify the matter? How much time is enough time?
4. What needs to happen with the students' meals if their meal bills are not paid up to date?
5. The school district promised that a student's meal will never be taken away again.
6. There were during that time of the incident two employees who were placed on paid leave while the incident was being investigated by the school district. Is that the answer to such a serious matter?
7. So the district decided that they would communicate directly with parents about meal balances, making weekly phone calls when balances fall below $10.00 and daily ones if there is a negative balance.

After the story broke with the media,

1. Two Utah State Senators ate lunch with the school's students.
2. A Utah Jazz basketball player gave free tickets to a student and stated that he would make a contribution to the school lunch program.
3. A Houston, Texas humanitarian, settled the lunch account balances and deficits of 60 local elementary school students.

What Did Parents Have to Say?

1. Parents were heard during a school board meeting citing the actions against the students by taking their lunches were wasteful, bullying, and stigmatizing.
2. Others shared the seriousness of shaming students for something that they definitely had no control over. The unpaid balance was an adult matter and not the child's.
3. This school district with its 23,500 students during that time carried an estimated $15,000.00 in unpaid lunch fees. However, the district was expected to spend approximately $13 million dollars on student nutritional programs. Wow, this caught the parents' attention!

Does Anyone Know Why Meal Bills Go Unpaid?

1. Family financial struggles
2. Layoff of parents or termination of their employment
3. Miscommunication between school and parents
4. Weaker local and statewide economic conditions
5. Family health problems causing financial burdens

In one survey of 521 nutrition leaders, 79.7 percent stated that there was a consistent or increasing status of unpaid meals.

Sadly, school districts have responded in several ways with much disagreement among those concerned about the effects on students.

a. Adopting easier online payment methods
   b. Setting up payment plans
   c. Hiring collection agencies to retrieve payment of unpaid meals

Some Actions:

1. The federal Healthy, Hunger-Free Kids Act of 2010 required the USDA to:
   a. Review state and local policies on extending credit.
   b. Provide alternative meals to students with unpaid balances.
   c. Prepare a report that is looking closely at whether there is overt identification of affected children whose bills may be unpaid.
   d. Providing assistance for families who are eligible with free or reduced lunch enrollments and are not in the program.
   e. Giving an updated financial support on the financial impact these actions will have on the local level as more information is being sought for national implementation.

Resources on Unpaid Meal Balances

Utah Incident Revives Debate on Handling Unpaid Lunch Debts, Feb. 19, 2014
"Utah Cafeteria Leader Placed on Leave After Taking Student Lunches" (Rules for Engagement Blog), Jan. 31, 2014.
"Cash or Card? The Answer May Affect Students' Waistlines" (Rules for Engagement Blog), Jan. 17, 2014.
"School Lunch Could Hit Skids if Shutdown Persists" (Politics K-12 Blog), Oct. 11, 2013.
"USDA Rules Give School Meals a Healthy Makeover," Feb. 1, 2012.

Source: Trump Administration Loosens School Lunch Nutrition Standards by Evie Blad, May 1, 2017

Chapter 10

So What Is Going on with Recess Time?

Well, most of us grew up in a period of time when recess was a much accepted and needed part of the school's curricula. I remember we had just as much fun with outside playtime as we did inside the school.

I am still trying to recall in my mind as to whether or not our teachers understood the need for children to have a break outside of the classroom and time for more movement and active play. I do not recall recess being a major form of punishment or privilege taken away as I hear of it today.

Of course we realized that playtime was a special privilege and we did everything that we could to make sure that we kept and maintained our privilege to go outside.

There was a scheduled time for all children to go outside and play. Believe it or not, even as we look back today and think about how we used that time, someone might say that it appeared that we did the same thing everyday. If we did, it did not seem to bother us at all. I really couldn't say that I heard any children complaining about the activities that we did or played day after day. There were some things that happened back then that were acknowledged as that is the way it is.

Recently, I read an article about "Recess as a Radical Proposition" in Educational Exchange that made me reflect on the times then and what I see happening with children in educational institutions today.

Recess As a Radical Proposition

February 28, 2017

In the state of Florida, there is a coalition of parents who decided to step forward and take a stand on this very important issue on the well-being of children. This group of parents are recognized as "recess moms."

In the state of Florida these recess parents had as their main goal to fight for the passing of legislation that guarantees that all elementary school age children will have 20 minutes of recess/free outside/physical play.

There was a similar activity in the state of New Jersey. Legislation passed, but later was vetoed by the governor who said it was "stupid."

Alia Wong wrote an article, "Why Kids Need Recess" (The Atlantic, Nov. 17, 2016)

The question continues to linger today in regard to what has happened to recess and allowing children the time and opportunity for free play. So as Ms. Wong mentions in her article, when did recess become such a radical proposal calling for the need for legislation to be passed?

1. So what are some of the challenges as to why recess is coming to the forefront of needing parental involvement and legislative actions?
2. So what do teachers and administrators have to say about the pros and cons of recess? Do they feel that it is important for these elementary age students to have a required recess period?
3. Why is it that in reporting the results of a survey school district administrators stated that about a third of their districts had reduced outdoor play as far back as the early 2000s.
4. So what justification did these school districts have for reducing recess and outside play during times such as they are today?
5. Theory 1—Decreasing recess and outside free play times would or should decrease any bullying.
6. Theory 2—Decreasing recess would complement the "No Child Left Behind Mandate." It is a known fact that for the pressures exerted by the requirements to successfully complete this, they chose to result in cuts in time to play.
7. The results are also showing that children from low-income families benefit tremendously from recess.
8. According to a 2003 study, just 56 percent of children living at or below the poverty line had recess. While 83 percent of those above the poverty line had it.
9. There were similar disparities in regard to the inequities of recess/play time that was noted between black and white children.
10. There are so many benefits to allowing the children to have recess—one is to help children become more cognitive, learning more easily.

The Benefits of Recess Time

1. A benefit for allowing children to run, explore, and have some physical free time is key to academic success.
2. Physical activities enhance and boost cognitive performance.
3. There are many studies that support the fact that regular physical exercise and activities improve mental abilities as well as academic performance.
4. Studies that focused directly on recess found a positive correlation between students' physical activities and their ability to concentrate in class. Thus will recess decrease the number of children who are diagnosed as having attention deficit disorder?

Recess Research Experiments

There were several experiments conducted by researchers who provided differential scheduling of childrens' recess of variant times and days.

Series 1—On some days, children were let out at 10:00 am and on other days at 10:30 am. *They saw that children's attentiveness/attention spans* decreased on the days when the children had to wait longer for recess (the 10:30 time). But they tended to bounce back after that participation regardless of the time. But the recess was critical.

Series 2—Fourth-graders in a school where children had no recess were given a weekly recess on an experimental basis. When they were given this recess researchers found that they had an easier time staying on task and were much less fidgety and distracted throughout the school day.

These experimental findings were enhanced by the analysis of 10,000 questionnaires filled out by third-grade teachers: Even a single 15-minute daily recess was correlated with more positive ratings of classroom behaviors.

Other Important Values of Recess

1. One of the most important values of recess is that children are allowed to create and design their own games.
2. Recess allows children to test their abilities and skills such that they had to increase their challenges and opportunities to challenge.
3. Recess allows children to role-play and portray various roles in their interactions with others. Some are leaders, game organizers, score keepers, etc.
4. Recess allows children to mediate their own conflicts—such as the rules of the games, violations, winning status, team players, etc.
5. Recess allows children to develop necessary lifelong social skills.
6. Recess allows children to learn how to navigate and pave their way through complicated conditions, circumstances, and situations as they arise.
7. There were early results from an ongoing study in Texas that suggested that elementary school children when given four 15-minute recesses a day are significantly more empathetic toward their peers than are children who don't get recess at all.

Should We Follow Finland As a Model for the Positive Effects of Recess?

Finland is a highly ranked and recognized school system and it is internationally known for its effectiveness with its students. The children in Finland get more than an hour of recess everyday.

What about China's School System and Recess?

It is very surprising to learn East Asian countries like China have 9-hour school days and weekend cram classes. Many educators are surprised to learn that in most schools, the children are granted a 10- or even 20-minute break after each class, or about every hour. Researchers wonder if they are onto a model plan that truly has implications for children in United States schools.

Resources on Recess and Outside Play

Burris and Burris, "Outdoor Play and Learning" (*International Journal of Education Policy & Leadership*, Nov. 2011)

Roth et al., "What Happens During the School Day?" (*Teachers College Record*, Apr. 2003)

Etnier et al., "The Influence of Physical Fitness and Exercise Upon Cognitive Functioning" (*Journal of Sport & Exercise Psychology*, Sep. 1997)

Centers for Disease Control and Prevention, "The Association Between School-Based Physical Activity, Including Physical Education, and Academic Performance" (July 2010)

Pellegrini et al., "The Effects of Recess Timing on Children's Playground and Classroom Behaviors" (*American Educational Research Journal*, Winter 1995)

Jarrett et al., "Impact of Recess on Classroom Behavior" (*The Journal of Educational Research*, Nov./Dec. 1998)

Barros et al., "School Recess and Group Classroom Behavior" (*Pediatrics*, Feb. 2009)

Pellegrini and Bohn, "The Role of Recess in Children's Cognitive Performance and School Adjustment" (*Educational Researcher*, Jan./Feb. 2005)

Texas Christian University LiiNK Project, "End of Year Report" (2015–2016)

Chapter 11

Do School Uniforms Make a Difference?

The issue of school uniforms is not new, but somehow it seems to be surfacing from a different perspective from days past and gone. I clearly remember growing up in the south and we were quite accustomed to some children wearing uniforms.

So somehow those students who attended Catholic schools or religious-based schools, those attending private schools and/or those whose parents chose to send them to some type of military post secondary or designated/specialized schools wore uniforms. So back then, it certainly did not seem to be an issue for most of us attending public schools. Somehow, I do not ever remember the conversation even coming up about us wearing uniforms in my elementary, middle or high schools.

But as public schools in the United States began to focus on ways of improving standardized test scores and school safety, many school districts began requiring students to wear uniforms as an answer to some of the school-related matters. Schools began requiring their students to wear uniforms. Although the numbers vary, it is estimated that approximately 20 percent of students in the United States wear uniforms to school.

So now, there seems to be heated debates about school uniforms all over the United States. To be honest, I am not aware of the fact of whether it is an issue outside of the United States. For some reason, this discussion has become an ongoing one. In many school districts, it has become one of the most heated debates.

For at least the past decade, it seems that school districts, families, as well as students seem to have fought a long, hard, and sometimes tumultuous battle about uniforms. The reason the road has been so rocky is that there seems to be two major issues at the forefront:

1. Do schools have the civil rights to regulate student attire?
2. Do schools have any evidence that dress codes and policies have any impact on student performance/learning?

Some school districts decided upon uniforms for what some term to be haphazard reasons. Some wonder if some of the recommended decisions were made as a result over some freedom rights such as cases involving the wearing of t-shirts that may be offensive to some individuals or groups of individuals. Some of the researchers cite examples such as anti-political actions, anti-gay or gay rights protests, etc. Often these types of protests lead to bigger protests, sometimes with judges having to render decisions on the side of the school or on the side of the student in certain situations. Often, many of the decisions rendered are unexpected or unanticipated.

Very interestingly, most researchers who study school uniform issues tend to view results from the basis of student learning, school safety, or academic performance.
Noted findings:

1. Uniforms do not improve school safety or academic discipline/achievement.
2. But in some Ohio schools, uniforms seem to have improved graduation and school attendance rates.
3. Despite the improvements in the aforementioned two areas, there was no known improvement in academic performance.
4. Therefore outsiders can be recognized quickly.

The Big Question Today: Why Do Some Public Schools Have a Uniform Requirement?

Taking a retrospective view back to the 1980s, believe it or not public schools were compared in unfavorable ways to Catholic schools, in particular. While there were no real known facts, the message was sent out that those uniforms were beneficial to the students attending Catholic schools. Therefore, some public schools decided to follow suit and started requiring uniforms.

Many feel that President Clinton added to the enhanced movement of encouraging school districts to move toward uniforms when in his 1996 State of the Union Speech he stated, "If it means teenagers will stop killing each other over designer jackets, then our public schools should be able to require their students to wear school uniforms."

Taking a Closer Look at the Pros of School Uniforms

Those who advocate on behalf of children enrolled in public schools wearing uniforms cite such critical factors as:

1. Stop and/or decrease gang formations on school grounds
2. Because of the similarities in attire, some feel like there is more overall stability in student discipline?
3. Help students not feel pressured in having to buy name brand or highly recognizable trend-type clothing.
4. Help identify those who are not a part of the school environment as an administrator, teacher, staff, or student.
5. Help decrease the labeling of the haves and have nots in schools reflecting economic statuses.
6. Increase student's interest in school, school-related experiences, pride in school and their education.
7. Improve student attendance.
8. Advocates state that students will pay more attention to their school work if they are not distracted or preoccupied with looking at or trying to keep up with the latest fashion.
9. Along with decreasing fashion distractions, it is believed that the students will show improvements in their school behaviors.

Taking a Closer Look at the Cons of School Uniform

Those who oppose uniforms cite the following:

1. The uniforms violate students' right to dress as they desire.
2. The uniforms hinder students from expressing themselves creatively through dress.
3. The uniforms are merely a surface cover-up when looking at the true realities of school violence.

4. The uniforms can make students a real target by those who attend other schools and decide to bully them.
5. A financial burden for low-income families.
6. An additional burdensome expense for families who feel that they already pay taxes for a free public education.
7. Enforcement in public schools is difficult for various reasons.

While school districts and boards have been looking at the issue of school uniforms for years, very seldom have they taken the time to look at any of the academic research on this topic before putting this issue on the table for consideration.

Media, including journalists, often have done some homework by reviewing some of the reports written on uniforms in public schools, especially those of the National Center for Education Statistics (NCES) which collects data and reports on school uniforms and dress codes. Still, school districts seem to lack making efforts to review the same or similar reports on school uniforms.

Many parents as well as students feel that students are being forced to dress alike, thus suppressing their freedom of individual expression.

While some families share that uniforms help financially by limiting the amount and types of clothing that they purchase for their children, others claim that they are not saving money because they have to purchase uniforms as well as other clothes for their children, thus costing them double expenses.

Others have complained in the past that it was difficult to find places to purchase uniforms, but now that more large chain stores like Wal-Mart and Target carry them, it makes it easier to locate them.

Is There an Issue or Dispute between School Uniforms and Dress Codes?

There have been many stipulations in regard to whether schools can really make all students comply with uniforms in uniformity? So even when wearing uniforms, are we truly looking for them to be alike? Or are we looking for them to be the identical same because they are supposed to be dressed in uniform. We must admit that there is the concept of uniforms, but does this mean the same to everyone?

Let's Take a Closer Look at School Dress Codes

It is believed that school dress codes are not as rigid as school uniforms. In many public schools, throughout the United States, there has been much resistance to school uniforms by the entire student body and for some teachers and staff.

For example, a middle school in Napa, California, required all students to wear solid colors and no images or logos on clothes worn. This became a major concern when a student was sent to detention for wearing socks that had Tigger on it as violating the school's dress code policy. In return, this particular student's parents sued the school citing that they violated the student's freedom of speech.

In response to the outcry, the school district superintendent decided to relax the dress code saying that students could wear clothing with images and logos on them. But while the dress codes were being relaxed, he announced his intention of moving in the direction of school uniforms.

Important Notation: Administrators seem to agree that it is certainly easier for them to enforce uniform requirements more so than dress codes, because of all of the individualization issues.

Important Notation: There are many school cases about involving freedom of speech/free speech where the courts sided on the side of the students against the schools.

Student Assignment
Check with your school or another school to find out what the dress code rules are. Some of the dress codes are very strict and seem unrealistic.

Dress Codes, Then What about Those Uniforms?
It was recommended that a close look be taken in regard to what really is a uniform? Do all people think of uniforms in the same way? Can there be some individual deviations from what everyone is supposed to be wearing?

Well it has been discovered that the rules are simply unreal in some cases. There are so many variations in what one school perceived as the definition of uniform versus what another might have.

School #1's Definition:

1. All boys must wear white button-down shirts and ties. (So can the ties all be different colors?)
2. Girls are required to wear pleated, plaid skirts, knee-length with jackets with the school logo on it.
3. All boys wear khaki pants with a shirt with a collar.

Taking a Look at an Elementary School's Sample of Diverse Wear
In Toledo, Ohio, an elementary school allowed students to have a limited number of colors that they can wear as a part of the uniform requirements. Such colors are white, light blue, dark blue, or yellow on the top half, and dark blue, navy, khaki, or tan on the bottom half.

So how uniform are these? Girls are allowed to wear a variety of dress items, but limited to blouses, polo shirts with collars, turtlenecks, skirts, jumpers, slacks, and knee-length shorts and skirts. Boys have almost as many choices such as dress shirts, turtlenecks, polo or button-down shirts, pants or knee-length shorts. Then when they enter middle school, another color is added to their color selection.

The Research Aspect of School Uniforms
Yes, there are marked differences in some schools who have uniform policies in place!

Most of us have our personal opinions about school uniforms. We have these for varying reasons as people of all backgrounds seem to think about uniforms. So what can we learn from what research says about school uniforms?

Virginia Draa, assistant professor at Youngstown State University, researched the areas of attendance, graduation, and proficiency pass rates at 64 public high schools in the state of Ohio. She shares as a part of her research that as she initiated this research, she really did not think that uniforms made a difference. But to her amazement and others, she found that uniforms do make a difference. Or she clarifies that at least at the schools where she conducted her studies, uniforms did make a difference.

Her study found that the schools that did have uniform policies showed improvements in school attendance, graduation, and suspension rates. But she was not able to make any connections between school uniform policies and academic improvements. The reason that this could not be determined is that there are too many factors related to the varied approaches used in implementation of instruction and curriculum.

No, there are no differences in schools with uniform policies and those that do not!

While Virginia Draa at Youngstown State University found that there were differences, David Brunsma from University of Missouri did not reach the same conclusion. In his 2004 book, *The School*

Uniform Movement and What It Tells Us about American Education: A Symbolic Crusade, he reviewed some past studies on the effect of uniforms on academic performance.

He did a personal analysis of the 1988 National Educational Longitudinal Study and the 1998 Early Childhood Longitudinal Study. Thus he concluded that there is no positive correlation between school uniforms, school safety nor academic achievement.

- Important Notation: In the United States, there has been a major move toward uniforms in public schools. About one-fourth of all elementary schools have developed uniform policies, thus requiring all students to wear uniforms daily to school.
- Important Notation: The number of middle and high schools with uniform policies is about half the number of elementary schools.
- Important Question: Experts studying the subject of school uniforms are pondering the question that is very important. So if uniforms are indeed supposed to help decrease and/or defer some of the school violence and improve academics, then why are there not more middle and high schools with uniform policies? Is it not true that these policies are just as important as they are in elementary schools?
- Important Notation: Researcher Brunsma states that it is much more difficult to implement uniforms in high schools, in particular and middle schools as well. Student resistance is prevalent among middle and high schools and usually very forceful in communities.
- Important Notation: Most court cases that were the result of school uniforms have been in grades K-12, but fewer in elementary grades.
- Important Message: Many feel that the uniform issue is such that experts who challenge as well as support school uniforms ask the question, Is the debate really about children's rights and will their voices be heard?
- Important Message: Is this debate about a group of adults who misunderstand the real issues and find a band aid approach for dealing with some more underlying school issues such as violence?
- Taking a closer look at school uniforms, what do students think about required school uniforms?

The Students Speak Out about School Uniforms

Students speak out about school uniforms expressing viewpoints of the advantageous and disadvantageous to wearing school uniforms daily?

It is very interesting that much of the discoveries and research were conducted after uniform policies were implemented and put in effect in schools.

The Students Speak Out Loudly Through Data Gathering by Researchers

- Student Message #1: After a school uniform policy was implemented in three Nevada middle schools, researchers from the University of Nevada at Reno wanted to find out what students thought about school uniforms.
- Fact #1: 1,350 seventh and eighth graders were asked about their thoughts about the change from not wearing uniforms to being required to wear them.
- Result #1: 90 percent of these students reported that they disliked wearing school uniforms.
- Result #2: 54 percent of these students shared that they still felt that they had their identity even while wearing uniforms.
- Result #3: 50 percent of these students agreed that uniforms helped save their families money.
- Result #4: Only 41 percent of students agreed that there was less gang activity at their school after they were required to wear uniforms.
- Comparative Facts: When researchers who collected data from students from these three schools looked into school discipline and local police records, comparing them to the previous year of not wearing uniforms they found:

Result #5: Discipline referrals were down by 10 percent.
Result #6: Records showed 63 percent fewer police log reports.
Result #7: Gang-related activities, graffiti violations. and fights were all down.

The data also demonstrate the discrepancies in efforts to establish the real effects of school uniforms as they relate to school experiences involving students.

If Students Are Required to Wear Uniforms, Should Teachers Also?

There are a few schools that I know of personally who require the teachers to also wear uniforms. Personally, I have not heard them complaining about wearing the uniforms but that doesn't mean that they don't. From the surface, it appears that the teachers shared in dressing like their students as a form of unity as well as uniformity. Some districts feel that the uniforms are beneficial to teachers also. They are also hopeful that this will decrease the need for administrators to have to deal with teachers wearing too revealing clothes, sometimes not appropriate for school.

Mere observation alone seems to help students accept the fact that if the teachers can wear them, they can also. It appears that children are thinking about the personal impact on their daily lives more than we are able to determine.

For example, the girls in the Shining Stars Girls Project at the University of Northern Iowa, Cedar Falls, Iowa, who are girls in kindergarten through eighth grades shared some light on what children are thinking about uniforms even when they are not at school.

Weekly about half of the girls bring extra clothes to change in, taking off the school uniforms as they begin participating in the afterschool program.

Each week when we go to the University's Dining Center for supper, the continual question they ask me is, "they don't have to wear uniforms?" For those who dislike uniforms, I am hopeful that their being able to see a large number of university students wearing clothes of their choice may motivate them to surely attend a college or university.

Summary, Implications, and the Realities about the School Uniform Debate

1. More and continual research needs to be conducted to see if there are indeed positive effects of students wearing uniforms versus not wearing them.
2. Is there evidence from parents that the uniforms save them money on school clothing/attire?
3. Many schools have a wear and share closet where, as students grow out of their uniforms, they can be passed on to other students who may need them.
4. In the beginning of the school year, many schools have established a school uniform fund to help those families with multiple children or who may not have the funds to purchase uniforms. Other community agencies and organizations have also donated funds to assist with this.
5. Most schools keep extra belts for the boys, so that there will be no "sagging pants." These are made available to students who may have not worn a belt to school that day. This is done so that punishing students for uniform violations would not become a disciplinary matter.
6. Schools are encouraged to have additional attire available for students whose families may be struggling with getting them to school or other issues related to uniforms so that children do not miss school.

7. Some schools do set aside a "jean" day or wear your own clothing as a reward day for students. Some children really enjoy this variation and change from the uniformity of students.
8. There is seasonal attire for uniforms and now there are more colors available for shirts, pants, skirts, and jumper dresses for girls also. The issue of shoes is one that many schools try to stipulate, so again students would not be able to have the discrepancy issues related to name brand items. Or if they are dealing with the name brand issue, it would mostly be for one seemingly unnoticed item. The other parts of the uniform seem to detract from items like shoes.
9. Schools really should seriously survey students and their parents prior to the implementation of school uniform policies requiring all students to wear uniforms. It appears that research data and assessing the wearing of uniforms happen after the policies are in place. Some data should be collected prior to implementation of the policies.
10. School districts should do everything in its power to not have parents and students feel as though they do not have a voice or that they have nothing to say about the school uniforms issue in general. Efforts should be made to include them in the process before, during, and after getting inputs from them on a continuous basis.
11. School districts must be prepared for parents as well as students who may protest and decide not to comply with the implementation. Administrators should strive to be proactive, planning ahead, and meeting with those who may be dissatisfied.
12. School administrators must be prepared to make public statements about why the school or the district changed its policies requiring all students at all grade levels to wear uniforms daily.
13. Are students required to wear uniforms to all school activities such as afterschool events, sports, or special school programs? Some say that the uniforms help them identify who belongs in the school and who does not.
14. The question about whether there is any correlation between school uniforms and student's academic achievement is one that is questionable because there is not uniformity of curricula, teaching–learning styles, etc. But it appears this is the most valuable data if it can be researched without bias.
15. If there is evidence of less gang activities, police loggings, and fights/violence, procedures need to be established in each school for how the data will be collected and kept. Even though some of this may not be as evident as a result of school uniforms, the before and after numbers do tell a story. Have university professors and students engaged in collecting and gathering the data to enhance the rationale for why the district decided upon uniforms.
16. When appropriate, allow students to share in discussions about the pros and cons of wearing school uniforms. Video and audio recordings from both the pros and cons should be a part of school media in the school. Students across all grade levels should be able to participate in the discussions to get a representative sample of grade levels and ages.

Summary

This chapter in this book only touches the surface of school uniforms. There is so much more that I could have included in this chapter, but I do plan on writing additional information about school uniforms.

This debate about school uniforms is definitely one that will linger on for a while because all schools are not requiring them. Then the question continues with why are some schools requiring students to wear uniforms and others are not?

A more serious and in-depth look needs to happen as all efforts should be made to answer some of the unanswered questions. Many are hopeful that this is not another method of segregation by race, income, or locale. Some feel that middle-class Whites have been able to stay the course, therefore keeping this topic away from their options at this time.

Once it is established that the debate over school uniforms or not is not merely what children wear as a part of their daily school attendance, but more so on issues like school improvements, the right to freedom of expression, and recognition of cultural and ethnic differences that must be respected. Until these matters are recognized and dealt with, this debate will linger on a little longer.

Student Assignment

1. Write a one-page summary of how it is perceived that school uniforms impact student behaviors and achievement.
2. Write a one-page opinion on whether you agree or disagree with the following:
   a. Uniform adoption improves secondary school attendance.
   b. Uniform adoptions in elementary schools generate large increases in teacher retention.
3. Class Debate:
   a. Group 1: Divide the class in half with half of the students expressing the points in favor of how school uniforms make schools safer, improve attendance, and student achievement.
   b. Group 2: Divide the class in half with half of the students expressing the points against how school uniforms make schools safer, improve attendance, and student achievement.

1. Take a look at the longitudinal study of 1988, respond to:
   a. School uniforms have no direct effect on substance use, student behaviors, or attendance. State whether you agree or disagree with the findings.
   b. Uniforms have no impact on student academic achievement. State whether you agree or disagree.
2. There is some confusion in regard to correlations between uniforms and achievement with both negative and positive data. Tell why and how this is confusing for those taking a closer look.
3. Write a four-page opinion on uniforms, student self-worth, and student–staff perceptions of gang presence in regard to school climate!

Additional Resources

Brunsma, D. (2004) *The School Uniform Movement and What It Tells Us about American Education: A Symbolic Crusade.* Lanham, MD: Rowman & Littlefield Education.

Cruz, B.C. (2001) *School Dress Codes: A Pro/Con Issue.* Berkeley Heights, NJ: Enslow Publishers.

Gentile, E., & Imberman, S.A. (2012) Dressed for Success? The Effect of School Uniforms on Student Achievement and Behavior. *Journal of Urban Economics*, 71. doi: 10.1016/j.jue.2011.10.002.

Yeung, R. (2009) Are School Uniforms a Good Fit? Results from the ECLS-K and the NELS. *Educational Policy*, 23. doi: 10.1177/0895904808330170.

Brunsma, D.L., & Rockquemore, K.A. (1998) Effects of Student Uniforms on Attendance, Behavior Problems, Substance Use, and Academic Achievement. *The Journal of Educational Research*, 92. doi: 10.1080/00220679809597575.

Bodine, A. (2003) School Uniforms, Academic Achievement, and Uses of Research. *The Journal of Educational Research*, 97. doi: 10.1080/00220670309597509.

Wade, K.K, & Stafford, M.E. (2003) Public School Uniforms: Effect on Perceptions of Gang Presence, School Climate, and Student Self-Perceptions. *Education and Urban Society*, 35. doi: 10.1177/0013124503255002.

Norum, P.S., et al. (1998) The Effect of Uniforms on Nonuniform Apparel Expenditures. *Family & Consumer Sciences, 26(3),* 259-280. doi: 10.1177/1077727X980263001.

Chapter 12

Achievement Gaps: What Role Does Absenteeism Play?

The concern of achievement gaps and the widening of them between races, sexes, as well as socioeconomic statuses continue to plague educational systems throughout the United States.

As we continue to assess and review some of the perceptions and rationale for the continuation of achievement gaps, we still feel that we have found some of the main highlights of this current and ongoing issue.

Educators, teachers and administrators included, continue to look at their schools, school districts, environments, and supportive programming for all students looking for openings about what needs to change to close these gaps.

Schools all over the United States are struggling with gifted and talented programs as well as special education programming for students who are classified as having a disability or special needs. As they look at these programs, data points to the fact that students of color and low-income students seem to disparately overpower the special education end of the educational hierarchy, but are almost absent or nonexistent on the top of the tier-gifted and talented programs.

So with these issues at the forefront for students present in schools on a daily basis, this seems to be even more devastating when we think of present vs. absent when we take school attendance. So who is looking at what is called excessive absenteeism and what impact should the definition of excessive absenteeism have on a student's overall school performance?

When it comes to the university levels, as college professors we have been made to develop classroom policies that address the issue of what each faculty member deems excessive absenteeism. I must admit that I was quite shocked and surprised at the different faculty attitudes, beliefs, and practices in regard to university-college students' absenteeism. I can certainly cite some of the challenges that I have encountered as it relates to absenteeism. Because a high percentage of our students transfer in from a 2-year college, they no doubt often tell us professors at the 4-year institutions that they were not required to come to class each time. They report that it was important for them to show up to take a test or a special assignment. But they also add that they were doing much higher in-the-field hours than our students in the 4-year institutions. I found myself saying to the students how important it was in my class for all students to be present in class. Much of what they needed to learn happened during class sessions. So being absent meant that they missed out on learning what they need to learn in this course. Merely passing a test does not account for the interactions, in-class participation, and in-class sharing that notes or individuals cannot adequately relate to. So this was a change of behaviors for these students.

What Is Excessive Absenteeism in Some College Classes?

For some reason, most of us have latched on to the number three as the determinant for excessive absenteeism or not. So many professors' syllabi include a statement like, "Three or more absences are considered as excessive absenteeism."

Then after we get past the three, we found that there was also a need for further stipulations and clarification. Then there is the need to help make distinctions such as excused absence, unexcused absence. Excused absences include, but are not limited to, contacting the professor by e-mail, phone call, or in person prior to the absence or extenuating circumstances, medical, death of a family member, a family crisis, or other situations as determined by the professor.

Unexcused absences are when a student is absent and does not communicate with the professor at all. Some of these absences are simply, oversleeping, didn't go to class or other personal reasons that do not fall under extenuating circumstances or justifiable actions such as sports, speech or other university-sponsored events that the student may participate in.

It seems obvious while including this information in our syllabi, but when the professor verbally or in written format does a reminder, students know that they may have surpassed the number and wonder if there is anything that can be done to rectify the situation. One thing that can be done is to not add any additional absences to the already excessive list.

I must admit that I really was surprised when one of my colleagues said that she does not want to know why they were absent. She does not want them to give her any reasons. So that one seems to be an isolated case in that while most professors are not trying delve into students' personal affairs, if there are no reasons given, then it will be more difficult to determine excused or non-excused absences.

So after monitoring absences for several semesters and conversing with some of the other professors, I learned that it is a good idea to give points for in-class participation, which means that if a student is absent, they will miss the class content of the day as well as points for in-class participation. So students often want to do the assignment independently to see if they can get the points for in-class participation, even though they were not in class.

So just as university students pose challenges for professors in regard to absences, so do elementary, middle, and high schools.

There are some big education policy decisions that are connected to student absenteeism that needs to be dealt with. So as we begin to look at some of the real educational issues such as teacher evaluations, homework, student engagement, student lunches, etc., Sarah Dock invites others to join in with what they call bug policy debates! It is time to stand up and speak out on some of these critical educational issues. School days are standing at the crossroads: Where do we go from here?

To better understand the realities that exist among students and their involvement with success, it is valuable to look closely at attendance and finishing school. Does it make a difference in graduation rates, successful learning experiences and achievement in our schools?

Wow, when it comes to student achievement, many educators advocate the lowest of all possible accomplishments is to move that disparities point by getting the child to school. Boosting and increasing student school attendance can and will make a difference in overall performance. If the parents/guardians or family members are not able to at least get the child to school, it has been determined that nothing else matters.

There is some new research that delves into the major differences in overall achievement based on whether students are present and in class or not.

IMPORTANT POINT: The Every Student Succeeds Act has caused districts to take a look at chronic absenteeism of students in schools. States are now required to report chronic absenteeism rates, which allow districts to use this as another form of school accountability.

Almost all of the states included chronic absenteeism data when submitting their Every Student Succeeds Act plan, including data on chronic absenteeism as a part of their school's accountability.

Research has indicated and confirmed that chronic absenteeism does contribute to lower test scores and the achievement gap.

Chronic absenteeism across school districts in the United States poses a very complicated, multi-dimensional problem. However, there is hope that there are solutions.

Here are some facts that we know about chronic absenteeism:

1. Chronic absenteeism contributes to school dropout rates.
2. Chronic absenteeism contributes to achievement gaps disproportionately affecting low-income and minority students.
3. Approximately 5–7.5 million students are missing almost a month of school. About 10 percent of kindergartners and first-graders are absent for this number of days.
4. Chronic absenteeism is detrimental to reading skills.
5. Chronic absenteeism impacts lower graduation rates.
6. Chronic absenteeism occurs as a result of health issues. Asthma and oral health needs are among the leading matters.
7. Chronic absenteeism is a result of lower test scores. Students who were absent for more than 3 days in the month before the administration of the National Assessment of Educational Progress exam (NAEP) scored 12-1 points lower than those who did not miss days.
8. Minority students have a higher rate of absenteeism than White students.
9. Blacks and Latinos were more likely to be absent than their White peers.
10. Students with disabilities have higher rates of absenteeism.

Source: Student Absenteeism: Three New Studies to Know by **Sarah D. Sparks** on May 8, 2017, 1:42 pm

Source: 7 things to know about chronic student absenteeism by Karen Yi, Sept. 1, 2015

For further information, see:

http://www.attendanceworks.org/wordpress/wp-content/uploads/2015/07/Mapping-the-Early-Attendance-Gap-Final-4.pdfz

Chapter 13

Invented Spelling Can Improve Reading Skills

It is highly recommended that educators make every effort to encourage students, especially kindergartners who use invented spelling.

Helping kindergartners who attempted to spell words that were unrecognizable to put meaning to them is a positive approach to use.

According to a recent study, it is proven that when we encourage kindergartners to attempt to spell unknown words on their own, it helps them to become better readers.

Gene Ouellette, an associate professor of psychology, Mount Allison University, and Monique Sénéchal, a psychology professor at Carleton University, did a number of studies on how invented spelling contributes significantly to literacy learning.

These researchers found out that over the years, there seemed to be something with those children who are independently doing invented spelling or doing it on their own that really helps them learn how to read. These researchers state that they think this is the missing piece of the puzzle.

So as educators begin to look for even more answers as to some strategies and approaches that empower children more with reading skills, they are looking closer at invented spelling.

Having been a preschool-kindergarten teacher, it was always an amazing experience when we could see the progress and growth in young children's literacy skills. Recalling the days from when they moved from writing to reading, it was always like magic to see what they started doing with letters, letter combinations, and other literacy-related experiences.

Then it was never long after that I would begin to see and hear them actually reading sentences and/or simple phrases.

Thus, it can be assumed that every opportunity should be made to give children paper, pencil markers, etc so than handing them something like an iPad. This is not in opposition to young children using an iPad or other technology, but allowing the students to use their skills in inventive spelling. The question remains, what then do we do to enhance these young children's literacy skills such that by the end of first grade, they are reading. The reading that we are talking about is not through a drill and skill approach.

There has been much controversy regarding best practices and helping young children develop skills needed for maximum literacy and reading experiences. It has been suggested that invented spelling is better than the rigorous Response to Intervention (RTI). This is an assessment that starts with kindergartners. It is also an intervention practice used to assist students with strengthening literacy skills.

As a practicing teacher and a researcher, I am in agreement with the new research findings that promote the individualization and control of children's own learning. The focus that makes it a highly recommended practice is because it is developmental and allows for children to grow from where they originally started from and move to higher levels.

The Definition of Invented (or inventive spelling)

The definition seems to have continued from when children would begin writing letters, at first with what did not seem as though there was a pattern to it or what many thought as not having any real meaning.

But the definition that is being used by researchers to share that is when students write words that are not familiar to them and do so based on how they sound to them.

What's So Important about the Process?

1. Writing unfamiliar words based on how the child thinks they sound.
2. Writing unfamiliar words based on how the child thinks they sound, even when they are incorrect.
3. Writing unfamiliar words based on how the child thinks they sound, even when incorrect, they over a period of time learn to break the code.
4. Writing unfamiliar words based on how the child thinks they sound, even when incorrect, they over a period of time learn to break the code and learn how to spell the word correctly.
5. When the child learns to spell the word correctly, this is when the effective approach is demonstrated at the research-proven levels.

More Magic about Children Using Invented Spelling

1. Young children gain additional experiences by writing these words on paper.
2. Young children gain additional experiences because of the magic of the kinesthetic movement which reinforces the neural pathways of the child.

One Invented Spelling Study with Increased Attention

Two researchers, Gene Quellette and Monique Sénéchal, have been studying the literacy-early reading-writing concept of invented spelling for years.

They found that:

1. Invented spelling influenced the child's reading skills after the initial stages.
2. Longitudinally, invented spelling influenced alphabetic knowledge and served as a connection between phonological awareness and early literacy-reading skills.
3. Longitudinally, invented spelling influenced the development of conventional spelling and phonological awareness.
4. Longitudinally, invented spelling influenced the development of strong alphabetic knowledge.
5. Longitudinally, invented spelling adds an explanation to the variance to literacy-reading outcomes that have not been fully explored relative to codes and language literacy-related skill development.

So What's So Good about the New Findings on Invented Spelling?

1. Believe it because it is true that children feel good about themselves and their accomplishments when they are able to write their own words.
2. Children feel more confident about their literacy skills because they are not consistently being corrected or told that what they wrote is not correct.
3. Testimonials from children verify that it is fun.
4. Children feel more positive about learning because of not being forced to repeat nonsense syllables that have no real individualized meaning to them.
5. Children feel more positive about invented spelling rather than being assessed by the RTI.
6. After a period of time, children learn to self-correct their own individual writing of any incorrectly spelled words.
7. If it appears to be appropriate that after practice over a period of time, parents and teachers can kindly help the child with the correct and proper spelling of words. This can be done if it seems like the child is stuck or not moving forward as perceived by the adults.
8. Yes the child is gaining phonological knowledge while using invented spelling.
9. Yes the child is gaining phonological knowledge while using invented spelling because of their deciphering the sounds of those letters on an ongoing basis.

The Other Perspective on Invented Spelling

For many parents and others who normally do not work with younger students, there is disagreement about allowing children to use the process of invented spelling. Some of the arguments include:

1. They feel that it is wrong for us in the educational process to allow children to spell words incorrectly.
2. They feel that it is wrong for us in the educational process to allow children to spell words incorrectly and allow them to do so for a period of time as they move to the stage of self-correcting.
3. Some feel that if a child learns to spell the word through the process of invented spelling, he or she may continue to spell the word incorrectly because that is the way they will recall it as the way to spell.
4. Some feel that there are major spelling difficulties and challenges to students in the United States.
5. Some feel that there is no developed approach or program to teach spelling in the United States.
6. Some feel that they cannot endorse invented spelling when we have so many students and even adults who cannot spell properly because of the complexity of the English language.
7. Invented spelling has been intertwined negatively as an anti-whole language concept.

The Anti-child-centered Approach

The educational system is such that too many school districts are not totally in support of the child-centered approach.

So many feel that we should not allow learning to children. This theory is that they cannot think properly without the leadership of an adult. Thus, the invented spelling approach is one that children lead the way with their own ways of spelling words.

The opposite of the child-centered approach is that of a scripted, structured, and highly managed curriculum that maintains control over children in the learning process. They believe that this controlling approach is the most effective even when these children are learning to read.

Phonics—Still a Lot of Questions?

Some who believe in all-phonics feel that too many children are introduced to this too early. The thought behind it is that when children are introduced too early, they miss out on the opportunities to explore words from their own perspective of how they look when writing and how they sound to them.

With too early formal phonics introduction, these children also miss out on the fun of drawing favorite and familiar pictures, scribbling, and moving to the actual printing of letters as they begin to experience the sounds of words.

Still others believe that there are some children who will need the formal approach to phonics. But they quickly add that there must be a pre-assessed and predetermined time, if at all.

1. For some advocates of other approaches to reading, invented spelling seems too simple.
2. For some advocates of other approaches to reading, invented spelling doesn't cost anything when reading series do.
3. There is a lack of understanding in regard to all of the high-powered brain work that goes into the child's use of invented spelling.
4. For many of the adults, they grow more and more doubtful when they are not able to visually see the child's growth in writing, reading, and literacy experiences.
5. There needs to be additional training so that those who work with young children learn to understand the importance of the sound–symbol relationships to children.
6. There needs to be additional training on invented spelling so that there will not be an inappropriate push to make children read earlier.
7. Research also shows that students with disabilities in middle and high school are taught through use of invented spelling.
8. The research focused on invented spelling words, but it is also noted that sentences can be used with older students.

Summary

It is important that strategies and approaches be used with young children that decrease guilt feelings, embarrassment, and taking a substantial amount of time correcting student spelling.

In order to experience student success, students should be allowed the freedom to write while exploring the approaches leading to their own self-corrections of spelling.

It is very important that teachers use encouraging approaches with students as they learn about word approximations, obtaining assistance from teachers in ways that are constructive, encouraging and rewarding when and if needed.

So regardless of how we may have felt about inventive spelling over a period of time, new research shows that for those who had taken invented spelling out of the curriculum, the time has come to put it back in.

The most important point to remember from this study is that it is our role to provide space and time for students to grow, develop, and feel good about their own writing. While helping them feel good about their writing, it is important that caution be taken when and if there comes a time for assisting with corrections. The approach of invented spelling helps a child to learn to read.

It should be recognized that while other literacy-reading programs are important, this new research gives educators a different perspective on approaches that work.

Source: The Power of Invented Spelling: Giving Children Control by Nancy Bailey, May 16, 2017.

References

Gentry, J.R. Landmark Study Finds Better Path to Reading Success. *Psychology Today.* Mar. 30, 2017.

Loewus, L. Invented Spelling Leads to Better Reading Study Says. *Education Week.* May 5, 2017.

Sénéchal, M. (2017) Testing a Nested Skills Model of the Relations Among Invented Spelling, Accurate Spelling, and Word Reading, From Kindergarten to Grade 1. *Early Child Development and Care,* 187 (3-4), 358-370.

Quellette, G., & Sénéchal, M. (2017) Invented Spelling in Kindergarten as a Predictor of Reading and Spelling in Grade 1: A New Pathway to Literacy, or just the same Road, Less Known? *Developmental Psychology,* 53(1), 77-88.

Chapter 14

The Effects of Low Teacher Expectations on Students of Color

Teacher leaders all over the United States speak openly about the importance of teachers having a positive attitude and believing in their students. Once they have high expectations for their students, they make it known to them.

Students share openly that they appreciate and believe in teachers who believe in them and want to see them succeed.

All of the data show that teachers who are aware of students who may come from environments where they may not have as much access to people who demonstrate successful characteristics either have negative expectations or either attempt to counter the beliefs of failure for too many of these students.

While there seem to be indicators of teachers having lower expectations of students from perceived disadvantaged environments, there is no evidence showing that these teachers are systematically biased.

But a study at American University and Johns Hopkins University questioned whether there is a systematic bias in teacher expectations of Black students' educational success.

Teacher Expectations of Black Students' Educational Success Study Results

Non-Black teachers have significantly lower expectations for educational attainment of Black students than Black teachers when assessing the same students.

1. Research question: Are Black teachers too optimistic in their expectations of Black students?
2. Research question: Are non-Black teachers too pessimistic in their expectations of Black students?
3. Or is there a combination of these two expectations when assessing Black students?

The answers to these questions are very important because teacher expectations are to

A. impact as well as develop student outcomes;
B. impact systematic bias in regard to teacher expectations related to student success; and
C. may contribute to academic achievement gaps and minimal academic attainment.

IMPORTANT MESSAGE FOR ALL TEACHERS

Teachers should maintain a positive attitude while relaying the message of high expectations for every student.

The Role of Systematic Teacher Bias in the Study

Data from a national survey of tenth graders in the United States where two teachers per student were asked how much education they expected their students to attain.

Research Design: The design is centered around the idea that if two teachers disagree about the expected educational achievement of a student, that at least one of the teachers must be wrong.

1. There are possibilities that the differences in opinions could be random by nature based on encounters/relationships between students and teachers but
2. If these differences in teacher expectations are such that they are impacted by demographic match between students and teachers, then it suggests that teachers have systematic biases for at least some students and their teacher relationships.

Example to think about

When a Black student is evaluated by a Black teacher and by one non-Black teacher, the non-Black teacher is about 30 percent less likely to expect that the student will complete a 4-year college than a Black teacher.

It is hoped that studies such as this one will begin correspondences between educators and others to

1. take a closer look at teacher expectations and how lower teacher expectations are formed;
2. look at possible interventions that might eliminate some of the biases found in teacher expectations;
3. take a closer look at how students might be affected in a long-term manner, especially when influenced mostly by teachers with low expectations; and
4. work to make the teaching staff more diverse and representative of the student population.

Source: Teachers' Low Expectations for Students of Color Found to Affect Students' Success by Madeline Will, May 18, 2017

Study Two

Another study conducted by Hua-Yu Sebastian Cherng of International Education at New York University's Steinhardt School of Education analyzed data from approximately 10,000 high school tenth graders and their teachers from the Education Longitudinal Study of 2002.

After analyzing standardized test scores and homework completion, Cherng found that math and English teachers were more likely to have lower expectations of students of color.

Source: http://www.nyu.edu/about/news-publications/news/2017/may/teacher-racial-bias-matters-more-for-students-of-color-.htmlMay 18,

When looking at teacher expectations, it was found that when the same Black student was evaluated, White teachers expected significantly lower academic success than did Black teachers. It was further discovered that it was especially true for Black boys. White teachers are about 40 percent less likely to expect Black students to graduate from high school.

The Journal of *Economics of Education Review* (May 30, 2016) included an article inclusive of the fact that the more modest expectations of some teachers could become self-fulfilling prophecies for students. These low expectations could affect the performance of students, especially students from environments where they lack access to role models who could counteract a teacher's low expectations, says study coauthor Nicholas Papageorge. He is an economist in the Johns Hopkins University's Krieger School of Arts and Sciences.

IMPORTANT FACT: "What we find is that white teachers and Black teachers systematically disagree about the exact same student," Papageorge says. "One of them has to be wrong."

"If I'm a teacher and decide that a student isn't any good, I may be communicating that to the student," he adds. "A teacher telling a student they're not smart will weigh heavily on how that student feels about their future and perhaps the effort they put into doing well in school."

IMPORTANT FACT: These findings go beyond just education and may be applied to workplaces, industries as well as the criminal justice system. These similar low expectations of systematic biases can be found in societal issues/matters.

IMPORTANT FACT: In the Educational Longitudinal study of 2002, 8,400 tenth grade public school students were followed. In that survey, two different teachers taught a designated student math or reading to predict how far that student would go in school.

When it came to White students, the ratings by both teachers were the same. But when it came to Black students, especially boys, there were huge differences.

IMPORTANT FACT: White teachers had much lower expectations than Black teachers when predicting how far Black students would go in school.

IMORTANT FACT: White teachers and other non-Black teachers were 12 percent more likely than Black teachers to predict that Black students would not complete high school.

IMPORTANT FACT: Non-Black teachers were 5 percent more likely to predict that Black male students wouldn't complete high school more so than Black female students.

IMPORTANT FACT: Black female teachers are significantly more optimistic about the abilities of Black boys to complete high school than teachers of any other demographic group.

IMPORTANT FACT: Black female teachers were 20 percent less likely than White teachers to predict that Black male students wouldn't complete high school.

IMPORTANT FACT: Black female teachers were 30 percent less likely than Black male teachers to predict that a Black male student wouldn't complete high school.

IMPORTANT FACT: White male teachers are 10–20 percent more likely to have low expectations for Black female students.

IMPORTANT FACT: Math teachers were significantly more likely to have low expectations for female students.

IMPORTANT FACT: Black students in 10th grade, especially Black boys, showed that they were less likely to enroll in a subject taught by non-Black teachers. The Implication: Biased teacher expectations have long-term effects on students.

IMPORTANT FACT: Teachers' belief about their students' academic attainment is an important point and is linked to students' own beliefs about how far they will progress in school, their attitudes toward school, and their academic achievement. Teachers' belief in their students' academic capabilities has long been understood to be a vital ingredient for student success and has been linked to students' own beliefs in how far they will progress in school, their attitudes toward school, and their academic achievement.

IMPORTANT FACT: According to Cherng, when a teacher expects a student to do well academically, then the teacher's behaviors are also shaped and determine body language, teacher behaviors, assignments given, as well as spending time with the student.

IMPORTANT FACT: Students respond to these high expectations by internalizing them and having the interest and desire to learn, thus boosting their own academic performance and expectations.

IMPORTANT FACT: Teacher expectations may be especially important for students of color, showing that when teachers have confidence in the performance of students of color, those students benefit more so than their White peers.

IMPORTANT FACT: Student expectations were also measured by how far high school seniors expected they would go in school such as would they graduate from college or whether they would obtain a graduate degree.

IMPORTANT FACT: The greatest gap was found for Black students with teachers reporting that their class was too difficult. In math, it was more than twice the percentage (18 percent) and English (13 percent) compared to White students.

IMPORTANT FACT: Teachers who underestimated their students' abilities had an impact on both students' academic expectations and their GPAs.

IMPORTANT FACT: Teachers who underestimated their students' abilities caused students to have lower expectations of themselves as well as their school completion. (Cherng)

IMPORTANT FACT: Teacher underestimations affected student GPAs, but for Black students, the relationship rather than the underestimation impacted Black students' GPAs. (Cherng)

IMPORTANT FACT: Teacher underestimations are harmful to Black students.

IMPORTANT FACT: Cherng concluded that opportunities should be provided for teachers to learn to how to deal with these biases and help eliminate the variations by focusing on student success.

Source:

https://www.fcd-us.org/assets/2016/04/Watching_Teachers_Work_0_0.pdf
http://cdn2.hubspot.net/hubfs/617695/premium_content_resources/pla/PDF/PLA_Fueling-th
http://www.voiceofsandiego.org/topics/education/no-school-district-in-the-country-has-ever
https://hub.jhu.edu/2016/03/30/racial-bias-teacher-expectations-black-white/
http://www.pbs.org/newshour/rundown/teachers-expect-less-students-color-study-shows/
http://www.huffingtonpost.com/2014/10/07/pygmalion-effect-study_n_5942666.html

IMPORTANT FACT: Researchers found that students whose teachers expected them to graduate from college were significantly more likely to do so.

IMPORTANT FACT: Teachers had lower expectations for students who were disadvantaged and of color.

IMPORTANT FACT: Teachers thought that a college degree was 47 percent less likely for Black students than for Whites.

IMPORTANT FACT: Teachers thought that a college degree was 53 percent less likely for low-income students more so than for students of non–low-income families.

IMPORTANT FACT: Teachers thought Hispanic students were 42 percent less likely than White students to graduate from college.

IMPORTANT FACT: Data from the National Center for Education Statistics showed that White students are almost twice as likely to graduate from college in 4 years compared to Black students.

IMPORTANT FACT: Students whose teachers had high expectations were three times more likely to graduate from college. (Boser)

IMPORTANT FACT: Teachers and students from different backgrounds may misunderstand each other based on race. (Boser)

Source: Ulrich Boser https://www.americanprogress.org/press/release/2014/10/06/98317/release-teachers-have-lower-expectations-for-students-of-color-and-students-from-low-income-backgrounds/Oct 6, 2014

Summary:

The study states that Common Core State Standards may be a possible solution because it requires states to raise educational standards while holding all students to the same benchmarks.

The United States needs to raise its expectations for students as well as educators. This may help children succeed in college and life.

Source: The Alarming Effect of Racial Mismatch on Teacher Expectations by Brown Center Chalkboard, Aug. 18, 2015

Chapter 15

It's Not Just Preschool, But Are Black Children Being Dehumanized?

The messages continue to ring with clarity when it comes to issues relative to Black children. Why are the messages similar in nature? While so many of us hope for a better and brighter future for children all over the world, somehow, it appears that Black children suffer at the hands of the educational arena. While there is definitely more diversity in educational settings, for many it appears that African-American children continue to lag behind in almost every area.

As urgent cries are heard all over the United States, groups of researchers and educators continue to ponder over what are some of the best approaches, strategies, and goals to help decrease the achievement gaps and to deal with some of the social-emotional dilemmas of Black children. So what needs to happen in homes, schools, and other programs to show progress, growth, and development for Black children?

Some experts wonder why there are children who seem to continue to linger behind in educational attainment, while others seem to continue to excel and pass them by. The answers are complex when it comes to Black children. There are many theories circulating that may fall under the category of truth while others may appear to linger under a category of myth or unproven evidence/documentation.

Recent studies show a theory of the intentional dehumanization of Black children. But could this be true generations after the ending of slavery? Could this be true years after an active civil rights movement with the marching of racial and cultural changes throughout society? Could this be true when it appears that some believe Blacks have more than they have had ever before in their lives?

Behavioral Dehumanization

As questions continue to pour in relative to how Black children are treated educationally, the scariest part of the entire ordeal is that this begins very early in the lives of young children. So many ask, how could this be when these children are so young, cute, and should be given attention so that they can grow and develop?

Others ask the question of this as a form of intentional continuation of the hidden form of slavery being imposed on the youngest of families? Or is this part of what some perceive to be misinformation of the truth about what is actually happening among educators and young Black students/children.

So where does the concept or practice of dehumanization come in for these children? One of the greatest forms of dehumanization begins with Black infants and toddlers and the suspension/expulsion of them from childcare and preschool programs. So questions are asked about what did these very young children do that the institution saw the serious need to suspend/expel them from their familiar environment of an educational setting?

The answers vary:

1. If these very young children show any aggressive tendencies or other than perfect behaviors, without much hesitation the answer or solution to the problem entails suspensions/expulsions. So many feel this is a major form of dehumanization because why would you treat such a young child in this manner?
2. If these children do not meet the "normalcy" standards, especially for behaviors, then their families need to find a different type of program for them, thus they are not welcome to stay at the current location.
3. There are some who have biased or prejudicial beliefs about certain races of people whether it is based on facts or hearsay. Thus the mere fact that some children are from a certain race, if bias, especially implicit bias becomes a part of their beliefs and thoughts about certain children, then the self-fulfilling prophecy takes over.
4. There are some who have the belief that if some children do certain unacceptable things, they are then treated as if they are representative of historical treatment or actions of a group of people.

While these may be some of the factors related to very young children, there is some evidence pointing to the fact that these early years are merely the beginning. These beginnings continue throughout the school years and for many through their post-secondary years. So for too many it is the beginning of what many consider to be the beginnings of the dehumanization pathway.

The Long-term Effects of Early Dehumanization Experiences of Black Children

So African-Americans make up about thirteen percent of the American population, yet they comprise about half of all prison inmates. How could this be, without what some call a racial conspiracy forwarded to Black genocide. Now this belief or theory seems harsh, but researchers are struggling to find other rationale as to why this practice of dehumanization has continued for such a long period of time. Is not a part of a planned program that a certain percentage of this group will not move beyond a certain level? In order to maintain this, certain practices must prevail and incarceration takes care of the surface part of the plan. For having one or more members of the immediate family being incarcerated at the same time, thus leaving many families struggling and in need of regrouping in attempts to make the lives of children more positive and humanistic.

The School to Prison Pipeline Is Real

Just thinking aloud about how much the theory of the school to prison pipeline has become so real. When first learning about it, one may hesitate about the true facts. But once there is in-depth research, it is easily recognizable. I was quite amazed at how the predictions of who would be in the pathway can now be determined at birth. Then by age two, it is believed that many feel that they have a very good handle through their predictions of who will remain on the prison pathway. I must admit that there are some defined characteristics that are being used to determine who will be going to prison in a certain number of years. Some of these predictions are based on the family background, especially that of the child's mother. So the time has come now, where the backgrounds of some of these mothers must begin to be improved and more on a path of upward mobility to give their children a possible chance. Besides the predictions made about the parental backgrounds, there is the deep funneling of young Black children into the pathway of the criminal justice system that merely begins through the suspension and expulsion procedures in educational settings. Thus when reviewing many of the school districts' data, regardless of the number or percentage of Black children enrolled, they continue to represent inequities in the school discipline policies that seem to be nationwide. Also these discipline policies seem to lack the scrutiny to look at issues such as inequality and equality. These actions are recorded and documented that show that Black children could do the same policy violation as other peers, but they will be channeled into the criminal justice system while many others are not.

A 3-year study shows how Black boys, especially, are perceived differently from others in the educational system. (Arnett Ferguson, Bad Boys: Public Schools in the Making of Black Masculinity) The following are some of the highlights of her studies:

1. It was well documented that educators and school administrators channeled Black male students, in particular, into the juvenile justice system. Thus she was able to cite that there were perceived differences about Black males and other students.
2. The trend of suspending and expelling Black male students continues today. Much of this has been continued by schools' "zero tolerance" policies. With the increase in these policies, school districts have added or increased the number of school police officers and are assigned the task of arresting students who are noncompliant and considered to be insubordinate.
3. Another major discrepancy and inequity of justice is found in the fact that what could have been construed as fights, or acting out behaviors, in schools turned to the criminal side for Black students.

Fact: Black students are usually suspended from schools than any other race of students.

Fact: Black students face disproportionate expulsion and arrest rates.

Fact: Children who enter the juvenile justice system are more likely to be arrested as an adult.

Fact: The United States Justice System, under the Obama Administration, realized that there is a serious matter in the United States. Thus a new set of guidelines were issued to halt or curb the discriminatory practices of suspensions in schools.

Fact: The discriminatory and negative discipline patterns and actions impact Black children as young as 3 years of age.

Fact: Black children face discrimination as early as preschool.

Fact: Suspending any preschool children is disturbing.

Fact: Although Black children make up about 18 percent of preschoolers, 42 percent of them were suspended at least once.

Fact: Although Black children make up about 18 percent of preschoolers, 48 percent were suspended multiple times.

January 8, 2014

U.S. Department of Education, press@ed.gov

U.S. Department of Justice

Collaborative Efforts to Make Changes

A discipline guidance package was released jointly by the U.S. Department of Education and the U.S. Department of Justice. This package is designed to help states and school districts to develop policies, plans, and implement practices to make school climate more positive, thus complying with the federal law.

1. Schools need to make the climates more positive for all students.
2. Schools need to make sure that their practices for responding to misbehaviors by students are fair, equal, and nondiscriminatory for all.
3. A significant number of students miss class because of suspensions and expulsions.
4. A significant number of students miss class for what might be considered as minor violations of school rules.
5. Sadly, students of color and also having been diagnosed with a disability are impacted in a very disproportionate way.

There is a guidance package that was developed by the U.S. Department of Education and the U.S. Department of Justice to be a resource to assist schools in creating a more positive school climate, boosting student academic success and decreasing the achievement gaps.

Former U.S. Secretary of Education, Arne Duncan, stated: "Effective teaching and learning cannot take place unless students feel safe at school." "Positive discipline policies can help create safer learning environments without relying heavily on suspensions and expulsions. Schools also must understand their civil rights obligations and avoid unfair disciplinary practices. We need to keep students in class where they can learn. These resources are a step in the right direction."

This resource package that is aforementioned consists of four components:

1. The Dear Colleague guidance letter on civil rights and discipline tells how schools can meet their legal obligations under federal law to administer student discipline without discriminating against students on the basis of race, color, or national origin.
2. The Guiding Principles document shares research and best practices of three key principles and related action steps that can help guide states to improve school climate and school discipline.
3. The Directory of Federal School Climate and Discipline Resources provides indexes of the federal technical assistance and resources for school discipline and climate.
4. The Compendium of School Discipline Laws and Regulations is an online catalogue of the laws and regulations on school discipline in each of the 50 states, the District of Columbia and Puerto Rico, and compares laws across states and jurisdictions.

Those in positions of authority in the Departments of Justice and Education agree that the school discipline plan should send a student with a violation to the principal's office rather than to jail.

All efforts must be made to provide for fair and effective discipline that will make schools safe, thus providing support and inclusion for all students.

This guidance package is the result of the serious realization that there was a great need to address the school to prison pipeline and discipline policies that push students out of school straight into the criminal/juvenile justice system. Therefore, the Department of Justice is able to enforce Title IV of the Civil Rights Act of 1964. Title IV prohibits discrimination on the basis of race or national origin in public schools.

Title VI of the Civil Rights Act of 1964 prohibits discrimination on the basis of race, color, or national origin by schools, law enforcement agencies, and other agencies/institutions receiving federal financial assistance.

The guidance package is also a result of President Obama's Now is the Time proposal to reduce gun violence in connection with Social Security Disability Insurance (SSDI) and fulfillment of the administration's commitment to this package was developed with additional input from civil rights advocates, major educational organizations, and philanthropic partners in the hope of meeting the needs of students.

Studies Confirming Dehumanization?

Annie E. Casey Foundation found that African-American children are on the lowest end of almost every measured index, including proficiency in math and reading, high school graduation, poverty and parental education. The report, titled Race for Results, shared that the index scores for African-American children should be considered as a national crisis.

There are two other recently published major studies that cite specific evidence of how Black children are so disadvantaged at an early age. One research project was published in the *Journal of Personality and Social Psychology*, titled: The Essence of Innocence: Consequences of Dehumanizing Black Children by Goff et al.

Study 1: This study examined how college students and police officers estimated the ages of children who they were told had committed crimes. Both of these groups were more likely to overestimate the ages of Black children compared to non-Black children.

So what did this imply? The implication was that Black children were seen as "significantly less innocent" than others. The authors wrote:

Critical Fact:
We expected... that individuals would perceive Black boys as being more responsible for their actions and as being more appropriate targets for police violence. We find support for these hypotheses... and converging evidence that Black boys are seen as older and less innocent and that they prompt a less essential conception of childhood than do their White same-age peers.

Study 2: Another study by researchers at UC Riverside found that teachers tended to be more likely to evaluate Black children negatively than non-Black children who were engaged in pretend play.

Psychology professor Tuppett M. Yates, who led the study, observed 171 preschool-aged children interacting with stuffed toys and other props and evaluated them for how imaginative and creative they were. Yates shared in an interview that during her observations, independent of the teachers, she noted that all the children, regardless of race, were "similarly imaginative and similarly expressive."

Critical Fact:
This researcher noted that when the children's teachers evaluated the same children at a later time, there was a discriminatory effect. Yates explained, "For white children, imaginative and expressive players were rated very positively [by teachers] but the reverse was true for black children. Imaginative and expressive black children were perceived as less ready for school, as less accepted by their peers, and as greater sources of conflict and tension."

Researcher Yates' Findings:
"It was clear that negative behaviors were magnified through 'race-colored glasses.'" Yates, in her study of children engaged in pretend play found that "there is also potentially a systematic devaluing of positive attributes among black children." She expressed concern about how "very early on, some kids are being educated towards innovation and leadership and others may be educated towards more menial or concrete social positions."

This is the same type of racial bias expressed by many researchers adding to the fact that many people believe that Black children are under the constraints of dehumanization.

Yates also reflected on the book, *Bad Boys* (2001) and how little seems to have changed since then. Yates affirmed author Ferguson's beliefs that Black children are given a "hidden curriculum." Yates too believes that this hidden curriculum persists today and is now starting much earlier than it could have been anticipated.

Critical Facts:

Fact 1: These researchers are expressing that with the continuation of hidden curriculum and discriminatory beliefs and practices, this type of inequality is being promoted generation after generation.

Fact 2: These researchers also commented on the Goff study that showed police estimates of Black children as older than they are. They believe that as a function of race here that Black boys are noted through a trend of "adultification." An example was shared that when a White student failed to return a library book, he/she was seen as forgetful, but when a Black student failed to return a library book, he/she was considered as a "thief" or "looter."

Summary

All of these studies consistently show that African-Americans have the walls of prejudice stacked against them from early childhood to adulthood. This certainly makes a case for the preschool to prison pipeline as the dehumanization of Black children.

Yates points out that through these studies that Black children are viewed differently, given less access to the kinds of venues needed to advance and progress in society. Therefore, they become less valued as a part of our culture.

Chapter 16

Tantrums: Growth and Development for Young Children

Tantrums

I am asked daily as to why and how temper tantrums can become such a crucial part of a young child's life? What happened? Are these new behaviors or old, long-term survival ways of communicating when the words are just not there yet?

For generation after generation, we have become accustomed to hearing parents talk about the terrible-terrific twos. So when they refer to this topic in their conversation, much of it is the same and yet much of it is different? How much of it relates to the behaviors of many of them?

Some parents frown when told about there are some positives that can come out of the positions that children and families find themselves in.

Although tantrums can surely be unpleasant, we should try to see them as opportunities for children to learn—about rules, why we have rules and the beginnings of limits. It is also very important that we begin to teach young children about words, especially words that will begin to help them describe their feelings. The issue of tantrums becomes challenging for us most of the time because of our lack of understanding the communication process for young children. Yes, we do know that many of them do not yet have the words to express their needs, interests, or feelings. So often part of the tantrum behaviors are exasperated because of what seems to the child like the adults misunderstanding of their communication skills. Often, we find ourselves saying to the child, "use your words." Well that is good teaching as we are trying to get them to express themselves, but if we stop and put ourselves in some of the young children's places, we will find ourselves saying, "what words?" "I can't find the words to say what I am feeling nor thinking, especially the way I am feeling right now." Well, I think about the many times as adults we have found ourselves in positions when we had to communicate with others when we have been placed in some very stressful situations. So let me pause for a moment to let us adults know how we respond like toddlers in tantrum situations even when we are not aware of our actions.

1. How about the times when someone we are familiar with questions our abilities at expressing ourselves?
2. How about feelings when we are in situations where we cannot truthfully find the words to tell someone how we are really feeling at the time about something?

3. How about our actions when we are angry and the person seems to be getting under our skin the more the event continues?
4. How about a time when we found ourselves totally out of control? We had not planned to be out of control, but some say we lost it.
5. How about a time since we do have words, we found ourselves using inappropriate words like name-calling, profanity, and other mean forms of communication?
6. How about a time when we have felt rejected and in reality no one was really rejecting us?
7. How about a time when we unfairly rejected or mistreated someone when the truth of the matter is that they had done nothing to us?

Why Do Tantrums Seem to Cause Adults the Greatest Nightmares?

Is it that tantrums have become such an issue not only for childcare providers, teachers, and parents, but for those in the general public who find themselves having to observe this embarrassing behavior? So, why are these tantrum-like behaviors so embarrassing? Is it because we are not accustomed to seeing children act like this?

Are we ashamed because of the reactions of the adults with the child? Are we thinking private thoughts about if this was your child how you would certainly handle it much differently? Or are the adults thinking about going over and giving a helping hand? Or some adults may find themselves interceding and trying to distract the child?

So knowing some of what we know, let's take a closer look at tantrums and behaviors that may make us shriek, want to scream, or possibly punish a young child.

Situation 1: An 18-month-old is in the shopping cart with mom, as they have been grocery shopping. The trip seems to have been a positive one as mom had a list of items to purchase and talked with the child about what was on the list. But now they are at the checkout counter, which has caused tantrum nightmares for many parents. So as I, the author, observed the interaction since I was in line right behind them, I knew what was causing this child's abrupt change in behaviors. I asked myself then and so many other times, "why are these stores putting all of the tempting candies at the checkout counter?" Then I stopped in my tracks because I already knew the answer—to sell. They knew that if they put the tempting candy right there that children would cry, scream, and have tantrums right at the checkout counter.

What happened next certainly depended on individual parents/adults and how they wanted to handle the situation. Another important factor that so many of our merchants don't want to take time to be fair about is whether the shoppers will have enough money to pay for their groceries and whether they had any spare money to buy some of the wishes of their children at that time? So that could be part of the decision, but it also depends on whether the parent felt as if it was advantageous to give in to the child this time, for fear of repeat behaviors the next time?

This case: The mother decided to allow the child to have one candy bar. The child wanted another, but she was direct, firm, and calm, and said, "Do you want this? You are not getting another one. Take this or you will get none." The child consented.

Situation 2: My son was around 20 months old when he started falling out on the floor. I would always observe what he was doing as I was trying to figure out what brought on that particular tantrum. I noticed one of the things that made me always observe children during tantrums. As he would fall out on the floor, he made sure that his head never touched the floor. As a matter of fact, each time he fell out on the floor, as the body approached the floor, he carefully took care of his head. To be honest, I was very grateful to know that he cared enough about his head not to hit it on the floor. That is one thing that does disturb me about observing children who are having a tantrum. I always hoped that they did not hurt their heads such that it affected them in the long term or short term for a matter of fact—related to a head injury. But one thing I heard a pediatrician say once was the head was the toughest part of a young child's body.

So as my son would fall out, he seldom would say the words, if he had any to express his feelings; instead, he would pout and cry. He wouldn't have the tantrum long and would not stay on the floor long, so once he settled down after getting up, I was able to delve a little further trying to inquire at the issue at hand. So sometimes he would point or go near where my attention needed to be drawn. He was a very meticulous child, so many of his tantrums were related to this. So he had a little toy truck and a toy car, he had placed them on the two blocks which were like tracks. His brother had moved them when he wasn't in the room. So he noticed right away that they were not where he had put them. So I called his brother into the room to put the two toys back where they had been: Mission Accomplished!

Situation 3: This 22-month-old was fine and came to the table to eat in a very nice calm manner. So I had mashed potatoes and put gravy over the potatoes. He began to scream loudly at the table and pushed the plate away. So again, I was puzzled and began to ask the child, "what's wrong?" Of course he could not tell me what the problem was. So my sister-in-law who was older and was of the "old school child rearing approaches all the way, was over to our house." She immediately told me what the problem was. She said, "he doesn't want that gravy on his potatoes." I was like you got to be kidding. So sure enough, I went in the kitchen and got a different clean plate. I came back with just the white mashed potatoes on his plate and nothing else. I put the plate in front of him and said, "here you go Jawanza." He started eating immediately, ate all, and wanted more. So that was another lesson that I learned as I began to deal with more children in the tantrum-toddler stages, that things must be right, all the way down to the aesthetics of their food.

Situation 4: This 3-year-old's mom asked me to take her and her sister to the park for some playtime. The girls loved the outside and certainly enjoyed all of the toddler level play equipment at this park. Their behaviors were so exceptional for their ages while we were there for playtime. So we stayed for an hour and a half, which gave them additional time to play on various equipment, play in the sandbox, and the other creative play areas at this park. Well, now, I started preparing them for leaving soon because it was time for me to take them home for their dinner. The 2-year-old didn't seem to fully understand that we would be leaving, so seemed to behave in a cooperative manner.

Well the 3-year-old began screaming and kicking wildly. She was screaming so loudly that I am sure all of the neighbors around or nearby could hear her. I really felt bad because it appears that everyone is looking at me as if "what did you do to her?" I tried to calm her down by repeating that her mom wanted us to come home so she could eat her dinner. I then told her that she was having chicken nuggets and French fries, her two favorites; she finally stopped crying and kicking. I held both of their hands and we walked back to the vehicle, strapped in car seats and whew, was I glad for that. Mission Accomplished!

So Questions Continue about the Existence of Tantrums and Development

When coming home from the hospital or having your baby delivered by a midwife, most of the time, parents and family members realize the significance of our roles because these children are our total responsibility. Their lives are in our hands. I will never forget how scared I felt when I first became a mother. I was in the hospital and certainly the stay was not very long. In between the hours of post-birth tiredness, caring for the new baby and hospital staff checking on the baby and new mom, there is not much time to feel so scared because help is right there at the fingertips. I remember them showing us how to give the baby a bath, wash their hair, changing their diaper, and breastfeeding.

I had decided to breastfeed all four of my children because I had read about all of the values and benefits to the child and especially to their health. So I quickly learned that the baby depended totally on me for their care, protection, and well-being. There are so many things that can cause a mother to be nervous and afraid.

I remember all of the research and information on sudden infant death syndrome when infants seem to die suddenly. Being in the field of early childhood education, I had studied a lot about this happening to babies. I felt so nervous, praying that this would not happen to my beautiful baby. I was so glad that someone had given me a baby monitor as a gift, since our apartment was an upstairs duplex and the bedrooms were upstairs. I could hear every move, grunt, sound that the baby made, and today I am not sure if that scared me more, but I was glad that I could hear sounds and movement and knew that the baby was okay and alive.

Soon as a mother, we began to observe the baby's pattern for eating, diaper changes, and of course sleeping. Also, a mother is one of the first ones to discover the child's personality developing and as their demands grow, the work for the parents, mom, dad, and other caregivers increases.

So what confuses many families is why some children have tantrums and some do not? Others wonder is there really something that parents can do to keep their children from ever entering the tantrum stages? But the truth of the matter is that as these children approach and enter into the terrific twos and many prefer to refer to them as the terrible twos, we find some new wonders about these children.

We learn very early that the youngest children will let us know right away that they have some things they like and others that they do not like. So some wonder how is it that a child that young could possibly know the differences. Not only do they have the likes and dislikes, but they have very clear viewpoints on what they will do and what they don't want to do—problem for parents, caregivers, and others.

What we need to know:

1. Children in these age ranges onward are feeling empowered to exert any control over their environments and those in them. This is the beginning of us as adults realizing that a child who is engaged in the powerful struggles of control has progressed developmentally to moving into a new stage of life.
2. Children are just beginning to gain some control over the spoken language. They are learning to communicate more with use of words. But we must remember that their vocabularies are limited and they don't have the full development of words to express all of their ideas, feelings, needs, and interests. Thus, these children can become frustrated very easily because of their inability to communicate verbally. Because of this, they use their bodies to express their needs.
3. It helps us to know that intellectually the young toddler's brain is not yet developed to realize how to stop doing some of the things that they are doing when asked to do so. The adult has to take extra steps and precautions to help these children find alternatives to any behaviors deemed inappropriate. Thus, it may be difficult for the child to figure out why hitting another child is inappropriate because he/she wants the toy that another child has.
4. It is important that we understand even a child in the toddler stage may begin to repeat back to us what is said to them, they still do not have the brain ability to recall that same rule when a situation arises again. As the child enters 3 1/2 to 4 years of age, the brain is better developed to begin to put restraints on these types of behaviors.

Important: What Can We Teachers, Parents, and Caregivers Do to Prevent Tantrums

How to Prevent Tantrums:

1. We must face the realities of the fact that a child's tantrum behaviors do not mean that as parents, teachers, caregivers, etc. we have lost full control or that the child has overpowered us in such a devastating manner.
2. We must get beyond the "shock" of how our own flesh and blood birth child is behaving. We must get beyond the blaming of ourselves or the thoughts about our children are born to be deviant or that the long-term effects will be that they may be deviant as they get older.
3. We realize now that for many children during the toddler years, this is a major part of their beginnings of demonstrating their growth and development rather than thinking of this stage as a negative reflection of this child.
4. We need to become familiar with the behaviors and actions that a child may exhibit so that we can be prepared to help them prevent having the need to have a tantrum. We need to use a similar approach as we do with children who are sometimes biters.
5. We must be prepared to separate the child's behaviors from adult perceptions of the situations before they arise.
6. We as adults must get beyond the mind-set that the reason that the child is behaving by tantrums is because the parents did something wrong.
7. We as adults must seriously get past the thoughts and ideas that the child is behaving through tantrums to embarrass or shame the parents.
8. We as adults must remember that the child needs a time frame to settle down because they may be having trouble coping with what is going on around them.
9. Try not to be distracted by observers, bystanders, or those who may cause you to feel negatively about how you personally deal with your child prior to them getting ready to have a tantrum.
10. Even when it is extra difficult, remain calm—try not to get upset with the child.
11. Try to support and guide your child through the process. "Let's go over here and see if we can find your lost toy. You look under the chairs and I will look in the toy box."
12. You have to make a decision about whether you will set limits in every situation where you feel that your child is about to have a meltdown or if it is best to choose the times when you will give attention to the child's actions or are some of them the ones that you will ignore. We must remember we have preferences and so do they. One mom was upset because the child chose to wear mitch-match socks. So she decided to let that one go and let the child wear those socks, even if others looked at her suspiciously.
13. Begin to better understand your child's interests and needs so that you can be prepared for what may have been eliminated and the child is seeking to find them.
14. Be prepared to give the child advance notice of what is about to happen. Parents, teachers, and caregivers must be prepared for the fact that it may work and sometimes it might not. "Tell the child when the bell rings, that it will be time to get ready for bedtime."
15. Make statements with the child rather than asking questions so that the child can answer with a refusal to the question. Do not ask a young child, "do you want your snack before the movie or after the movie?" In reality, the child may not know the answer to the question. So in some cases, it is easier to bring the snack when the movie is halfway through, rather than posing the question. Do not ask a child a question like, "would you like to pick up the toys now please?" What will you do if the child says "No?" So instead say to the child, "It is time for you to pick up the toys now."

16. Give young children age-appropriate choices and not those that are not in their range. "Would you like to go to the Chicago Cubs game or the Detroit Lions?" The child is probably not familiar with either team and if he/she is, this is a family-adult decision and not a young child's.
17. When beginning to establish limits/boundaries with a young child, use a kind, but firm voice without a lot of emotions. Anger or crying in front of the child may cause the child to lose focus of what is expected of him/her.
18. Use as few words as possible when guiding the child or establishing ground rules and limits. Giving the child too many tasks or too long sentence structures/commands may go unheeded because the child may be overwhelmed.
19. Talk to the child in a calm lower tone with positive nonverbal body actions as well.
20. Your facial expression, body language, and a calm approach can send the message needed to let the child know that you love him/her, care about them, and you are not upset with them. This may instill in them more the desire to do what is asked of them.

How to Help Your Child by Intervening

1. Some may agree while others disagree about how to and whether we are truly able to calm a child down. So some make no efforts to engage in this part of the child's actions.
2. Others may think that there is something that can be done to help the child once they seem to be out of control or may be in need of assistance.
3. Instead of focusing on the adult trying to make or help the child to calm down, the focus should be on what can be done to help the child find independent ways of pulling themselves together to deal with the situation at hand. We must remember that sometimes children are overwhelmed about what is going on around them.
4. In order to positively help a child, begin to pull themselves back together—the adults in the child's life again must remain calm while in the midst of the tantrum. Families try different approaches and some may work at times and during other times, they may not work.
5. If the child is having a difficult time during the tantrum, believe it or not they are truly relying on the adult to help them pull themselves back together. Remember that even though they are having a tantrum, they are observing the adult's reaction toward their behaviors.
6. Try even when it is very difficult to refrain from getting very upset with the child. Try to avoid yelling, shouting, expressions of anger, or frowning facial expressions. These may cause the child to become even more upset, causing the tantrum stage to escalate and/or last longer.
7. Again, some agree, while others may disagree on the adults confirming the child's feelings and perceptions when having a tantrum. Sometimes the adult may say, "you were upset because Jamie had the toy you wanted, but Jamie was playing with that toy, so let's see if we can find one like it or to see if Jamie is done playing with that toy." It is important that the adult walk the child through these suggestions to see which one might work. For merely stating them may cause the child to become even more upset.
8. Respect your child's expressions, but hold the limit. Calmly let the child know what you will help them to not do. For example, "I will sit here with you because you are upset now. I will stop you from throwing toys."
9. Although some people think it works. Do not shame the child, even when you think it might be the best.
10. When working with teachers on the "time-in approach versus time-out," some disagreed with this approach, but it does work for us to provide comfort such as a favorite toy, soft, soothing music, a calming-relaxing area, or a hug. These will provide alternatives to tantrums and outburst behaviors.

11. Many experts recommend that parents, teachers, caregivers, etc. recognize when it is best for a parent or staff to take time away from the child and the situation. When possible and if appropriate, have another adult take your place.
12. Provide a safe place for the child to be able to take a break to calm down and to be away from the situation that may be causing or adding to out-of-control behaviors. It is recommended that this be an area with soft materials such as pillows, bean bags, stuffed animals, and soothing music. Other materials can be added as deemed appropriate.
13. Offer the child some ideas for ways to get their anger out. It is recommended that vocabulary words that are descriptive of some of their behaviors may add to their growth. "You seem to be angry." "You seem to be irritated." "You seem to be upset." "You seem to be frustrated about not getting that extra cookie that you wanted." Since you seem angry, you can hit the bean bag, the pillow, or stomp your feet, if it is going to make you feel better." You are helping the child see these acceptable ways of expressing anger rather than other non-acceptable actions.
14. Over a period of time, if young children are guided properly, they learn how to self-regulate, calm down, and soothe themselves.

IMPORTANT: Even though tantrums can be unnerving and often devastating for adults who have to deal with them, the message that we would like to leave is that children are growing, developing, and learning about their feelings, the importance of having limits and boundaries because they are skills that all of us need to become successful citizens.

Message to remember: Tantrums are actions/behaviors that happen mostly when toddlers become overly frustrated, overwhelmed, and not knowing how to cope with what is happening in their environments. Adults such as parents, teachers, and caregivers can help support the child by showing that they care and understand and that they want the best for them.

Chapter 17

Black Lives Really Do Matter

As we ventured into our 6th Annual Conference on African American Children and Families at the University of Northern Iowa, Cedar Falls, Iowa, we could not have chosen a better keynoter/speaker/presenter than those who joined us in February 2017.

Last year, I had the privilege of hearing our keynote speaker do a presentation on why "Black Lives Matter." I am sure that there are many who may read this and perhaps have the same questions, doubts, and disagreements as so many others. Please take a moment to read this chapter because it will certainly help you to be better able to help students understand the true meanings.

Many people wonder why this topic ever came up and even why it is still being mentioned today? There will be those who question why there will be a distinction made about "Black Lives Matter" from "All Lives Matter."

Urgently Important

All Lives Matter, Children's Lives Matter, etc., yes! Not until I really listened to the historical context and rationale for why this message surfaced nationally within the last year for certain, did I begin to look at this matter closer than I had done previously. As a matter of fact, it sounded like a slogan, theme, or new topic of discussion. We repeat, we honor, and respect all lives.

Once one studies and seeks answers to questions as to why this issue of Black Lives Matter seems to cause some to cringe in their seats, more clarity will be realized. This message of thinking there is a blatant racist prompting to deter from the need for us to respect all people is far from the truth. I am very hopeful that those who joined us at the 6th Annual Conference learned and turned over a new leaf in life. It is also our hope that you gained more insights and a better understanding of the plight of many African-Americans who came before our time.

Growing up in Charleston, South Carolina in all Black elementary and high schools, little did we know that years later there would be a public outcry for why Black Lives Matter. Our teachers, administrators, and counselors all were Black. So for some us we were shielded from some of the walls of racism and segregation because of the safety net of protection built around us that allowed us to not fear some of the things that are definitely on some of the radars of children and families today.

Well, I really can't truly say that, but it just seemed as though it is because our teachers lived among us, knew our families, knew each of us, and we felt like we had the support from those in the "village."

Then as life would have it, I was able to matriculate to one of the best historically Black colleges and universities in the world, Fisk University, Nashville, Tennessee. Fisk's small, private, 99 percent

Black student and faculty population again seems to have built a wall of protection and support for those of us who were privileged and honored to be enrolled there. For me, it was especially special since my counselors told me that I wouldn't be able to go there. Yes, they were Black and told me the truth. But God had something different to say about my future and where I would be destined to go. So, yes I would not have been able to go there because my parents like many today could not afford to send me to college for 1 day if there were to ever have been such a thing. But I was blessed that a recruiter came to my hometown and some family and friends from the "village" encouraged me to go. What a blessing, I took my transcript and the person looked at it and said, "I am going to go back and get you a scholarship." Wow, I thought is he really telling the truth? Well he told the truth and 3 days later I received an official letter offering me a 4-year full scholarship! Wow, was I blessed and wow was I forever grateful and wow, did I want to go to college, do well and make my family, friends, and teachers at my schools happy if I succeeded! Wow, would I make myself so happy if I could go to this school and do well in my classes and keep my scholarship.

But little did I know that all of those experiences and more among those that would become real experiences today that would bring about the message of "Black Lives Matter." Like when I went to the Woolworth Store, not knowing anything about segregation, discrimination, racism or prejudice, I was at the beginning stage of seeing life from a different perspective. The reason I term it as a different perspective is because it was truly different from any experiences ever shared in our neighborhoods, schools, and churches on the east side of town. We were divided by the railroad tracks as in so many other areas throughout the United States.

I learned quickly that there truly was another side to why Black Lives Matter. When I asked the lady at the Woolworth food counter, in Charleston, South Carolina, "can I get a hotdog?" (I had the money that mama had given me.) My friend (another year-old) and I had never heard the "N-" word before when the lady behind the food counter told me that they didn't serve "N-s," I just thought she couldn't understand what I said as a young child, so I repeated the request. "Can I please have a hotdog?" The second time when I repeated the request, she seemed to get very angry with me. My friend stood quietly by and did not request an order of food. This is when I think the lady behind the food counter called me a double "N" "Nig---Nig---." As the lady's face showed so much anger and hostility, it didn't take me long to realize that whatever was happening that she was not going to give me a hotdog, nor was she going to serve us at all despite the fact that we did have our money that our parents had given to us.

My friend was still quietly standing there, where her face moved from one of a question mark to one of fear. So I decided that it was best for me and my friend to get away from there. I, Gloria, and Effie were too young to understand that "Black Lives Didn't Matter" when segregated lunch counters throughout the south refused to serve Blacks.

But then as I left the counter and we ventured to the back of the store where the water fountains and the restrooms were, I saw what has never left my mind from my childhood days until now. I have heard relatives and adult friends speak of some of life's experiences that dig down so deeply into one's soul that cause one to have some inner memories that seem to never leave the mind. The truth behind the story seemed to have been heart, soul, and spirt torched with the staunching smell and touch of a deep piercing. I am sure that the images that I am about to share will follow me to my grave—I say this because of how many years have transpired since the day of these events. While I do not think about these experiences regularly, they cross my mind too often when another horrific event calls for what I term the "mistreatment" of Blacks. I call them horrific because they cannot be forgotten, no matter how I try.

Then I remembered this other horrific time, when "Black Lives Didn't Seem to Matter." Somehow at a very young age, we had learned to read the words, "Colored" and "White." I cannot recall if our teachers and parents made sure that those were among our first reading vocabulary words or not, but

I sure am grateful that I learned them and never forgot them. Little did I know that those two words would be such a critical part of literacy. But that's when I realized that Black Lives Didn't Matter when our great-great grandparents and grandparents were denied the right to an education and that it was against the law for Blacks to learn to read.

So what I am about to share in that I was so young to be a brave soldier and help fight a battle that I did not know was a real battle for Black people until I witnessed it firsthand. When we arrived at the back of the Woolworth Store, there was an elderly Black man and I am sure he was very thirsty because it was a very hot and humid day like so many days in South Carolina. While we had learned to read the words "Colored" and "White," especially for water fountains and restrooms, I'll call him Mr. Ferguson, had not. I'm sure when he saw those what seemed like cold, icicles coming from the outside of the "Whites only" water fountain that he thought about how he could get a cool drink of water. During that time the stores had security guards or police officers working there. As soon as Mr. Ferguson drank from the wrong water fountain, two officers were right there, storming upon him. This was a usual tactic when Black people got out of line, out of order or crossed that racial line that you dare to trod. I thought about how our hidden life's teachings, experiences, and words or hint to the wise never really shared with us—the "what could happen to us." Looking back, I am not sure if this went on the side of their teaching us to love everyone regardless of race, color, or creed or not wanting to put so much fear in us, that we were too afraid to go about our daily lives.

So they started beating him over his head with what we called a "Billy club." Mr. Ferguson started to bleed so much that on impulse and without any fear, I ran in the "Colored only" bathroom and grabbed some paper towels and started cleaning his face and head. The sight was so unbearable as I could not see any reason why someone could legally beat this "old Black man like that." After all he certainly was not stealing anything. Only when I got older did I realize that "Black Lives Didn't Matter" if you drank out of the wrong water fountain or mistakenly went in the wrong restroom because of one's race. Today there is a much bigger fight about the restrooms and whether it should be designated for one sex, individualized recognition of sexual orientations, etc. Still today, I tremble at the thought that I could have been hurt by running to Mr. Ferguson's aide.

But if you came to the Conference, you didn't hear my story about "Why Black Lives Matter." When we take a retrospective view about what brought the real issue to the forefront, we find why. But we must realize that there is another important issue:

The Educational Side of Black Lives Matter

http://www.thestranger.com/slog/2016/10/19/24630108/two-thousand-seattle-teachers-wore-black-lives-matter-shirts-to-schools?utm_content

About two thousand teachers in the Seattle, Washington area showed their support for some of the injustices perpetrated upon Black students by wearing their t-shirts declaring "Black Lives Matter Day."

Teachers decided to respond to bomb threats that almost caused a negative experience for a Black student empowerment event that was to be held at John Muir Elementary School.

While this planned event was scheduled at the elementary school, there were educators who realized the importance of teaching their high school students about institutional racism. Institutional racism and implicit bias are some topics that come to the forefront in many lives today in the quest for bringing about change and more recognition of the need for equality.

The teachers received support from the Seattle Educators Association, Mayor Ed Murray, and King County's Equity and Social Justice Inter-Branch Team. Support from others can be critical when stepping out on faith in the "Black Lives Matter" events. Standing alone can be very difficult for those who may not garner the needed support. This form of movement and action meant a lot to the students and teachers because the time had come to stand up for justice. The Black Lives movement is about justice, fairness, and the treating of everyone with dignity and respect. It is about not selecting any individual based on race as a standout example for what could or should happen to others if specific directives are not heeded or if actions of individuals are misinterpreted, misjudged, or dealt with out of preordained fear.

At the national level, former MSNBC host Melissa-Harris Perry, Olympic medalist John Carlos, and Black Lives Matter co-founder Opal Tometi also publicly backed the teachers. The action was also endorsed by the Seattle Educators Association, Mayor Ed Murray, and King County's Equity and Social Justice Inter-Branch Team, Seattle Hawks Defensive Lineman, Michael Bennett. Teachers from elementary, middle, and high schools participated.

This show of support by these leaders was very powerful.

Chapter 18

Placing Educational and Cultural Values on the Lives of Blacks, Latinos and All Children

Attending some professional events, it was more than obvious that those who were in attendance felt that this was a very critical time in life for Blacks and Latinos. They wanted to make sure that they emphasized that there are major concerns for values as a part of the educational and cultural curricula for all children, but especially for Blacks and Latinos.

Approaching the Group: Is It Really an Emergency or State of Emergency on the status of Blacks and Latinos in Educational Systems in the United States

Throughout the United States, there have been many protests as a result of Black people's treatment by law enforcement and other criminal justice unfair practices.

Yes, those who have studied and researched systemic practices in schools throughout the United States find that for some reason there were those who opposed Blacks and Latinos. It was found that these negative attitudinal treatments carried through on an ongoing, consistent, and regular basis.

1. These practices are such that these students are ignored, minimized, demoralized, and are placed in circumstances and conditions that seem to have them look as though they are in harmful environments.
2. The real focus of what is needed to improve educational and cultural experiences of students should be the focus of teacher preparation and training programs.
3. Why is it that teacher preparation institutions have so many gaps in what future teachers are being taught to teach them to be more effective with all students?
4. Future teachers are crying out and asking for teacher preparation institutions to provide them with more curricula and field experiences so that they can learn more about how to close achievement gaps between various groups of students.

Emergency! Emergency! Emergencies Are Prevalent among Schools Serving African-American and Latino Students

1. Who is responsible for the blind eyes and nonvisual underrepresentation of Blacks and Latinos in gifted and talented classes?
2. Who is responsible for the blind eyes and nonvisual underrepresentation of Blacks and Latinos in Accelerated classes?
3. Who are the major key players in why there seem to be ongoing, consistent suspensions and expulsions of the same students?
4. What's really behind the "School-to-Prison Pipeline?"
5. Are we beginning to experience a decline in school dropout rates for Blacks and Latinos?
6. Are we beginning to experience any evidential changes in graduation rates for the said group of students?
7. Are we configuring the unemployment rates of dependents of Black and Latino parents?
8. When configuring the unemployment rates of Black and Latino families, are there any provisions being made for improving the life conditions of these families that are impacted by unemployment issues?
9. Are these students steered toward college readiness classes and experiences?
10. Are there evidential backings that show Blacks and Latinos being pushed toward the criminal justice system and away from the advanced educational and post-secondary experiences?

The answers to any of these questions can definitely impact whether students are declared to be in a state of emergency!

Does Statistical Data Tell a Story or Do the Students Tell the Story?

As I began to take a closer look at how these students are faring in our educational systems, I am sorry to say that there is no way that anyone could truly look at this without statistical data.

1. African-American students are four times as likely as White students to attend schools where 60 percent or fewer of the teachers meet all state certification and licensure requirements.
2. Latino students are twice as likely as White students to attend schools where 60 percent or fewer of the teachers meet all state certification and licensure requirements.
3. Almost one in four school districts with two or more high schools reported that there is a teacher salary gap of more than $5,000.00 between high schools with the highest and lowest Black and Latino student enrollments.
4. According to the United States Department of Education and the U.S. Office of Civil Rights, one-fourth of high schools with the highest percentages of Black and Latino students do NOT offer Algebra II. (Why?)
5. According to the United States Department of Education and the U.S. Office of Civil Rights, one-third of high schools with the highest percentages of Black and Latino students do NOT offer chemistry. (Why?)
6. Black and Latino students represent approximately twenty-six percent of students enrolled in gifted and talented programs in schools. But they comprise forty percent of enrollment in schools that offer gifted and talented programs. It should also be noted that not all of them offer gifted and talented programs.

Chapter 18: Placing Educational and Cultural Values on the Lives of Blacks, Latinos and All Children

A State of Emergency That Calls for Ongoing Improvement Assistance

Those who truly research the topics of educational reform and needed changes in our school system continue to ask the same questions.

1. Despite what is called educational reform that has been at the forefront for more than a century, U.S. public school systems continue to underserve a great number of African-American and Latino students.
2. Despite what is called educational reform that has been at the forefront for more than a century, U.S. public school systems continue to underserve a great number of low-income and other underserved populations that are historical representations of the sameness.
3. So many feel that the lack of the call to action by the systemic plan of not providing a strong quality education for Blacks and Latinos shows that this is not a priority in U.S. educational matters.
4. So what needs to happen in order for the needed eradication of inequality and unfair practices in U.S. school systems? One must speak out, step forward, become more knowledgeable, become more aware of some of the needed strategies to fight for the students.

It Is a Known Fact That There Are Some Very Harmful School Practices

What is meant by harmful school practices? Despite the fact that there are some who are listening to the voices of those in need of assistance, there are some practices that are haunting certain populations of students. So why is it that such a great nation has nurtured practices that are harmful to certain populations in our school systems? Does that sound like something is wrong, broken, and needs to be fixed?

So what are some of these known harmful school practices?

1. Stereotyping- Why is it that we find ourselves and others in our school system who have stereotypical attitudes? Have they personally experienced these stereotypes or are they assuming certain things based on their personal opinions?
2. Placing negative labels on students and their parents/guardians- Think about whether you know students whom teachers, administrators, and/or staff seem to have negative attitudes about certain students and their families regardless of what they may try to do? Well it happens every day. People who do this seem to hurt students more because they feel pain from the unnecessary bias.
3. Academic tracking- Some people have difficulty believing that this really happens. There are those who tend to put some students on an academic tracking path—stating whether the student is not doing well, but no real efforts are being made to help them improve—rather it is that's the path that they have been placed on.
4. Low expectations- This one is a big factor in the harm process—it is very painful to have a teacher or other educational staffer say something like, "That D is good for you, you should be proud of your work." Positive, higher expectations work best.
5. Grade inflation- This is when a grade's real meaning is not the same for all students. Instead, this grade is granted but it has underlying factors that those granting the grade understand very well.
6. Use of ineffective instructional strategies- There are too many students for whom the practices used in school do not work, yet they are still being used.
7. A refusal or inability to differentiate instruction- There are students who needed to have differentiated instruction in order to have their individual needs met.
8. To assist struggling learners in working hard to do well- These are the reasons that some educators ignore these students in the educational environment or refuse to help them move forward.

Even More Harmful

1. A boring non-culturally relevant curriculum that students show no interest in. Are teachers willing to work a little harder or spend a little extra time finding activities and experiences that are relevant to these students as well as others?
2. A preoccupation with high-stakes testing- It is sad and so amazing how schools in America seem to have become obsessed with the focus on what is called high-stakes testing. The reason that it is called high-stakes testing is that there are so many possibilities of what could be lost or gained by students' performance on these tests.
3. Ineffective, unfair, and overly punitive classroom management strategies- Research is showing how Blacks and Latinos are being severely punished in comparison to other students of different backgrounds and ethnicities. While students of these ethnic groups are punished greater than others, the cry is for those in positions of authority to look at them.
4. Zero Tolerance Policy-related practices that result in tracking students into the prison pipeline- This one is very serious and so very scary because it is so real and we know that too many Black and Latino students are being channeled into the prison pipeline.
5. Rudeness, hypocrisy, and sending mixed messages to parents/guardians- Parents and family members are becoming more and more discouraged with the system each day because of what they say are major communication issues. Many express feelings of being alienated from the mainstream school population and activities because of the attitudes of school personnel toward them. They share that they often feel isolated as well as alienated. With these feelings of alienation comes the feeling of non-inclusiveness, many expressing that they do not feel that the school welcomes them.

So what does Dr. Gail Thompson say about the serious issues facing schools and their preparedness and expectations for students of Latino and African-American backgrounds.

The Teacher Confidence Study—Out of 239 Teachers

When interviewing teachers about their confidence when working with students of color, she found that:

1. 70 percent of the teachers shared that they were very confident about their ability to effectively teach White students.
2. 67 percent of the teachers expressed that they were confident about their ability to effectively teach Asian-American students.
3. 63 percent of the teachers expressed that they were confident about their ability to effectively teach Latino students
4. 58 percent of the teachers expressed that they were confident about their ability to effectively teach African-American female students.
5. 55 percent of the teachers expressed that they were confident about their ability to effectively teach African-American male students.
6. 42 percent of the teachers expressed that they were confident about their ability to effectively teach students who are considered to be low achievers.
7. 40 percent of the teachers expressed that they were confident about their ability to effectively teach students who have poor math skills.
8. 36 percent of the teachers expressed that they were confident about their ability to effectively teach students who read below grade level.

Chapter 18: Placing Educational and Cultural Values on the Lives of Blacks, Latinos and All Children

The Teacher's Voice

In one of her findings from the study, one White female high school teacher with 3 years of teaching experience shared the following:

1. She was worried that she felt afraid of Black students, especially the boys.
2. She shared that they are so loud that she cannot determine when they are talking in class because of their loud tone of voice.
3. She further shared how challenging it is because of the difficulties of trying to make a decision in regard to when and if to respond to their questions because of not knowing if they are being confrontational or combative with her.
4. She further expressed that Black students seem to be more argumentative.
5. She further expressed that Black students seem to have a sense of entitlement that other races did not have or lacked.
6. She further expressed the fact that the type of discipline that she used seemed to incite a battle of power between her and the students. So all efforts are made to decrease or wipe out this one because she could not risk losing the battle.
7. Seventy-five percent of the students she sends to the principal are African-Americans.

The Teacher's Voice #2

A White male middle school teacher with more than 15 years of teaching:

1. I have more to learn about classroom management.
2. I still have more to learn about treating students fairly.
3. I need to get more confidence.

The Teacher Confidence Study Results (continued)

1. 43 percent of the teachers expressed that they were confident about their classroom management skills.
2. 60 percent of the teachers expressed that they were confident about their ability to work effectively with Latino parents.
3. 59 percent of the teachers expressed that they were confident about their ability to effectively work with White parents.
4. 56 percent of teachers expressed that they were confident about their ability to work effectively with Asian parents.
5. 26 percent of the teachers expressed that they were confident about their ability to work with ESL parents.
6. 43 percent of the teachers expressed that they were confident about their ability to incorporate racial issues into their lesson plan

The Teacher's Voice #3

A White female elementary school teacher:
I have not been able to figure out how to communicate with ESL parents

The Teacher's Voice #4

An Asian American middle school teacher shared that:
She lacked the confidence in dealing with African-American, Latino students, and their parents.

The Mindset Study—Out of 237 Teachers

93 percent said that most teachers do not know how to work effectively with African American students

60 percent said that most teachers do not believe that most African-American students are capable of doing outstanding academic work.

77 percent said that most teachers don't treat or view African-American students in the same way that they do to non-Black students.

80 percent said that most teachers don't believe that most Black parents care about their children's education.

75 percent said that most principals don't believe that African-American parents are very concerned about their children's education.

55 percent said that most principals don't believe that most African-American students are capable of doing outstanding academic work.

54 percent said that most teachers don't believe that African-American students are as intelligent as non-Black students.

When asked why many African-American k-12 students underperform at school, the most frequently cited reason was low expectation from adults in the educational environment.

Teacher Voice #4

White male teacher:

Often felt frustrated when confronted with issues related to race because so often people bring up the idea of color blindness. But he shared how he realized that anyone who thinks that race is not an issue isn't really seeing through the right lenses.

Dr. Gail Thompson, author of the book *Up Where We Belong*, also conducted the Up Where We Belong Study

She collected data of:

121 questionnaires from teachers

268 questionnaires from high school students

146 from student focus groups

What Did Teachers Say about Their Students?

91 percent said that they made the curriculum relevant to their student's lives.

63 percent said that the majority of their students could not read at grade level or above.

51 percent said that students who do poorly in school "are largely to blame for their failure."

17 percent believed that a student's aptitude is determined by the student's race or ethnicity.

Chapter 18: Placing Educational and Cultural Values on the Lives of Blacks, Latinos and All Children **121**

What Did Teachers Say about Their Students' Parents?

64 percent blamed parents for students' low achievement.

34 percent said that the majority of their students did not have parents who cared about their academic welfare.

What Students Said about Their Teachers

Latinos (79 percent) and Blacks (70 percent) were less likely than Whites (84 percent) to label their teachers as "good" teachers, but Black males were the least likely to do so.

Blacks (58 percent) and Latinos (54 percent) were more likely than Whites (38 percent) to say they wished that they had better teachers.

Latinos (58 percent) and Blacks (51 percent) were less likely than Whites (66 percent) to say that their teachers were fair about discipline

Blacks (32 percent) and Latinos (28 percent) were more likely than Whites (4 percent) to say that their teachers were unwilling to answer questions when they didn't understand an assignment.

Latinos (38 percent) and Blacks (34 percent) were more likely than Whites (28 percent) to say that their teachers wouldn't give them extra help during class time.

Latinos (57 percent) and Blacks (56 percent) were less likely than Whites (70 percent) to believe that their teachers cared about them, and Latinos were the least likely to believe this.

Student Voice #1
African-American student
    I think that a lot of the teachers misuse their authority

Student Voice #2
There is a P.E. coach that threatens students, making negative statements like, If I was younger, I would beat you up. The student continued by saying that this teacher gets a lot of students suspended

Student Voice #3-
Female high school student
    In the school, tutoring is available after school, but no one wants to go because the teacher is mean and students are afraid of her.

Student Voice #4
If you don't understand something that is being taught, the teacher gets frustrated and asks us "Why don't you understand? And makes us feel real stupid.

Student Voice #5
Teachers need to learn different ways of teaching because too many of them are stuck in their same old outdated ways. They should realize that there are different ways of student learning and there

should be different ways of teaching. That would allow teachers to teach all of the students and not just the ones with a certain learning style.

What Students Said about the Curriculum

Blacks (66 percent) and Latinos (57 percent) were more likely than Whites (48 percent) to say that their classes were boring.

Latinos (61 percent) and Blacks (60 percent) were more likely than Whites (50 percent) to say that most of their classes weren't preparing them for the real world.

Seventy-five percent of Blacks and nearly 60 percent of Latinos said they wanted to learn more about their culture in class, in comparison to 36 percent of Whites.

Student Voice #6

African-American male student

You learn about negative culture. You learn about slavery. You don't learn about positive Black people.

Student Voice #6

African-American high school student

They act like slavery is all that Blacks come from when we also have great Black poets, we also have civil rights leaders, black lawyers, authors, and all kinds of people and all they act like all we come from are the cotton fields.

Student Voice #7

Latina high school student

Shared that she had learned a lot of American history because she lived in America all of her life. She was asking about learning a little about her culture also as a part of the history being taught.

Chapter 19

Placing Educational and Cultural Value on Latino and African-American Students Part 2

This chapter is a continuation of the statistical results mentioned in Placing Educational and Cultural Value on Latino and African-American Students. This chapter will present an analysis of some of the findings as examined by Dr. Gloria Kirkland-Holmes, based on the findings and research highlights of Dr. Gail Thompson, Wells Fargo Endowed Scholar.

Research Highlights Analysis

1. One of the obvious findings is that students can attend the same school and share, perceive, and/or have dramatically different schooling experiences. If the students' experiences are being reported as negative, schools should make every effort to find out the reasons why some school experiences are being perceived as negative.
2. Some do not believe that those who are in the decision-making roles such as our policy makers, Boards of Education, State Departments of Education, administrators as well as teachers are often not demonstrating evidence of being committed to making any changes to enhance the educational experiences of some African-American and Latino students. Some express the importance of so many obligations and responsibilities that they admit to not taking any special time for improving diversity experiences in their respective schools. The negative conditions persist more devastatingly in low-income communities.
3. One of the more serious issues that educational systems are faced with today is ineffective teacher training in institutions that prepares our teachers. During teacher education reviews and assessments, the topic of teacher training may be included, but very seldom is there enough detailed questions related to diversity and preparing teachers how effectively to work with students and parents/guardians of color.
4. Note how the perspective of beliefs that some teachers have presented itself surfaces to the forefront in that somehow those who can make a difference denote that they do not believe that Latino and African-American students deserve the same or as much as White students.

5. It certainly seems to be a continuous cycle of what Dr. Thompson calls unaddressed "mental baggage." The data show that these views are shared by many who should be in leadership roles and helping and supporting students more effectively. Because the baggage is most often unaddressed, we tend to see the continual perpetuation of harmful practices being imposed upon African-American and Latino students.

How Teachers Can Improve the Schooling Experiences of African-American and Latino Students When They Care!

1. It makes a big difference if there is a willingness on the part of the teacher to personally and individually become one who influences students through their actions of life-changing behaviors of support for these students who are in need.
2. Teachers need to learn what is referred to as the "Winning Formula." This means that the teacher has grasped what it means to make the best provision of opportunities for student successful learning experiences.
3. Teachers must learn to deal with their own mental baggage, gain a positive attitude, and function with a corrected and positive mind-set.
4. Teachers need to make sure that they make every effort to form a strong positive relationship with all students.
5. Teachers need to develop strong leadership and effective classroom management skills in order to meet the needs of all students.

How Teachers Can Improve the Schooling Experiences of African-American and Latino Students (2)

1. Teachers must learn, adopt, and implement the best practices of outstanding teachers.
2. In order to become effective teachers, each must assure students and families of a curriculum that is interesting, challenging, and culturally relevant.
3. A strong, supportive, and effective teacher is always self-reflecting and finding alternate options when needed, guaranteeing success for every student.
4. It is a MUST that effective, caring teachers form partnerships and positive relationships with parents and guardians of color. It is crucial that an understanding is developed that it is very difficult to separate children from families.
5. It is urgent that teachers who are looking to develop positive relationships with students have strengthened confidence. It is difficult to work with building the self-confidence of students when teachers themselves are weak in their confidence.
6. Teachers must commit to growing, developing, improving, and becoming more confident even when it hurts. Good teaching comes from the heart and soul and sometimes it is measured by the opportunities to help students to become better in learning experiences.

What School Leaders Can Do to Make Education Brighter for All!

1. School leaders need to demonstrate a true commitment to improving educational experiences and opportunities for all students and families regardless of race, ethnicity, or socioeconomic status. This must be a district-wide priority with a focus on each individual school.
2. School leaders need to "check themselves" individually and personally. If when so doing, it is found that there is some mental baggage that they are carrying around with them in regard to perceptions, feelings, and opinions about African-American and Latino students and families,

there is work to be done. This work includes finding some of the deep-rooted causes for negative feelings and examining what needs to be done to rid one's self of these.

Develop Short-term and Long-term Action Plans!

1. Everyone who has a role in the success or failure of students should make sure that they are holding themselves accountable for what needs to happen to make a successful experience for all. If a person finds themselves in a position that they are a part of a team that is hindering the progress of students, it is best to step aside and allow someone else who is in a more effective role to fulfill your position.

Help Teachers?

1. If we are truly going to help teachers identify and address their mental baggage about African-American and Latino students and their parents/ guardians in a safe environment, there must be some heart-to-heart and soul-to-soul one-on-one truth-to-consequences conversations. These must include genuine seriousness of teacher actions and how they impact the lives of others.
2. Teachers who find themselves thinking lesser of certain students than others or being a perpetrator of the "self-fulfilling prophecy" should take bold stands to make changes. These changes must include learning how to raise expectations such that every student is given an opportunity to succeed.
3. Teachers need to work diligently to improve their relations with African-American and Latino students and their parents/guardians through a variety of approaches and strategies. These must include finding ways of reaching out, building positive relationships, and thinking about how to put into place, "do unto others as you would have them do unto you."

Help Teachers

1. Develop the necessary skill set to effectively implement the standards-based culturally relevant lesson plan that includes engaging students in their own learning.
2. Learn how to more effectively implement instructional strategies and approaches that are especially designed for students who are labeled as lower performing students.
3. Become a part of a team that is able to model for students positive experiences as a part of "learning communities."
4. Learn realistic measurements of expectations and anticipation for how to deal with various types of student behaviors. One such approach is effectively learning how to deal with noncompliant behaviors.
5. Learn how to communicate with students who use nonverbal communication to relate to teachers. While some students may culturally use this approach more so than expected, accepted, or respected, teachers need to learn how to turn them into positives rather than negatives.
6. Learn how not to take students nonverbal actions as a doorway to sending them to the office or handing them over to school safety patrol officers. Both of these practices have proven to be discouraging and causing students to shut down their open relationships with teachers. Perceived overuse of nonverbal communication by some students may be a signal of the need for more encouragement and support.
7. Learn how to take students' negative behaviors and help them to turn them into positives. Learn how to distinguish when there are times to ignore, redirect, have a discussion, or to have a "let's talk short meeting."
8. Develop a plan for prepared ways of dealing with certain types of behaviors including when there is a need to implement stronger assertiveness skills, allowing students to know that teachers demand respect and that they will also respect the students. There will be a sharing when there is a two-way relationship: teacher-respect→student-respect.

Help Teachers

1. Differentiate and distinguish between minor problems and major ones. This seems to be crucial in school-related experiences. It can become catastrophic when a student perceives an action to be not that major, and yet the teacher perceives it to be major and serious. The discrepancy between the two ideologies can pose some potential and major challenges.

Develop a student–teacher cohesive contract to distribute to students on the first day of school:

1. The contract should include responsibilities and expectations with a listing for both parties

Teacher Responsibilities   Student Responsibilities
____I agree to_____   ____I agree to_____

Identify, be honest, and face up to any fears or misconceptions one might have about specific types of students, especially about Black males.

If you truly are a teacher who is afraid of Black males regardless of their age or grade levels, then there needs to be some serious self-examination of some of the root causes for such attitudes.

Learn to differentiate between what is considered to be realistic fears versus imagined fears. Imagined fears can overpower the thought process and may interfere in overall teacher effectiveness, again especially with certain students.

Helping Teachers Work with Parents

Many educators have expressed true viewpoints at all grade levels that it really is difficult to effectively communicate, teach, and work with students of African-American or Latino descent, without having developed a positive relationship with their families.

While some may or may not agree, teachers across grade levels continue to ask the question, "do I need to call or contact your parents?" Believe it or not, merely asking this question does solve some problems for teachers even if it is short term, while it works long term for some.

Help Teachers Learn Positive Ways of Communicating with Parents

Some feel that if teachers are inexperienced in dealing with some parents of color, then a more scripted approach may need to occur until the teacher gains more confidence. So as a part of the preparation, it is suggested that these teachers have index cards with examples of what could be said to parents in certain situations. Of course the written comments may not always be appropriate; but, teachers will gain more confidence as they interact more with families.

Prepare Weekly Correspondences to Communicate with Parents

Teachers who become aware of the value of positive notes, letters, cards, and certificates of encouragement to students also help develop positive relationships with their families. Thus, as student relationships improve at home, they also may become stronger at school because of the positive home–school communication.

What Should Teachers Do When and If Parents Accuse Them of being Racist or Unfair to Their Children?

Of course it hurts and will hurt anytime a parent feels strong enough to inform a teacher, staff, or administrator of their perception of a teacher being racist. Teachers must get prepared for the variety of approaches parents may use when they come to be the bearers of bad news.

So what about the irate, seemingly very angry parent or the calm accusatory parent? Each one will possibly deserve a different type of teacher reaction-response. It is very important that the teacher remain calm, no matter what happens. If a parent seems to be loud, boisterous or out of control, the teacher is not expected to behave in the same manner.

All efforts should be made to get the situation under control through use of a calming approach. Using a calming voice often helps to smooth things over, thus opening the doors for conversation.

One effective approach is allowing the parent to voice the concerns, issues, and their feelings about why they came to school. Allowing this in the beginning of the conversation will allow the parent to be heard. In such a case the teacher will be the respondent, thinking of some of the most effective approaches to use with the family. The teacher's response should be one of acknowledging and recognizing the parents' feelings, perceptions, and comments. Then it is also a good idea to discuss what could be some of the solutions to the problem at hand. It is important to hear what parents have to say as to the critical needs or crucial actions that need to occur to help with the resolutions.

English as A Second Language, ESL Parents, and Translators

With all of the changing populations in the United States, the needs are greater than ever before in finding effective communicative strategies and approaches that are best practices when dealing with parents/families.

Everyone should be engaged in finding out who could serve as interpreters to help with translation among parents and staff. If there are no available translators in the school, then the school leadership needs to come up with a plan for how to communicate with families who have English as a second language.

There should also be teacher/staff training on the pros and cons of online translation programs in case it needs to be used in some situations. This could help them learn some of the basic words and phrases that may be used in some families.

How Parents Can Improve the Schooling Experiences of African-American and Latino Students

1. Parents should emphasize the importance of education by providing learning experiences such as games.
2. Parents should teach your child about good manners.
3. Parents should teach their children about appropriate personal, casual, and professional attire. Dress attire and mannerisms go hand in hand.
4. Assure your child of your beliefs in their performance by encouraging them to develop strong literacy skills including comprehension and decoding. Children who learn to read well tend to succeed in other areas of their education.
5. It is a common sense research fact that those children who grow up in print-rich environments at home tend to develop better reading skills than those children who do not have the same at home. Show children that you truly value literacy and therefore give them books as holiday and birthday gifts.
6. Ask your child to read to you on a regular basis as a means of encouraging them to read.
7. Help your child create and design personalized books that include genuine information about the child.
8. In order to ensure that your child understands the reading material, ask him/her to tell you what the story or reading assignment is about.

9. Learn some of the recommended best practices to help your child grow in literacy learning and becoming a more avid reader. Use skills like helping your child problem solve on what to do if there are words that they don't recognize or do not know the meaning of.
10. Make weekly vocabulary word lists with your children. This will increase their vocabulary knowledge. These words may also be used for spelling, which is a great challenge in schools in the United States.
11. Be a great role model of reading by allowing your child to see you reading a variety of materials such as magazines, books, newspapers, etc.
12. Keep abreast of research on homework and how it can impact your child.
13. Make sure that your child is getting homework several nights a week. Learn the homework pattern of your child's teachers and the school. If your child needs help, do the best that you can with helping or try to get help from school, if needed.
14. Help your child develop good, strong math skills.
15. Find some of the most appropriate books and materials to help with the skills that need to be developed.
16. Work diligently with your child by guiding him/her to take courses on a track that will allow him/her to be prepared for college or other career choices by having taken the proper math courses during middle and high schools.

How to Dismantle the Cradle to Prison Theory

1. It is important that parents help and make sure that their child understands the class rules.
2. Talk with your child about appropriate behaviors so that they understand the school's no tolerance policy.
3. Help your child to learn how to treat others with respect if they want respect in return.
4. Teach your child to respect authority and not talk back to adults.
5. Teach your child how to use their time wisely, by finding out what options are available if they complete assigned tasks before others.
6. Teach your child about nonviolent problem-solving solutions when faced with conflicts.
7. Make arrangements for your child to be able to visit colleges and universities. This will serve as a conscientious effort to motivate the child to have an interest in attending college.
8. Make arrangements for your child to take advanced or college prep classes and to enroll in summer enrichment programs that are recorded as a part of the record that you are college-ready.
9. Take your child to visit local colleges and universiles. • Expose your child to college-educated individuals who are down-to-earth. • Enroll your child in college-preparatory and summer enrichment programs.
10. Help your child meet respectable role models who will support what you are attempting to instill in your child.
11. Stay abreast of current trends and resources for parents so that you can be a support and advocate for your child.
12. Keep empowering and encouraging yourself as a parent and in believing that you are the greatest supporter of your child.
13. Practice writing correspondences that may express parental support for your child directed to proper powers to be.

Parental Resources

National PTA: Contains Parent Guides and Tips http://www.pta.org/topic_getting_involved.asp.
Parents Association: Contains Links for Parents and Teens http://www.parentsassociation.com/.
Reading Rockets: Contains Strategies, Reading Guides, and Research for Teachers and Parents http://www.readingrockets.org/audience/parents.
Put Reading First: Helping Your Child Learn to Read: A Parent Guide from the National Reading Panel http://www.nationalreadingpanel.org/Publications/helpingread.htm.
Read, Write, Think (International Reading Association) Contains Valuable Information for Parents and Teachers http://www.readwritethink.org.

Chapter 20

The Legacy of My Own Second Language: Gullah

As I write this chapter, I do so with much emotion. For all of the years that I have been teaching and writing, I never really sat down to pen the real language that I grew up with from childhood!

Interestingly, we grew up speaking a second language but were never told that we were speaking a different language because it was our first and main language. But as we spoke the Gullah language, we learned "standard" English as best as we could with our teacher models. So when we think in term of today's English Language Learners, there has always been much that I knew when it came to young children in my classes.

I always found myself "going to bat" for these students because I guess I grew up having "standard English" as our second language.

Source: Lorenzo Dow Turner, A linguist who identified the African influences in the Gullah dialect by Jason Kelly

History and Background of the Discovery of the African Influences on the Gullah Dialect

Lorenzo Dow Turner, PhD'26 through his interest in becoming what was termed as a "linguistic detective" learned about the historical influences and connections of Africa on the Gullah dialect.

Turner, like then and like many others today, became inspired and interested when hearing the use of language of many who were from South Carolina, specifically and spoke the Gullah language.

Hearing two students speak, Dr. Turner became interested when two students at South Carolina State College in 1929 were speaking what he thought sounded like broken English.

To some, this language was what they thought were partials from an identified name of pidgin English. It was believed that slaves learned that language was influenced by Whites.

Turner had a master's degree from Harvard and a PhD in English from Chicago and he was able to hear something deeper in the language that he heard. He did realize that he could not understand what he was hearing.

When Turner asked the students what language they were speaking, they replied, "We're Gullah." When they said Gullah, they were referring to the slave descendants on Sea Islands in South Carolina and Georgia.

This prompted a research agenda that became a major area of study for Dr. Turner.

He started out by tracing the roots of the Gullah language and culture. There are other linguists who had studied the Gullah language, but their findings did not have African influences.

Some thought that the Gullah language originated when slaves deciphered and changed English heard from Whites. They then thought that they said the same words but did so with a different intonation, pronunciation, and grammar.

Guy B. Johns of the University of North Carolina believed that the Gullah language had no African influences, but instead represented a devastating effect of slavery on their lives. Thus this language sounded like their expressions through devastation.

Still learning what other linguists said when listening to and studying the Gullah language, Dr. Turner held on to his belief that there still were African influences. Dr. Salikoko Mufwene confirmed that while Gullah certainly is inclusive of the English language, Dr. Turner was the first to prove that "one cannot account for the languages that the slaves had brought from Africa."

So as Dr. Turner was used to the speech and patterns, he could definitely hear the English words, but what was so important were the words he heard were not English. He then began to think that those are probably African words.

Dr. Turner set out to learn more about what he heard. He began to interview residents of the islands where Gullah was spoken.

Growing up in South Carolina, I can confirm what Dr. Turner learned that some of the islands were so remote and the lifestyle of the residents was totally isolated from the mainland. As he could not do the interviews in their native area, he made arrangements for some of the residents of these remote areas to be interviewed. They were brought to areas where there was electricity for the 100-lb recorder used by Dr. Turner.

As he was making arrangements for the interviews of those speaking the Gullah language, he also gained some knowledge of how these slaves survived some of the conditions that seemed unbearable.

Other researchers who visited the islands spoke of the isolation or what some would call segregation. It was found that there was the White family that owned the island and the plantation. Everybody else on the island was Black. Thus, slave overseers as well as drivers were often also Black. Thus, this allowed them to maintain their African culture. Because of the isolation of those on these islands, those who were interested in meeting them had to spend time building relationships because the culture is a very closed one.

Interestingly, Dr. Turner came from a family with a serious commitment to education during a time when it was difficult for Blacks to get an education. Dr. Turner was born in 1890 in Elizabeth City, North Carolina. His father, Rooks Turner, started school at age 21 and went on to get a master's degree from Howard University. Two of his brothers also pursued degrees in medicine and law.

I have been so impressed with the educational track of this man and became even more impressed with him upon learning that he became the head of the English department at my undergraduate school, which is one of the oldest Historically Black Colleges and Universities, Fisk University, Nashville, Tennessee.

Thus, in 1929, he also founded the African studies program while there. He later moved to Chicago's Roosevelt College in 1946 and was the first Black professor hired by a White institution. This college had been founded in 1945 and was recognized as one of the institutions that would not discriminate based on race or religion. He also established an African studies program there.

With all of his professorial work, he was still very devoted to finding out more about Gullah. With his desire to learn more about Gullah, it became known that slaves had been brought from West Africa to areas in Charleston, South Carolina and Savannah, Georgia, where there were rice coast ports as a main product.

Thus the majority of the population became Black because most of the Africans were able to resist some of the tropical fevers that had plagued European settlers. Thus their African languages became interfused with English. Therefore, Gullah came about as a very distinct and unique language. It was noted by many that no one could take their language away from them.

Dr. Turner began to identify what he called "loanwords" which had African- and English-based identifiers attributing to the Gullah language.

Here are some of the loan words that he began to identify:

Cootuh—Turtle
Buckra—Whiteman
Nyam—Eat
Swonguh—Boastful

Dr. Turner's most evidenced list of 3,600 "basket names" showed the true influence of Africa on the Gullah language. He also showed the impact of what he called "grammatical number": da (boy), dem (the boys), and serial verb constructions—come kyah me home (come carry me home).

Dr. Turner had to further establish as a part of his studies that the Gullah language borrowed from African languages. Thus he began studying at the University of London's School of Oriental and African Studies. This was where he really found the connections to the Gullah language. They were stronger than he had thought. This was where he would truly discover the influences of the African language on Gullah.

Dr. Turner would play the recorded audio tapes that he had made in the United States to African students who were studying in London. They would listen and identify the African words as they heard them.

In 1938, Dr. Turner went on to study Arabic at Yale University where he learned of other sources of Gullah phrases. Thus, he also learned of a religious tradition called "ring shout." It was discovered that this shout originated from sha'wt, which was the act of circling the Islamic Kaaba building during the pilgrimage to Mecca. The word came from Muslim slaves who were brought to the Sea Island. It worked with a call and response that was a part of a dance, ring-shout practice.

The determination of this and to find what he called "specimens of the dialect" came after he put together a word for word document of the connections of African words and Gullah. He studied this for almost two decades and was able to put his work in a book that is still used and recognized as the reference text entitled, *Africanisms in the Gullah Dialect* (University of Chicago Press, 1949).

This man was so full of wisdom and knowledge that it is such an honor to read and study about his work after growing up in the locale of South Carolina. Not only was his work considered the honor and glory of the Gullah language and culture, but he also brought forth the recognition and need for African-American studies, still prevalent today. Prior to his delving into these longitudinal research-based studies, many felt that African knowledge had been erased by slavery of a people. Dr. Turner showed the world that was not true and he built a strong bridge of learning of the connections between African-Americans and their African past. He became known as the pioneer of this great maintenance of two valuable cultures.

His work continued between 1962 and 1966 when Roosevelt became a training site for the Peace Corps volunteers. He helped prepare secondary school teachers to go to work in Sierra Leone, Africa. He taught them Krio, the language spoken by 16 ethnic groups in that country during that time. He contributed to International Education and Exchange programs. He also had a collection of artifacts that were collected in Brazil and Africa. He also wrote two Krio textbooks before retiring from Roosevelt in 1966.

He died in 1972 at age 81 and will long be remembered for his hard work, perseverance, and consistency in discovering Gullah's African influences. He is also noted for his research into the origins of creoles and African-American vernacular English or Ebonics.

Yet with all credit due to him, and while his works are still being used today, the most important contribution that he made was that he was able to preserve a cultural heritage that many thought was lost. He proved, despite what some may say, that slavery had not erased the memory of Africa for those who were victimized and forced into slavery.

Source: A Language Explorer who Heard Echoes of Africa (New York Times, September 3, 2010) © 2010 The University of Chicago® Magazine 401 North Michigan Avenue, Sui

In this chapter, I do hope that the readers will find learning about the Gullah language and culture as interesting as it has been for me. While I was growing up as a child and attending schools, I still find it intriguing that none of our teachers or parents ever told us that we were speaking a different language. They didn't tell us we were speaking a different language nor did they ever let us think that there were only some people who spoke the Gullah language. It still puzzles me until today about how some of us learned to speak standard English and others did not. Some of us may speak some form of standard English, but the intonation, pronunciation, and distinct tongue still could make standard English sound totally like a different language. As children of the descendants of families in South Carolina, we as children certainly learned our language from family members. While learning it from family members, we had to have the ear to hear what they said, understood and reproduced much of their language even if it was a more modern or individual or creatively developed by each one of us. When we gathered in neutral or central locations, communication with each other was always like a reunion of all of the natives gathering together. While we were surrounded by Africans as well as native islanders, I still do not recall that we could so uniquely tell who was not from South Carolina. The reason is that our native people often lived on isolated islands and South Carolina is still known for them today. We realized that there were locale reasoning that separated us from so many of our people even though we were all African/African-Americans. We were never taught to discriminate against any of our people. We were all brothers and sisters and immediately loved each other when we met. The islands in South Carolina that made us so uniquely separated were done so by islands of water. The islands of water made it so that transportation to leave the island was a form of control and certainly allowed for little time to think about escaping or disappearing. It would only be by what was called a miracle that someone would discover that people were actually inhabiting some of the islands because some had determined that some areas were non-livable. But Africans who had inhabited these lands were strong, creative, and had perseverance and endurance skills. This meant that they were already survivors based on how they arrived on the sea islands of South Carolina and Georgia by force. So while there were hardships, there were joys of a people being allowed to stay together and still practice much of their African tradition.

Another great thing that is still powerful today for Africans and African-Americans is when there are numbers from the same or different tribes, but still there is this sense of unity that caused us to be separated. But even with the separation many learned how to connect those characteristics that were common among them enough that they became learning experiences for all. So how wonderful to see even today, despite separation, that many of us still delight in the common practices, linguistic tongues, and other uniqueness that we recognize immediately. No matter where we live, travel, or trod, somehow we always seem to recognize someone who reminds us of someone we knew or know from somewhere. The first few times that people would come up to me and ask me if I am one of Mr._____'s children, it would scare me. I would be scared because I always hoped that I did not look like someone who someone was looking for because they were in trouble. But as time would tell, the same thing started happening to me, I would see someone in a different neighborhood, state, or city and they would remind me of someone I knew back home. By the time I went to Fisk University, my undergraduate school, although 99 percent of us were Black, there was no convincing them that I was not from Africa or Jamaica. Sometimes I would get tired because of the struggle and settle for which of the two places they chose as my home. That was when I really realized how important my language and the sound of my language meant to them. I was proud though to be recognized for my unique language that I very quickly learned the name for the language as Gullah and the people were referred to as "Geechies." As a matter of fact, they still call my oldest brother "Geech" today as he is an older adult.

When we started school at a very young age, we were so impressed with our teachers and how "proper" they talked. I was always one who was keen for listening to language and how people talked. I became very skilled at recognizing people who were not from South Carolina by their language. So as we got older, we always dreamed of going to New York. But for me it was the language and what seemed like city-cool dress-attire. So as I went to school, I remember coming back home daily as a first grader, getting in the mirror and imitating how my teachers talked. I really think that is part of the practice that helped me to learn standard English. Then I moved away to go to college, first Nashville, Tennessee, Terre Haute, Indiana, and then Cedar Falls/Waterloo, Iowa. But in all of these places I remember struggling when friends, professors, and acquaintances would squinch their eyes, hold their ears, and looked at me strangely because they really did not know what I was saying. I remember during my student teaching in Nashville, Tennessee, with kindergartners who would correct me when I did not say a word the same way that they said it. So I started asking them, "how do you say it?" They would tell me and I would try to repeat after them. This again really helped me especially with pronunciation and intonation. Of course there were some Gullah words that there were no substitutions for. So words like pop, soda, I learned to try to listen for which word they used in different places and I would adapt to the word used. Then as I went on to college, many of my friends became interested in Gullah and started asking me how to say certain words and I thought that was cool. So as I began to go more on the speaking circuit in my career, I began to share more examples of the Gullah language because people were interested. Still today, I am always surprised by how many people are interested in researching and learning more about the language.

Some Facts About Gullah:

1. The Gullah people are descendants of enslaved Africans who lived in what was called Low country regions in the United States, specifically South Carolina and Georgia.
2. These areas also included the coastal plain and the Sea Islands.
3. Descendants of enslaved Africans from the Gullah tribe also comprise a majority of the current inhabitants in the Bahamas. They share almost identical dialects.
4. Historically, the Gullah region extended from Cape Fear area of North Carolina's coast, which is south of Jacksonville, Florida's coast. But today, the Gullah area is limited to Georgia and South Carolina Low country.
5. The Gullah people and their language are also called Geechee. This name derived from the Ogeechee River, located near Savannah, Georgia.
6. Gullah is a term that was originally used to designate the variety of English spoken by Gullah and Geechee people. But over time it has been used by Gullah speakers to formally recognize their creole language.
7. Gullah language granted distinction and unique identity of the people referred to as Gullah.
8. In the State of Georgia, the people are referred to as "Freshwater Geechee" or "Saltwater Geechee." This distinction is made based on the proximity of the people to the coast.
9. Because the Gullah people lived through a period of remote isolation on the islands, they were able to preserve much of their African language and culture, while learning about new experiences from this region.
10. The Gullah people speak what is termed an English-based creole language that definitely included many African loanwords.
11. Gullah language is influenced by African languages in grammar and sentence structure.

12. Sometimes referred to as "Sea Island Creole" by linguists and scholars, the Gullah language is especially related to and almost identical to Bahamian Creole.
13. Gullah arts and crafts, farming, fishing folktales, music, rice-based dishes, and storytelling traditions all show strong influences from Central and West African cultures.
14. The Gullah people have a rich tradition in storytelling. They are well known for their Trixter Tales. These are where animals, people, and God play key roles in stories that have been passed down for generations. They are usually humorous with human characteristics and showing different predicaments that people find themselves in.

Resources

Burch, A.D.S. Threatened by Change, Gullah Fighting to Preserve their Culture. *The Miami Herald*, November 30, 2003.

Burden, B. A Bible to Call Their Own: Gullah Speakers Put Verses in Native Tongue. *Atlanta Journal and Constitution*, June 11, 1993.

Creel, M.W. (1988) *A Peculiar People: Slave Religion and Community-Culture among the Gullahs*. New York, NY: New York University Press.

Crum, M. (1968) *Gullah: Negro Life in the Carolina Sea Islands* (1940). New York, NY: Negro Universities Press.

Curry, A. (2001) The Gullah's Last Stand? *U.S. News & World Repor*, June 18, 2001.

Glanton, D. Gullah Culture in Danger of Fading Away. *Chicago Tribune*, June 3, 2001.

Jacobs, S. The Sea Islands' Vanishing Past. *Boston Globe*, Mar. 24, 1992.

Joyner, C. (1984) *Down by the Riverside: A South Carolina Slave Community*. Urbana: University of Illinois Press.

Pollitzer, W.S. (1999(*The Gullah People and Their African Heritage*. Athens: University of Georgia Press.

Rose, W.L. (1964) *Rehearsal for Reconstruction: The Port Royal Experiment*. Indianapolis, IN: Bobbs-Merrill.

Turner, L.D. (1949) *Africanisms in the Gullah Dialect*. Chicago, IL: University of Chicago Press

Wood, P.H. (1974) *Black Majority: Negroes in Colonial South Carolina from 1670 through the Stono Rebellion*. New York, NY: Knopf.

UUUMeans: What is hidden can be very important.

UUUU is hidden can be very important

Use the Glossary of Gullah Words to help students create a story!	Source: The Black Border by Ambrose E. Gonzales
KETCH	catch, catches, caught, catching; took, take; as: "'E ketch 'e tex f'um de fus' chaptuh een Nickuhdemus." He took his text from the first chapter of Nicodemus Also for reach, reached; as: "Time uh ketch de ribbuh bank, de dog done gone"
NOMANNUSSUB	impolite,
BLE	without manners, rude
SHAWT	short, shawtpashunt," short patience or irritable, irritability
STUHSTIFFIKIT	Certificate

Chapter 21

The Realities about Unequal Education

For many, the questions, ideas, concerns, and realities about unequal education have been a long time happening in the United States. Being in the educational field for most of my career, there are many observations that are so obvious that it makes one wonder why have there not been some major changes when it seems so obvious to some?

1. One cannot help but think about whether our educational system have been so long term?
2. One cannot help but think about whether this has been a preplanned plot against certain groups or populations of students?
3. One cannot help but think about why some of the educational/academic achievement gaps have not decreased or changed?
4. One cannot help but think about our educational system will become any better for certain groups or will it be a programmatic suffrage for the rest of most of our lives?
5. One cannot help but think who are the educational leaders in our country? Why has there not been any major legislation pushing for these needed changes?
6. One cannot help but think about educational teams, State Boards of Education, National Education Associations and community agency resourceful boards, committees and those who can help with the promotion of changes are not pushing to do so?
7. One cannot help but think about what aspect of our inequities in education are so predetermined by local and community finances?
8. One cannot help but think about whether schools will ever show equity when they are located in different areas of the city, county, and state that are reflective of many characteristics.
9. One cannot help but think about whether schools will be better off with local control versus any federal regulations keeping close monitoring on school operations.
10. One cannot help but think about whether there is evidence of any changes that have been successfully implemented since the 1954 Brown vs. Topeka Board of Education ruling.

Ary Spatig-Amerikaner, Aug. 22, 2012

Source: Unequal Education- Federal Loophole Enables Lower Spending on Students of Color

"Students of color are being shortchanged across the country when compared to their white peers."

The Declaration of Public Education for All

One must recall the important ruling by the United States Supreme Court in 1954 in order to objectively begin to problem solve or think about the realities of inequities in our educational system.

One must certainly realize that this is not a new issue, and is resultant of the 1954 ruling of Brown vs. Topeka Board of Education.

The Supreme Court declared that public education is "a right which must be made available to all on equal terms." Many called this a landmark decision. Landmark, why? Some feel that the reason it is a landmark decision is that this decision was intended to change the focus, direction, future, and present status of educational equity in the United States.

1. So the ruling was intended to bring national attention to the fact that this decision was critical in the promotion of the fact that the federal government would no longer support nor allow states to provide unequal educational experiences/opportunities for people who have been historically denied equal access.
2. This ruling was voted on and was unanimous when these judges overturned the racist concept of the fact separate education to ever have been considered as equal.
3. This ruling also brought to national attention in the United States that the voices of people who had historically been oppressed can now be heard rather than hushed up.

Amazingly Have the Changes Been Made Since 1954?

Of course the answer that one might receive depends on with whom the conversation may arise/exist. But the truth of the matter is whether the person would be able to truly look at the realities of what is happening in our educational system today.

Having grown up in the south and attending segregated schools throughout my life, one must take realistic and objective views on what is really transpiring in our public schools in the United States. We must be able to look at the issues that were wondered about in the beginning of this chapter.

So after the ruling, school districts set out to see how they could make this work where schools were expected to demonstrate equality in educational systems throughout the United States.

Many talk about the strengths and the definite weaknesses of the whole concept of busing as a solution to dissolving the separate but still unequal concepts in most of the public schools in the United States. While this practice is still a key one in many school districts across the United States, there have been disadvantages as well as advantages.

Advantages to Busing Students

1. This was the one main idea/concept that was incorporated throughout America to try to end segregation of schools. For some, it was a band aid approach to get some students out of their neighborhood schools and going to new schools to help integrate some segregated schools.
2. This provided for students who were too far from the designated school of attendance that they would need transportation to go to a school that was not within walking distance. Some students are bused for longer distances than others, which opened the doors for them to learn other areas of their locale that they may have never had the opportunity.
3. Busing allowed students to meet new students as well as teachers from another side of the town that they may not have had the chance to had they stayed in their neighborhood schools.
4. Busing provided transportation for students whose family may not have been able to get the child to and from school.

Disadvantages of Busing

1. Many parents and students complain of the early hours of the day that they have to be ready to catch the bus to go to school. Some students cite the length of the rides to and from school as tiresome, boring, and often overwhelming for them.
2. Many of the rural schools in some states had to combine, closing some schools with fewer students and joining with others to increase the number of students. Thus this decreased the number of buses needed to get the students to and from school.
3. Many school districts must come up with annual reports of showing how they plan on decreasing the cost of busing. This may include combining pick up and drop off spots of students.
4. Many school districts find that it was appropriate for them to change the types of preschool and kindergarten attendance/programmatic options for students. Thus some school districts went to the full day kindergarten programs, while others thought that alternate days' attendance would save the district busing funds rather than offering an am and pm half day program option.
5. Many of the busing for school attendance purposes may be dependent upon the weather for going into certain areas. Like in a state like Iowa, when there is snow or the remains of snow on some of the rural roads, it is advertised on media stations that for some rural areas buses will cover hard surfaces only, so then those students may miss school based on the condition of the roads near where they live.

So today with nearly 60+ years after the Brown vs. Board of Education decision/ruling, schools tend to still be separate and unequal. Almost 40 percent of Black and Latino students attend schools where a 90 percent or higher student population is non-White.

On the other hand, most White students attend a school where at least 77 percent of the students are also White.

Experts studying as well as those monitoring school desegregation patterns are finding that schools are as segregated as they were in the 1960s before busing even came into existence. So, wow, what does that imply or tell us? It tells us that the methods being employed to gain integration/desegregation are not working, especially with busing as the major action.

Still others are saying that there are no designed plans for how to successfully desegregate our public schools in the United States. The truth of the matter is that our schools are located in certain areas that call for them to be schools that are hard to desegregate merely by its location.

A contributing factor to schools is the important fact that schools are "as segregated as they were in the 1960s before busing began." Based on where students reside, it is becoming more and more urgent that we recognize that the schools are separated not only by when, where, and how they were built. Breaking down those building walls of segregation can truly be difficult.

So in the Brown vs. Board of Education case, the Supreme Court had to take a real close look at the boundaries of what is known as legal separation of schools. The real segregation was representative of an oppressive and discriminatory status of Blacks in the United States.

Those looking at segregation patterns realize that while schools in America may not be operating legally under the jurisdiction of a local mandate, one cannot help but visually recognize the long-term effects of status differences between Whites and non-Whites. It is a separate but unequal school system that has a funding formula that shortchanges equal educational for students of color.

Looking more in depth at the Brown vs. Board of Education, one certainly would be looking at how there was this justified legal separation of schools by race. Why did this legal segregation reinforce and emphasize a demeaning degradation of the true status of Blacks in America? It is no secret that such a designated formula for legal operation of public schools emphasizes further funding differences with non-Whites being on the financial deficit end.

One fact that seems to have been truly determined as real is that separate will always be unequal, no questions about it. But then we need to ask ourselves, how unequal are the educational services we

140 Classroom Management and Effective Strategies to Motivate Students

provide for students of color today? So why is this such an important and lingering question, factor, as well as reality? The truth comes out in the formula of per pupil state and local funding for students of color.

Researchers cite the fact that for more clarity and understanding not only is the funding formula significant, but how the money is spent may be more important than the formula itself.

Experts studying desegregation factors and other related significant status matters realize that some newly found data may assist with further answers to significant questions. Thus, information is now available for further study in the actual spending from state to local resources.

With all of its reviewing of issues related to actual spending and school expenditure of funding, a very valuable data collection was added to the 2009 assessment of teacher salaries. Surprisingly, teacher salaries had never been examined as a part of the status inequities among Whites and non-Whites. This information was collected by the U.S. Department of Education.

So when reviewing the per student expenditure by schools, it was found that:

1. Students of color were shortchanged across the United States when compared to their White counterparts.
2. Significantly, there is a fallacy in that the variations in the schools per student funding formula were inaccurately thought to be based entirely on the differences between school districts' property taxes. But the reality is that approximately 40 percent of this variation was found instead of the entire per student funding being truly based on property taxes. Instead it was found that the property tax bases were WITHIN school districts and not between.
3. It has been determined that there needs to be a change in the federal education law in order to close this loophole in the inequity gap. Thus the school districts would make this a more equitable expenditure on students of color.
4. While this does not seem to be complex, school districts argue that the salaries of teachers were of no significance when looking at overall per pupil expenditures. Veteran teachers who have been in the school district enough years to be considered of such status decide to move out of a high-need school to a low-need school which is usually richer, whiter, and already of a higher status. Thus this veteran teacher's actions based on moving that salary into the low-need schools, the misleading fact has been that the per pupil; spending would be equal between both schools. This is NOT true and is referred to as the comparability loophole.
5. New teachers often tend to start their teaching careers in high-need schools that typically serve many students of color and low-income, earn noticeably less than veteran teachers. Thus this leads to a much lower per pupil spending in schools determined to have the highest percentage of students of color.
6. While this has become a known factor, this problem still has been difficult to measure because data are unavailable.
7. Some researchers explain the rationale in regard to the inequities by providing documentation of the said pattern of underrepresentation of fair and equal per pupil funding, thus, underinvesting in students of color.
8. In 2009, the Obama Administration recognized the importance of data on teacher and school level nonpersonnel by including them in the report of the actual state and local spending as a part of the American Reinvestment and Recovery Act of 2009. In 2011, the Obama Administration, for the first time, historically released this information to the public.
9. SIGNIFICANT POINT: A major question that needs to be answered is the federal policy that was supposedly designed to guard and protect against within-district inequities. Title I of the Elementary and Secondary Education Act is what is termed as the federal government's main educational contribution for students living in poverty. Typically, school districts report that they are meeting

this requirement. However, the law requires that districts EXCLUDE teacher salary differences as they are related to experiences. They MUST NOT include this information in determining whether the comparability compliance is being met. Please note that in order to receive this Title I funding, schools have to promise to provide equitable educational services to higher poverty schools that are "comparable" to those in the lower poverty schools.

SIGNIFICANT POINT: This law that requires teacher salary differences to be EXCLUDED related to experience when determining the comparability compliance. Note this is a major exclusion because teacher experience is a major determinant of teacher salaries. Thus this exclusion and prejudicial process also provides misleading results. So this allows districts to report and appear as if they are providing equal spending on high-need schools as well as low-need schools. The truth of the matter is that they are not receiving equal funding. Again, this has been cited as the comparability loophole. School districts across the country routinely tell the federal government that they are meeting this requirement. But the law explicitly requires districts to exclude teacher salary differentials tied to experience when determining comparability compliance. This is a major exclusion because experience is a chief driver of teachers' salaries. This misleading process leads to a misleading result—districts think they are providing equal spending on high-need schools and low-need schools, even though they aren't. This problem has been frequently called the comparability loophole.

Thus this comparability report requirement is no doubt similar to other federal education laws, full of unequal, noncomparable loopholes when it comes to students of color and those living in poverty because of the agencies' "silent treatment of race."

Thus inequities based on race and poverty continue to exist mostly because of predetermined exclusion of the significance of teacher salaries and the inclusion of per pupil funding differentials within school districts.

Student Assignment

After reading this chapter, choose one major issue that you think is a contributing factor to the long-standing continuation of inequities in the educational system in the United States.

Chapter 22

Real Teacher Shocking Experiences Part 1

*These are real teacher education student experiences that have been adapted so as to not have any identifiable information or experiences relative to the originators of the experiences.

Shocking Experience 1

I have had a lot of shocking experiences in my lifetime. But nothing was quite as shocking as finding out that one of my closest friends had died. It was my freshman year of high school. I remember that the hallways were filled with students and busy as usual. Then, one of my best friends walked up to me and hugged me with tears in her eyes. When I was able to finally get her to stop crying, she began to tell me what had happened. I was getting prepared that it was not going to be good news. She then told me that our closest friend's mom had called her and told her that our friend had died the night before. I was shocked and honestly couldn't even cry. I was in complete shock and denial. I stood there waiting for him to walk through the school doors as he had done everyday. He would always come and give me a big hug with the biggest smile on his face.

For some reason, I could not seem to get that smile out of my mind. The other students in our class could sense that something was wrong. By this time, it was like when you play that game, "telephone." My friend told another one of the boy's good friends. Thank goodness, he was strong enough to tell our whole class.

By now, questions were coming from everywhere as everyone started asking questions about what really happened.

As news reports started coming across various media wires, we learned that our close friend that we thought we knew so well suffered with serious depression. He gave up and didn't want to fight any longer. Everyone in our class seemed so shocked. It really was a sad day.

It was really difficult for us who were closest with him because he always seemed so happy. He always acted like nothing bothered him. So ever since that day, I often wish it was possible for me to go back in time and ask what I should have been asking all along, "are you okay?"

At night, sometimes I still hear the news reports like it just happened today. I pray everyday that the pain and shock of missing him will cease and eventually go away.

But one of the greatest things that happened is that my class grew closer and closer everyday. There was never a day that someone in our class did not mention him by name.

The teachers were also shocked. They could tell that our class needed some additional counseling or emotional support. They were so kind to us and decided to postpone the academics and let us share our feelings of grief together. We were so grateful to them because we really needed that time together.

Because our school was a private one, most of our teachers read the Bible to us regularly anyhow. Some of them chose to read the Bible and pray with us.

They were so understanding and sensitive to our needs. They would allow us to talk, cry, or just sit in silence if we needed to do so. They genuinely wanted us to be alright. They wanted to help us through the pain that we were feeling.

So as a teacher, I will always remember that if shocking things happen, and it affects my students, I will step back so that I can make my students' well-being a top priority.

I still think about those teachers who helped us through that experience and have the utmost respect for them. I want to pattern after them in my own classroom.

Shocking Experience 2

After I graduated from high school I went on a mission trip with my high school youth group. The place chosen was a religious camp in Wisconsin for adults with mental and/or physical disabilities. I was one of the counselors and each of us was assigned one camper. We were to make every effort to make the camp for everyone as much fun as possible.

If any of the campers needed help with mobility or hygiene care, that was a part of our job also. We helped the camper's play games, participate in camp activities, and took them to the chapel. This was a very scary time for me because of my imagining being responsible for a camper for a whole week.

I had never worked with anyone who had a disability and I was out of my comfort zone. By the end of the week I was very shocked about how much fun we had and felt sorry it was ending.

Shocking Experience 3

I think this can be helpful to others who are teachers or want to become a teacher. I learned how scary it can be when we find ourselves in situations that overpower or overwhelm us.

So many children are overwhelmed and scared to go to school. So I hope that I will be able to use my experience to help them to learn that things may appear scary at first. But it will get better after a while.

I was spending some time with a friend at another university. So when we awoke the next morning, we learned that our longtime friend that was going to college in Illinois had committed suicide.

He was one my closest friends while growing up. We did everything together such as working on farms and in school events. It was my responsibility to assure that our graduating class honored him at the funeral.

Losing one of your closest friends and classmates at age 19 is very difficult. I came from a very small town in Iowa, so this was a shock to everyone in our community. I realize how important family is, especially since this happened. The time that I spent at UNI before going back home was very rough for me. But the support that I received at UNI really helped me and made life easier for me.

Shocking Experience 4

When one of my best friends committed suicide, I believe that I truly learned so much from the experience. I know that it really helped me grow so much as a person. I am sure someone may be saying, how can a suicide help me grow as a person?

I think it will help me be a better teacher someday in many ways. Since my friend's death, I find myself being more interested in inquiring about people's feelings. I have been thinking about some of life's experiences that could cause one to think about taking their own life. I know that some children are different and feel that no one is listening to them.

I am very hopeful that I will go out of my way to make sure that students in my class will feel that I care and listen to them.

I am hopeful that I can make it such that those with whom I come in contact will not feel that they should be treated differently because of their backgrounds or where they came from. I want to be a very good teacher who cares.

Shocking Experience 5

I know some of you who might be reading this might be surprised that I am 24 years old and have a total of 14 sisters and brothers. In my family, this includes half siblings, step sisters, and brothers.

So when I was 22 years old, my dad and his wife (not my birth mother) made an announcement to all of us that they were expecting a boy. Being selfish, as some might say, I was not happy. Personally, I did not think they were prepared to have another baby at age 40.

But to my amazement, when he was born, it looks like all of the family problems went away. Everyone in our family seemed so happy.

So while we were all so happy, being in early childhood I noticed that he was so quiet, abnormally quiet compared to what I thought other newborns were like.

As he grew older, concerns in our family arose because he would not talk. He did what many children did, but did so strangely, he would point and whine. So we just thought that he developed slower than other children his age. When he turned 2 years old, these characteristics became more obvious because he would not say a word. Then members of our family began making statements like, "He is in his own world." It seemed that he was doing things that did not make sense to us for a child his age.

I was really shocked when my mom called me and told me that the specialists had diagnosed him as having autism spectrum.

We had been learning about autism spectrum in several of our classes, so when I heard this, I thought that's it. I should not have been shocked because of my education background, but I felt really bad because my dad went into shock and he is still in denial. He was not going to accept the fact of any of his children having any special needs. When you think about it, he is probably right in his beliefs. The child is very smart and just slower in some areas than other children. Well, truly many children with autism do have those characteristics.

I hope that I will maintain the attitude of encouraging him and believing like my dad that he can do anything that he wants to try to do. But I am afraid that society may cut his dreams short.

I have been learning in my course of study that autism does have many spectrums and I feel that having experienced the various phases during my brother's that I am able to recognize many forms of autism. Experiencing my little brother's personality will help me as a teacher to understand and have a better knowledge of teaching diverse learners.

It is important for teachers to be observant so that they can objectively view diverse learners. Each teacher should learn how to better understand each student and attempt to meet their individual needs.

A teacher who understands each student's learning style will help students grow besides helping the teacher grow along with the students.

Shocking Experience 6

A shocking experience that really affected my life is when my favorite uncle got divorced. During that time, I was a sophomore in high school. Now some people say they can see divorces coming, but I could not see this one. My aunt (his wife) engaged with our family often. Everything seemed to be normal to us, so we did not notice anything that looked like divorce.

Being as young as I was during this time, I began to wonder what drove them apart in hopes that it would help me in my own life. So while I was in high school, my uncle had a girlfriend. Next thing I know they were married.

Now, some might say it was none of our business, but it seemed extra hard for my sister and I because she had children. So these additional children seem to really intrude in our family because during the time, my sister and I were the only grandchildren. We were upset because the attention was not going to my sister and I; these intruders were receiving some also.

Shocking Experience 7

I was very disappointed when I realized how much people in our society really look at people based on how much money they have or don't have. But I believe that we must treat all students the same regardless of their socioeconomic status. I was so shocked when the people who work in the cafeteria came and collected the lunches of ten children in the lunchroom because their parents weren't up to date on their payments for school lunches. When they took the lunches away, all of the children could see. But what caught my attention was the youngest girl who was in kindergarten. She began to cry loudly, saying, "Give me my food, I am hungry." All of the children near her immediately tried to give her something off their plates so she could have some food. These children displayed such a caring attitude toward this child; it helped her to bounce back to what had happened to her. So by this time, the principal came around with a sack of lunch and milk for each of those students. I did hear him say to the crying child, "No one will take your lunch away again" (in the hope that she would stop crying).

I was shocked when I read the same thing had happened to some children in Utah and that it made national news. I couldn't believe that children were being treated like this in schools. As a teacher, I hope that I will be able to play an important role in the well-being of my students so that they are not embarrassed because of money. We make everything so commercial and we wonder why some of our lower income families do not like school.

Shocking Experience 8

There is a shocking experience that came to my mind right away. When I was a junior in high school, I had a cousin who was a sophomore in high school. Our school had away basketball games one Friday night. My cousin was with her boyfriend for the weekend. I played basketball for our girls team and then was a cheerleader when the boys played. Around half time at the boys game, my parents pulled me out into the hallway. They had tears in their eyes as they told me that my cousin's boyfriend had died.

The reason I was so shocked is because I knew she had just left to see him. I didn't want to doubt my parents, but I admit I was in denial hoping they had made a mistake with their information.

Of course without having any information, my mind was really twirling with questions everywhere. So as I began to uncover some of the details about what happened. I learned that it was a gun that caused the accident. And my mom shared that my cousin witnessed the whole event. So not only was it a shocking experience for me, but obviously extremely shocking for her.

As a future teacher, I learned that this situation can help prepare me for some of the situations that I may have to deal with. I hope to be an observant teacher who notices my students. I will always want to know my students well in order to notice any changes in their demeanor or the way they are behaving. There could be something going on at home that is affecting their performance at school. If there really is something going on, I want to be there for my students and being mindful of it.

Shocking Experience 9

The most relevant shocking experience I can think of would have to be something that happened to a friend of mine. When we were in the seventh grade she found out that her father was diagnosed with lung cancer. Now mind you, her mother was never a part of her life because she died when she was very young. So now she is about to lose another parent.

So how would most of us handle this? After my friend found out about her father's cancer, it was a devastating and shocking experience; it was a huge shock because he had been such a healthy, active person all of his life. It came as a shock to me as well because I have never had a family member with cancer and he was like a father to me because we were so close at this time. After sticking by her side until her father passed away and long after that as well, I think this experience could help me as a future teacher. It could really benefit me because I learned to not only try to understand what my friend was going through, but help her along the way. I know as a future teacher I will come across students who have lost a parent, sibling, other family member, or friend who may still be coping. It is important for me to help them in their time of need and be understanding of the situation as well.

Shocking Experience 10

I have cared for children in the same family for the past 4 years. Therefore, I have seen children experience a lot.

Last year, a new baby was added to the family and the two children and I were so excited about it. The children stayed with me while the baby was born and while the parents were in the hospital. When I took the children to visit their new brother for the first time, they were so excited. The 5-year-old girl could not wait to go to school and tell all of her other classmates about the new baby. However, by the time Monday morning rolled around and the children were getting ready for school, she was crying and saying she did not want to go to school. She did not want to take the treats she had made to celebrate her new baby brother. Nor did she want to talk about the new baby. I finally convinced her to go, telling her that we did not have to even mention her new brother if she did not want to. By the time we got to school, she had decided to tell her teacher again and was happy about her brother then because everyone wanted to hear about him.

This leads me to believe that sometimes kids do need more attention than we provide. In this case, she was upset because her new brother was getting all the attention instead of her. She had not seen her parents at home in the normal home environment for a few days. Even though I was normal and at her house all the time, she was not sure how this new baby was going to fit into the family.

As a teacher though, we need to be aware of structural changes in the family and how children may deal with this. Some children do have difficulties with new additions to the family. Teachers who are aware of the impact of family changes will be prepared and can help. This also lets me know that there are various behaviors that a child may display with ideas about coming to school.

Shocking Experience 10

I know there are other people who may have an experience similar to the one that I am about to share. When I was working in childcare, there was one child in particular who didn't want to listen to me. Well not only me, but the child wouldn't listen to any adult either. So when the child was asked to calm down, his behaviors erupted more. So we the adults took the next step because the child's actions were putting the children in the class in danger, we felt.

The next level action that we decided upon was to take him to the director to see if that would calm the child down.

While I was walking this child down to see the director, he bit me several times. To be honest, that was very shocking to me, especially since I had never been bitten by a child before. I never imagined a child biting a teacher.

What I learned from this shocking experience is that you should always expect what is not going to happen to possibly happen.

Shocking Experience 11

As I am thinking of shocking experiences, events automatically came to my mind, but they were ones that had not happened to me. School shootings come to my mind right away. It is so difficult to imagine that anyone can even think about shooting a child.

The real reason that I think this is so shocking is because it is so awful and to think about our time coming to the point that this is what some people think is alright.

As future teachers, it is important that we become prepared for such events in case they happen with us.

Shocking Experience 12

When it comes to shocking experiences, school shootings seem to be too real right now. Although they are looking at some of the details behind these school shootings, they have not stopped, although we pray that they do stop. It just seems so unfair for this to happen to anyone.

This scares me every time I think that it could happen in a school where I might be teaching. I feel that my role would be multifaceted if this happens. I would make sure that I am helping students, their families, teachers, and others by helping to find resources, including a counselor, when appropriate.

Shocking Experience 13

When I think about shocking experiences, I think about some things such as death or illness or sad events that happen in our community that cause sadness.

I think that sudden illness or terminal illnesses are shocking and can be devastating for families if not dealt with properly. Also, there should be support for the children who are a part of these events and family changes. We should not assume that all children understand what happens.

However, when these hardships are in relation to children I often feel that hearts are even heavier. I have had personal experience with this shock. As a young teen, my best friend's younger brother was diagnosed with leukemia. I watched as he went through extensive treatments, chemotherapy, transplants, and the long hospital visits. While these things were enough to break your heart a million times, I constantly found myself shocked in a variety of different ways. The first was the constant heartbreak, anxiety, and distress that I watched my friend and her family consistently go through. But the most shocking of the journey was watching the child in a hospital bed so full of life and love. While he knew his body was sick, he showed no signs of a broken heart. This was so shocking to me because I was watching everyone around him hurt, but not him. He found the good in all situations at such a young age. To me, it was a constant reminder that children have positive minds, big hearts, and the desire to see the good in all people and all things. While some students can be facing severe struggles either internally or externally, they are still anxious to learn and interact with us and their peers. We as teachers need to be prepared to help by helping our students find the good despite the circumstances that they are faced with.

Shocking Experience 14

It is so hard to find the words to describe illness, death, and losing someone at some point in their lives.

While we try to protect our young students, we realize that we cannot shield them from all of these shocking experiences. But we should be prepared to help students deal with sorrow, grief, and tragedy.

Shocking Experience 14

Children go through shocking moments, as do adults. When I was working in a childcare environment, I saw many shocking experiences regarding children and their families. Sometimes, I wonder about life and shocking experiences as a teacher. Does it get easier as time goes on? For children, I hope that as we teach about coping skills, they get stronger.

As educators, we feel that we are in more of a supporting role since we are with the same children on a daily basis. Children depend on us to keep them safe and teach them how to deal with some of the challenges of life. The adults in their lives and the environment that is supportive and encouraging make a big difference in how they deal with shocking experiences.

Chapter 23

More Real Shocking Experiences Part 2

Shocking Experience 2-1

Something that was shocking to me actually just happened a couple days ago. I work at a daycare center in a 2-year-old room. This is a time when we plan holiday activities for the children. So it was around Thanksgiving time when the teacher in the 2-year-old room decided to decorate the classroom representing Thanksgiving.

So she decided to decorate the door of the classroom and had a large cutout image of what she said was an Indian. I know we had been studying in my classes at UNI that we needed to make sure that we were teaching children accurate information when it came to the holidays. We had already had a controversial discussion about whether Christopher Columbus really discovered America.

When I arrived at the childcare center on this particular day, it looked like most of the children were already there. The teacher began telling me as she appeared to be frazzled and upset that one of the children's parents had approached her and told her that she had a very serious concern that she wanted to discuss with her. She said that the dad told her that the decoration on the classroom door would be offensive to many people. He further stated that it would be a disgrace especially to Native Americans.

She went on to tell me how the father had gone on to share his feelings with other parents, a few of the other teachers and then the director. During that time, he seemed to be overly responsive to this image on the door to the classroom.

After he left the center in the morning, he proceeded to go and write a Facebook post including photos of the offensive door.

Then there were some other public actions taken by this parent expressing his concerns. Shortly after these events, the child was taken from the center and we never saw the child nor parent again. This will truly help me as a teacher by trying to learn as much as I can about diversity and not using stereotypes of any group of people. If I do make a mistake about something that I didn't know, I will try to rectify it right away. I am hopeful that I will understand the feelings of all of my families.

Further Elaboration on Shocking Experience 2-1

I decided to come back and attempt to explain a little more detail since my classmates asked me additional questions. I agree with what most of my classmates wrote about how they would have handled the situation.

What I learned is that the picture, image of the Indian, would be a cute figure representing Thanksgiving. But when looking into the matter further, I learned that this is one holiday that offends Native Americans in particular because the information is not accurate. I remember my instructor giving us an example in class and I really felt bad. She started singing a familiar song, "One Little Indian" One little, two little, three little Indians, four little, five little, six little Indians; seven little, eight little, nine little, ten little Indians." So the teacher asked us would we take that same song and replace it with, One little, two little, three little White people? So that didn't sound too good to us, but helped us to take a different look at some things that we say without thinking about them.

So when we are dealing with holidays and different traditions, we really need to be objective and selective to information on religions, cultures, ethnicities, etc. We must learn to look for stereotypes and try our best to not promote them. As future teachers, we must be sensitive because I can see some of the misconceptions ruining our teaching careers. I probably would not have thought too much about the picture of the Indian, if our teachers had not taught us about some misconceptions to be careful about. Of course the teacher felt bad because had she known, she probably would not have put the picture up. She certainly did not put the picture up to intentionally offend someone. The teacher did take the picture down that same day, but I also feel like the dad went overboard with his handling of the situation.

Shocking Experience 2-2

I have had many shocking experiences, but I think I will share one that took place when I was doing my field experience at one of the local elementary schools.

I had a different type of placement/assignment. The special education classroom where I was placed was for students who just seem to need a little help and not much. But I was also assigned to a kindergarten classroom. My obligation was to follow one little boy from the kindergarten classroom to the special education classroom.

It became obvious to me after a short time that these children's home lives were quite different from mine.

The little boy that I work with has a twin brother and they live with their aunt. She was their main caregiver, but I am not sure where his mother is. For some reason, there was never any conversation about her.

I was getting so excited because my supervising teacher invited me to attend the student conferences. I felt like I would learn more about the children and their family lives. So I still learned somethings about my assigned child's family, but auntie did not come to the conference, but dad and his girlfriend came.

So the dad began by introducing himself and seemed to have such an outgoing personality. So he told us that his family was helping him to try to get the children back under his custody full time. He also shared how he really wanted to know how his children were doing in school.

I was very shocked when the girlfriend began to question the teacher about such matters as to why the child was crying so much at school, what did the teacher do to make the child cry, and why didn't the teacher let the child eat the pop tart that he brought from home. She continued to ask questions of the teacher, but in a rude way. I was so shocked to see "a parent" come into the classroom and speak with such disrespect toward a teacher. I had never seen this before. I was so proud of the teacher who immediately gave quick responses to all of the questions and proceeded to begin sharing about the child's work. I must admit I was shocked at how the teacher was able to stay so cool with a parent ripping at her with accusations.

I think this was really a learning experience for me because of people's lack of understanding about some of the experiences of teachers. It is important that teachers learn how to handle situations that sometimes seem impossible to deal with the right way.

Shocking Experience 2-3

For me a shocking experience happened during my field experience assignment. There was a first grade girl who had to be sent home with what they called a "take home lice package" every Wednesday (and any other designated days) when I was there. I was told that he continuously came to school with lice. This shocked me and I wasn't sure if I should have been so shocked because of what I noticed about how unkept this child was. He came to school daily without a shower or bath and never wore any clean clothes. To be honest, this really opened my eyes about some of the difficulties some children may have at home.

I had not had many experiences with low-income students but was learning quickly. In my preparation in becoming a teacher, I have been so shocked by some of these children's parents' reactions to their education.

The child's mother was the recipient of many of the backpack meals sent home by the school. The meals were for the child like many other children in the school. Despite being the recipient of these meals, the mother was always rude and disrespectful toward the teachers and others at the school.

When I sat in on the parent conference of this child, I was really shocked to hear a mother speak about her child the way she did. I was so used to hearing parents defending their children and protecting them. This really opened my eyes that all is not well at the homes of too many children. I must remember that school is the safest place for many children. I learned that we as teachers must be patient and try to understand each one of our students. Many of them depend on school as a place of safety. I also learned not to ever judge the students and their families, but try to do my best to make it a positive experience for the students in my class.

Shocking Experience 2-4

I had a shocking experience in my assigned class field experience. I was in Pre-K Special Needs classroom at one of the local elementary schools in Waterloo. I hope that no one reading this will misinterpret my true feelings about the teacher to whose room I was assigned. But personally, I did not feel like she tried to help me learn or explain anything that could have been important for me. I didn't want to say my experience was useless, but I feel like it could have been better. So one day while I was there, one of the students tried so hard to complete an assignment in his own way, because he had a special need. The teacher laughed at him as if making fun of him. I noticed that the child became sad and never said another word to that teacher the entire time that I was at this site. I now better understand why we see some children who freeze up, stop talking, and never communicate with others.

It was really shocking to me because these students should feel safe and comfortable in their classroom. It appeared that this teacher made him feel unsafe.

Shocking Experience 2-5

During the summer program, I became a co-teacher in the school aged room. We went on a lot of field trips, including once a week when we went to the public pool. I was so shocked when we took the children to the pool and upon our arrival, there were two men fighting. The pool was evacuated and the police were called. As the pool was being evacuated all of the teachers, children and myself were sitting on the side waiting and wondering what was happening. The children were scared. At the time we did not have any answers to their questions. Now, since I am confused, I just kept wondering what did we need to do to keep the children safe? I knew that whatever decision was going to be made, it needed to be done quickly. After a while when law enforcement arrived, we were cleared to go back in the pool. But I noticed some of the children appeared very nervous about getting back in and wanted to just wait and watch. As a teacher this taught me that even in what may seem like a safe public environment anything can go wrong and we should be prepared for anything.

Shocking Experience 2-6

At my summer job at a childcare center, I had a shocking experience when I got to work one day. I was working in the toddler room, and I came in to find all of the children screaming loudly. Then I noticed that there was one of them who had moved from a crib to a cot, but was screaming in a crib. This caught my attention right away. Then the lead teacher was screaming about how she "couldn't deal with [the child in the crib] anymore . . . ."

So I was able to get the children calmed down and get ready for lunch. This experience really stayed on my mind because in our training at the university, they always told us to know when there was time to step back and ask someone else to step in for us. We all realize that there could be some moments in our teaching careers that things just didn't seem to be going right.

I really did learn that in order to work with children, especially very young children, that you really have to have patience. Then I saw firsthand how the mood of the teacher can definitely affect the mood of the children.

Shocking Experience 2-7

While I was working with a student who is diagnosed as on the autism spectrum, he shocked me. He began to have a meltdown during a theater lesson. I had worked with him before, so I knew a few methods that worked to calm him down. As I began to initiate these different methods, I realized very quickly that none of them were working. He then began to lash out in frustration. He did not want to participate in the lesson; he wanted to go home. I had him for the full hour, so I knew that wasn't an option. I began to sit next to him and work on our project without saying anything. When he realized I wasn't paying attention to his outburst, he began to kick and flail even more. He bit me twice and slapped my leg a few times. Each time I simply prompted "Gentle" and touched his face lightly. Finally, after testing my patience, he held my hand and said "Gentle." One thing I learned from this experience is something that worked before isn't always going to work. Along with that, I learned that patience is so important when working with children who struggle to communicate their needs. It's important to stay calm, have a thick skin, and strong resilience!

Shocking Experience 2-8

Over the summer I was working for a childcare program. I was the lead teacher in a 4/5-year-old room. My shocking experience happened about half way through the summer. From day 1, there was a little boy who was very challenging. He never wanted to do anything that we were doing, he had a really hard time with transitions, and he HATED nap time almost as much as he hated going home at the end of the day. I'll call this little boy, A. So one day, during center time, we were getting ready to switch centers. I'm not really sure how the events all played out because it happened so fast, but next thing I know A is standing on top of a table yelling, "Listen up all my N******!!" I was in SHOCK! I didn't know how to react to A or what to say to him. My assistant teacher jumped in and distracted the other children while I got A off the table and took him out of the room. My first thought was to be angry and discipline A, but my second thought was, "Why did he do that?" Before I even said anything to A, we walked around the school together. When we got back to our classroom hallway I sat down with A and asked him why he jumped up on the table. His response was, "Nobody listens to me."

To make a long story short, after talking with this little boy and talking/knowing his mother, his behavior shouldn't have surprised me as much as it did. A has grown up in a "rough" home where he sees and hears things that are beyond him. Words/names we think are inappropriate are used in his household on a daily basis, so he doesn't know any better. If I would have reacted like I had initially wanted to, it wouldn't have had a positive impact on him. Instead, we sat down together and talked about the things that are appropriate at school and at home and how they are sometimes different.

Being able to sit and talk with A gave me a whole new perspective of working with him. This experience not only made me realize that sometimes kids honestly don't know any better. It also made me realize what it's like to talk with parents about something uncomfortable. After A jumped on the table and said what he did, I had to talk to his mother. It was the scariest moment I've ever had! I didn't know what or how to even bring that up to her! With the help of my supervisor, I made it! I also had to write a note home to the other parents talking to them about how this week in school we talked about the language we use while at school.

Shocking Experience 2-9

When doing my field experience at a local school in a first grade classroom, I was shocked to learn that this school did not have an art teacher. When walking to the classroom the walls are filled with artwork, from students in kindergarten through third grade. One day after being in the classroom for a few weeks, I asked her when they go to art. The teacher told me that there is not an art teacher in the school anymore and that all the teachers do art in their own classrooms. Also when there I realized that there was one child that was behind in math and reading, I asked her if he goes to another teacher for help. She said no, she is the one that takes the time to teach him. I was more surprised than shocked, but shocked nonetheless about this, because all of the teachers were taking time and coming up with ways to teach art to their students. From this I have learned that as a teacher you need to be prepared to teach any subject. I also learned that in the olden days teachers taught every subject themselves to every child in their classroom. I am not sure how this union thing is going to affect teachers in Iowa, but I know they are having a tough time in the Wisconsin schools. Being able to see a teacher doing so much in the classroom that she didn't train for is kind of scary and inspiring at the same time.

Shocking Experience 2-10

One shocking experience I had was in my field experience classroom. There is one student that is very disruptive and has very little self-control. He is one-on-one, and always has an adult with him. I was very shocked to find out that it wasn't unusual for him to just run out of the classroom. He gets very agitated and even violent when something does not go his way. I learned that they are creating a "safe room" for him. Now he has been taken out of the classroom, and is trying to earn his way back into the classroom. This was a very shocking experience for me, because I have never seen a child with severe behavior problems in the classroom with everyone else. I also have never seen a child become violent with not only himself but the adult that is trying to help. He is a very, very smart child. Seeing all the behavior problems he is enduring also makes me question other areas of the child's life.

Shocking Experience 2-11

I had a shocking experience when I did my field experience in a first grade classroom. A child who had a hard time concentrating on his school work would get frustrated when he couldn't figure a problem out. One time he looked to be really focused on his school work, but a minute later he got up and threw his desk and threw a temper tantrum. It was really shocking how stressed out he got and how he handled his stress. The whole semester that I was there I only saw him act out like that one time. I think it's important to know each child's stress levels and when they get to what some call out-of-control behavior that we as teachers should allow the child to take a little break and do something else for a while.

Shocking Experience 2-12

I had a shocking experience during my field experience. I was placed in a Pre-K Special Needs classroom. The students I observed had a wide variety of special needs. This was a shocking experience because I quickly learned that adapting and modifying your lesson plan to adjust to the needs of the students is a crucial skill to possess as a professional educator. It was also shocking to me to observe the different and unique strategies used to teach each individual student. With the little experience I had at the time, I had no idea how much time and effort goes into teaching and managing a positive classroom environment.

Shocking Experience 2-13

In my field experience, I was at a kindergarten classroom at a local school in Waterloo. A shocking experience that I had was during writing time when all the children would get out their notebooks and write about anything. Some days they had a topic to write about, but most days they could write about the weekend, something they liked to do, etc. As I was walking around and helping children think about what to write about, there was one student who was drawing a picture about what she did that weekend. She talked about what she and her grandmother did. She shared the picture was about the weekend. I was shocked by how she didn't talk about her mother or father, but just about her grandmother. I realized that not everybody will have a mother or father raising them, but extended family members, or even other family members living with them besides immediate family. This really opened my eyes to the realities of what life may be like for some of these students. I learned that I can take these experiences as memories for me to truly understand the meaning of diverse families and family structures. The good thing is that these children do have someone in the family who is trying to help them grow and develop.

I must really begin to build upon gathering titles and copies of books that show different families and not just the one with a mother and father.

Chapter 24

More Real Shocking Experiences 3

Shocking Experience 3-1

When I walked in the room, I noticed right away that the child was trying to warm up to the environment. A question that arose was "Should this shocking situation surprise anyone?" I think most of us recognize the fact that when a preschooler comes to school, there may certainly be some adjustment issues most of the time. Some think that their parents are being replaced by other individuals in the environment. But the truth is that there cannot be anyone to supposedly replace their parents. Of course for new preschoolers, these adults are people that the child has never seen before.

So when this same child ventured out to other areas—early childhood program areas—she seems to be fine. So some people were wondering why she was fine in one place and not so relaxed in others. When the student attended the YWCA she was fine, do we know why? No, we do not. Children have their own way of warming up to new things just like everyone else when put in new or different positions. This experience taught me something new, whether it was shocking or not. I have learned that you have to give young children their spaces in certain moments, then everyone learns at their own pace.

Shocking Experience 3-2

When I think about shocking experiences there are many situations that come to mind. One of the experiences was my first college job at an early childhood program.

I very quickly started saying, "WOW what an experience." Then after this initial college experience, I decided to transfer to UNI. So my first reaction to being at a new institution was that my field experiences were so interesting. So I was able to start working at a childcare center in Waterloo. While working there one summer, I didn't have just one shocking experience, but multiple. When I first arrived for the job, I was not really sure what to expect. I had a class of 30 children with me and two other teachers. I had been forewarned about a few of the children. But other than that all of the other children were new students.

One day at lunch I had my back to the table where my students were sitting (keep in mind the students in my class were either just entering preschool, going to kindergarten, or starting first grade). I was listening to a couple of the conversations going on when suddenly I heard a boy say, "Do you know where you came from?" This little boy went on to explain to the other children exactly what sex was and how a baby is made. I was horrified!

How in the world a child so young not only knows what sex is but how it worked and in detail? I had heard children before try to describe where babies come from, but none ever with the real knowledge and/or understanding of the details. So, not knowing what to do, I decided to stop the conversation as soon as I could.

Luckily the little boy was only sitting by one other classmate at the time. Trying not to panic, or make my concern so obvious, I immediately went to my supervisor because I had no idea of how to handle this shocking experience for me as a future teacher. After a long talk with her we decided it would be best to work one-on-one with the parents. This was certainly one of the challenges for teachers in determining the best approach and when it is best to speak with the parents vs. the child or vice versa. Of course in some situations, it is best to speak with both together. Tough call at times. When the boy's mother came to pick him up, we pulled her to the side and talked to her about the day's events. She didn't seem surprised and then continued to tell us why. After she left, we had to talk to the other child's mother. Well, she wasn't too happy about the situation that her child was placed in receiving this type of information that her family did not give to him. We talked with this mother and the child about appropriate conversations to have with our friends and tried to answer any questions the child had.

This experience was extremely shocking for me. I would have never guessed that this would be a topic that I would have to talk to my students and their parents about. Out of it all, I was able to learn a lot from it though. Never underestimate what your students might know because we do not know where they learned the information. I also learned that it helps to know how to communicate effectively with parents. I think this is the hardest challenge for many people when dealing with controversial issues. There are some conversations that we would rather not have with parents, but we know that they are essential. As I gain more experience, I learned that talking with parents is not all fun and games. It is even more difficult because we are not sure how they will react to the information that we have to share. This discussion made me realize that this was one of the scariest conversations that I had ever had with a parent. Some teachers choose not to bring up these topics with parents, although the events did happen. There are many things I wish I could have changed about how some of the conversation went, but it was a great/shocking learning experience for all!

Shocking Experience 3-3

A very shocking experience occurred while I was still in high school. My family and I were on our way home from vacation when my father received a call from his brother, my uncle Benjamin. My cousin, his daughter was being airlifted to the U of I Hospital due to a farm accident. Her arm twisted around a power takeoff shaft, from her hand all the way to her shoulder.

At first, they thought that it was necessary for her arm to be amputated. She was fully conscious throughout the whole ordeal, and my cousin refused to let them cut off her arm. Eventually, they were able to save her arm, but with tremendous tendon damage. Through years of physical therapy and surgery, she now has use of two fingers and her thumb. She missed months of school due to hospitalization. I was shocked yet amazed with her determination and will to keep her arm and gain full use of it.

The most shocking part of the aforementioned event was the courage and persistence that my cousin had. Even though with doctors' recommended amputation, she fought to keep her arm. Not only was she keeping her arm, but she was also going to keep her graduation day schedule despite the many times she was hospitalized.

I learned so much from my cousin that I as a teacher have a responsibility to my students. I will always provide opportunities for students to succeed and to ensure they will never give up. I want to be that motivator that helps them to strive to do the best they can despite the odds that may be against them. Recalling the events, my cousin had every right to make some of the greatest excuses for why she needed to stay home and may have needed an additional year to complete high school. But she didn't use any of these as a way of survival. So if we as future teachers can maintain the courage, strength, and hope to help some of our students to keep on striving, then we will feel as though some of our work is complete. As a teacher, I will instill pride, hope, self-confidence, and stamina so that they will be able to stand despite hardships and shocking experiences that may come their way. Teaching my students to have positive mind-sets and to know that no struggle they have with school can set them back is my end goal.

Shocking Experience 3-4

For my shocking experience, I would like to share about a couple of students that I observed talking about a sparkle tooth in the childcare center where I worked. The reason why it became a shocking experience for me was because the young boy wasn't fully grasping the idea of a "filling." He knew that it was where his tooth was, but he thought that the dentist had completely removed his tooth and replaced it with a shiny tooth. Also, the other boy who was asking about the sparkle tooth stated that he also wanted one. This showed how he didn't understand that we don't just want sparkle teeth! He didn't realize that something happens in order for us to need the sparkle tooth. I realized that as a teacher, part of our job is to help our students to fully understand information before the class moves on to either a different topic or level. I was pleased to learn when one of my classmates had sent me a message encouraging me for realizing that young children may need so many different opportunities to explore concepts when learning. I realize as a future teacher that my students learn best when we understand and accept their different learning styles. She also shared that as a teacher we can't let the simple things slip our minds because that is the process of learning and how children grow. My classmates and I agreed that we need to make sure that our students grasp the ideas and concepts before moving on. So many times because we have so much to cover that we can be skipping over some much needed information for learning.

Shocking Experience 3-5

I was lucky as a child to live in the same house from birth to college. My neighbors had this same opportunity, and so did most of the students that I went to school with. We lived in the country, so we all grew up together as neighbors and sort of like family. My closest neighbors had five children. There were two who were a bit older and three closer to my age. This was a very affluent family who I remember had so many "things" compared to what our family had. The family attended the private school in the closest town and was active in the Catholic church. Growing up, I always wanted to be part of their family. The oldest brother often complained of struggling to make friends. He attended college and never really decided on what to do as a career. He was teased by his siblings. I assumed this was part of normal family interactions, so I didn't think of any of their actions as mean. So my being young and inexperienced, it appeared to me that he came from a big family and had everything at his fingertips. So, while everything seemed so wonderful and perfect to me because of my focus on him, I was really shocked to learn right after graduating from high school that he had committed suicide.

His mother was like a second mother to me and she was devastated. This was very difficult for me to see how distraught she was. But now as I look back, I feel like I should have reached out to him. It shows that you could have all the money in the world and what appears to be a healthy support system and it just still may not be enough.

As a future teacher, I plan on helping my students find happiness, success, and purpose. I won't hesitate to reach out. I also learned not to take anyone for granted into believing that everything is alright. It is even more devastating to find out that everything is not alright. But I do believe that I would feel better in my heart and should if I knew that I had reached out to my students even if they decide to do something not so pleasant. I hope to live and teach my students about the things in life that money cannot buy, but how to find love within themselves.

Shocking Experience 3-6

A shocking experience that I had was losing my friend in a terrible car accident over the summer. As I write this, it is still difficult for me to think about it. I was on vacation with my family when I woke up to many missed calls from my Gamma Phi sisters. When I finally was able to call them back, I found out about this very sad news. I really had a difficult time because denial took over my thoughts. I had never dealt with the death of someone very close to me nor in our age range. I must confess I did not know how to handle this. Some very valuable lessons that I learned from this experience was that it is okay to grieve in different ways. Some people are very open about a loss and others are very quiet. Going into each shocking experience with an open mind and being ready to help each individual in their own way is very important.

Shocking Experience 3-8

A very shocking thing happened to me while I was nannying a few summers ago. I had nannied for a set of 8-year-old twins (1 boy and 1 girl). The shocking experience happened during the middle of August. Throughout my time taking care of these children, I got to know them really well. I learned of their interests, what they wanted and didn't want to do, their favorite places to go, etc. They had gone to a few camps throughout the summer and at the time of the incident, they were in an art camp.

As a person listed on the pickup/emergency contact list, naturally I was the second person they contacted (mother was at work). One of the camp counselors had noticed a picture that the girl had drawn. The counselor found it a little disturbing, and thought that it was only appropriate to contact the family.

She had drawn a picture of a girl standing over a big puddle of blood, with blood coming out of random parts of the body. Not only were the drawn images disturbing, but the written words were too. Next to the picture, the words stated, "I can't take it anymore, I wish I could just be free."

As the counselor described the drawings and read the horrid words to me over the phone, I became concerned. I began to think deeply recalling that I had never noticed any signs of what seemed like depression or deathly thoughts. She had always appeared to me to be a happy child. I asked the counselor to send me the picture to show her parents, and then asked him whether they had talked about the picture with her. He said "No," they wanted to call us first, so that we knew about it. He then proceeded to say that they were seeking advice from us as to how or if they should approach it while she was at the camp. I told him I would try and contact the mother ASAP to tell her the situation at hand.

Nervously, I was able to get hold of her mother pretty quickly and we discussed an action plan of how the pickup was going to go that day. Their mother called the camp back and said we were going to talk to her about it. So I picked up Josiah (the twin boy) and their mother picked up Josephine from camp that day. It was my understanding that Josephine and her mother had a long talk about why she drew the picture and how she was feeling. So a close family friend who is a child psychologist was contacted. The mother made arrangements for her to talk with Josephine the next day. It was said that she did not share much. So the psychologist recommended taking her to the suicide/depression wing of the hospital as they could better work with her through therapy, medication, and suicide watch. That night, her parents admitted her to the hospital where she stayed for 4 days, getting her the help she needed, and started her on antidepressant medication.

Of course this was so shocking to me until I almost could not handle it. First of all I had read about childhood depression, but it was difficult for me to visualize a young girl at that age being depressed.

I had never thought about this kind of situation until it was right there in my lap. I never noticed any warning signs and still think about whether I missed any key actions. I quickly learned how children put up a front and don't always show how they are really feeling on the inside. I also learned how important it is to have an action plan for crisis and emergencies. We as teachers must always be prepared for any situation as they arise. Seems a little unrealistic, but the truth is that we must. Wow, she was having those kinds of thoughts and sadly, there are children younger than she was who were also having similar thoughts. As a future teacher, it is SO important to really get to know your students on a personal and emotional level. They could be suffering from various mental health issues that we are not even aware of. We must be prepared; there is no other way.

Shocking Experience 3-9

A shocking experience that really sticks out in my mind is my grandfather passing away when I came home for the summer. Somehow, I thought that he was waiting until I got out of school so that he could say his goodbyes to me. My grandfather and I were really close and always had been since I was an infant. He had been diagnosed with cancer about a year prior to his departure. For some reason he never really seemed sick until about a month before he passed. He was such an amazing and loving person. I really miss him every day. The reason this event is so shocking to me is the fact that I was the last person who was able to actually say goodbye to him. He had not woke up for up for couple of days. So when I arrived, I gave him a kiss, said goodbye, and left for home. But on my way home, I got the call to come back right away. It was so hard to see all of my aunts, my mother, and my grandmother so torn apart as a result of his death. However difficult this experience was, and still is, it has given new light as to what students may be dealing with in their lives. Prior to grandfather's passing, I really didn't know what it was like to lose someone so dear until now. As a teacher, this gives me more insight into how I can help students. I realize that the only thing that helped me was talking about it even though I really didn't want to.

Shocking Experience 3-10

The most shocking experience that I can think of was during the summer of my sophomore year of high school. It was the beginning of August and I had brought some friends up to where my grandparents live for the weekend. We spent our weekend at the lake which was nothing out of the ordinary. But on Sunday we decided that we wanted to go tubing, but we couldn't decide which three of the four of us would be going tubing first because the tub said it only holds three people. But we decided that all four of us would go at the same time because we were pretty little. Well about an hour later, the four us of got thrown off the tub. I come up from the water and my face is throbbing and I couldn't figure out why. Then I ran my hand across my chin and looked down and I saw blood and started screaming. And when I started screaming I realized that I had lost off of my teeth because I hit my friend's hip when we went off the tub. Well after my friends and I got back into the boat we realized that I had gashed her hip open with my braces and that I was missing my front left tooth. From this situation I learned that anything can happen at anytime. So when something major happens in a classroom, it's important to just stay calm and everything will be alright. That's what we did despite the tragedy because we knew it could have been worse.

Shocking Experience 3-11

My shocking experience happened over the weekend. My hometown made the news because the football team used slurs against a gay male who was nominated for homecoming court. This was shocking to me because I know the victim in this situation and was very close to him. I felt so bad because they should not have treated him like that. He did no wrong and is a kindhearted person. So now we are awaiting justice. We are hopeful that some action will be taken against those who were involved in this hatred as some of us continue to provide support for the victim. No one deserves to be bullied, but instead should be treated with dignity and respect. As teachers, we should make sure that these topics are included in our curriculum.

Shocking Experience 3-12

This past summer, I was so happy that I landed in a job working at a day camp for children. I was a counselor in the 5-year-old age group. I was shouting and telling everybody that it was the best experience ever. One day for an arts n' crafts activity, we chose to have the children draw what they want to be when they grow up. After they finished all their drawings we met in the large group and shared what we all wanted to be. The children were sharing their pictures and occupations such as rock star, policeman, singer, princess, etc. These seemed to be the trend or commonality among peers. However, one young boy went up and shocked us all. This 5-year-old boy got up in front of the group and stated that he wanted to be a paleontologist when he grew up. He knew exactly what it was and what they did.

This experience taught me to never underestimate children. Their brains are bounces, and as educators we need to fill them with as much knowledge as we can, because they are capable of retaining the information; it isn't merely going in one ear and out the other like many think. Beyond that, it taught me that we need to listen to children and hear what they have to say. Their input may be the missing piece we need.

Shocking Experience 3-13

My shocking experience would be a few moments that happened this last summer. I nanny for a family here in Cedar Falls and their 4-year-old cracks me up. I was helping him get dressed one day and he says to me "your belly looks like a butt crack." As I was completely caught off guard, I kind of giggled. Somehow my boobs became my belly that looked like a butt crack. A second moment was when he randomly asked me when I was having my baby. I was shocked at this moment because it had seemed that he had mistaken my tummy fat for a baby belly. I have known him for almost 2 years and this was the first time he had asked me that, so all I can think is that he thought that I was pregnant this whole time. Kind of hilariously shocking.

Chapter 25

Hip Hop-Rap That Teaches

Hip Hop into the Alphabet
Hip Hop Animal Rock

F is Fish
I squirm my body like a wiggle fish
And shake them as I go,
Through the water with a fish
So fishingly to and fro.

S Is Six Big Fish

Six big fishes swimming in an ocean
The first one says, "This ocean is wide."
The second one says, "This ocean is deep."
The third one says, "This ocean is a great landslide"
The fourth one says, "This ocean is a big bleep."
The fifth one says, "This ocean is full of fun."
The sixth one says, "This ocean is fun in the sun."

Can You Wiggle To and Fro?
Can You Wiggle To and Fro?
Do your shoulders sway high and low?
Can your hands clap a lot?
Can you turn them like polka dot?
Can you throw your fingers over your head?
Can you toss a ball behind your head?

Pa-lunk

Pa-lunk, pa-luk went the little frog
Pa-lunk, pa-lunk went the little frog
Pa-lun, went the kittle frog on today
And his eyes went pa-lunk, pa-lunk, pa-lunk!

B-Alligator

B-Alligator , B-Alligator , where are you from
B-Alligator, B-Alligator, show me your tongue
B-Alligator, B-Alligator, moving around the log,
Splish, splash, splish, splash, splish, splash
And away swims the big – B-Alligator, B-Alligator

Bees Swarming All Over

Bees swarming all over the place
Bees swarming all over the place
Hiding away, so no one can see the face
Soon they come crawling out of a hive
Looking to see how many are still alive
One, two, three, four, five.
Bees swarming all over the place
Bees swarming all over the place

Biggety, Biggety, Biggety, Bubmble Bees

Biggety, Biggety, Biggety, Bubmble bees
Who can say Biggety Bumble bee,
Count one, two, three
Who can play Biggety Bumble bee,
Let's play hide n' seek
Biggety, Biggety, Biggety, Bumblee bees
Touch your head, touch your toes and knees.
Bigget, Biggety, Biggety, Bmble bees

Come on Baby Bumble Bee

Come on Baby Bumble bee,
Will you come and play with me?

Come on Baby Bumble bee,
Zzzzzzzzzzzzzz, you stung me!

Girly Eyes

I see the world through my girly eyes,
And my friends are on my mind.
I'm walking around some pretty roses,
I'm walking around some pretty roses,
I'm walking around some pretty roses.

I'm talking on my cell phone, only they are gone
I miss talking to them after they left me alone.
Now I'm just playing games by myself
Now I'm just playing games by myself
Now I'm just playing games by myself
Now I'm just playing games by myself

I'm reading my favorite book until bedtime
Wonder when the clock is going to strike nine?
I'm thinking about my great day at school
I'm thinking about my great day at school
I'm thinking about my great day at school
All through my beautiful girly eyes, cool!

My Monkey See, My Monkey Do

My monkey sees me clap,
My monkey claps, claps, claps
My monkey sees me jump
My monkey jumps, jumps, jumps

My monkey taps his head
My monkey taps, taps, taps.
My monkey stomps his foot
My monkey stomps, stomps, stomps

My monkey slaps his knees
My monkey slaps, slaps, slaps
My monkey swings from trees
My monkey swings, swings, swings

Five Little Monkeys Jumping on the Couch

Five little monkeys jumping on the couch,
One fell off and said "ouch."
Four little monkeys jumping on the couch,
One fell off and said "ouch."
Three little monkeys jumping on the couch,
One fell off and said "ouch."
Two little monkeys jumping on the couch,
One fell off and said "ouch."
One little monkey jumping on the couch,
He fell off and said, "no more monkeys jumping on the couch."

Two Little Bluebirds

Two little blue birds
Sitting on a wall,
One name Peter and the other Paul.

Two little blue birds sitting in the mall,
One name Susan and the other Saul.

Two little blue birds sitting in a chair,
One name James and the other name Claire.

Two little blue birds sitting in tree
One name Tommy and the other Mickey.

Blue bird Blue bird Through My Window

Blue bird, blue bird through my window,
Blue bird, blue bird through my window,
Oh Susie, I'm tired.
Take that little girl, pat her on the shoulder,
Take that little girl, pat her on the shoulder,
Oh Mary, I'm tired.
Blue bird, blue bird, through my window,
Blue bird, blue bird through my window,
Oh Jamie, I'm tired.
Take that little Jamie, pat her on the shoulder,
Oh Jamie, I'm tired.

Hey You Little Chick

Hey you little chick, cute as can be
Peck, peck, peck, peck feeling so free
Hey you little chick, yellow shiny feathers
Strut, strut, strut, strut, head held high
You shine where ever you go with the weather.
Hey you little chick, you are a special one,
To be remembered by all those who meet
you on your way to the place of chick greet.

Move and Turn

Move and turn
Move and turn
Clap and turn
Clap and turn
Wave and turn
Wave and turn
Put your hand in the air
Put you hand in the air
Bend and touch the ground
Bend and touch the ground
Hand on head
Hand on head
Hand on hips
Hand on hips
Touch your lips
Touch your lips
And let your backbone slip!

Five Wobbily Ducks

Five wobbily ducks went out to play,
Over the hill and far away,
Father duck said, "Stay, stay, stay."

Our wobbily ducks came wobbling back.
Four wobbily ducks went out to play,
Over the hill and far away,
Father duck said, "stay, stay, stay."
Four wobbily ducks came wobbling back.
Three wobbily ducks went out to play,
Over the hill and far away,
Father duck said, "stay, stay, stay."
Three wobbily ducks came wobbling back.
Two wobbily ducks went out to play,
Over the hill and far away,
Father duck said, "stay, stay, stay."
Two wobbily ducks came wobbling back.
One wobbily duck went out to play,
Over the hill and far away,
Mother ducks said, "stay, stay, stay."
Five little ducks came wobbling back.

Seven Little Ducks

Seven little ducks that I once knew,
Tall ones, funny ones and jumpy ones too,
But the one little duck
With the streak on his back
He led the others with a quack, quack, quack.

Down by the lake they would go,
Wobble, wobble, wobble, wobble to and fro.
But the one little duck
With the streak on his back
He led the others with a quack, quack, quack.

Quack, quack, quack.
Quack, quack, quack.
He led the others
With 4 quack, quack, quack.

L-I-N-G-O

There was an old lady who had a horse
And Lin-go was his name-o.
L-I-N-G-O
L-I-N-G-O
L-I-N-G-O
And Ling-go was his name-o.

2. (Clap) I-N-G-O
3. (Clap, clap)-N-G-O
4. (Clap, clap, clap)-G-O
5. (Clap, clap, clap, clap)-O
6. (Clap, clap, clap, clap, clap)

Old Mrs. Mickey D.

Old Mrs. Mickey D. had a farm, E-I-E-I-O.
And on her farm she had a cow, E-I-E-I-O.
With a moo-moo here and a moo-moo there.
Here a moo, there a moo, everywhere a moo-moo.
Old Mrs. Mickey D had a farm, E-I-E-I-O.
And on her farm she had a duck, E-I-E-I-O.
With a quack-quack here and a quack-quack there.

Pig- Oink-oink

Kitty- meow-meow

Dog- ruff, ruff

Chicken- cluck-cluck

Horse- neigh-neigh

Add favorites!

Have You Ever Seen an Elephant?

Have you ever seen an elephant go like this and that.
He's very big,
He's very tall,
He's very heavy,
He has no fingers,
He has no toes,
But wow, does he have a great long, nose!

Monika's Camel

Monika's camel has five humps,
Monika's camel has five humps,
Monika's camel has five humps,
Boom, boom, boom (move hips side to side with each boom)
Go Monika go.

Monika's camel has four humps
Monika's camel has four humps
Monika's camel has four humps,
Boom, boom, boom (move hips side to side with each boom)
Go Monika go.

Monika's camel has three humps
Monika's camel has three humps
Monika's camel has three humps,
Boom, boom, boom (move hips side to side with each boom)
Go Monika go.

Monika's camel has two humps
Monika's camel has two humps

Monika's camel has two humps
Boom, boom, boom (move hips side to side with each boom)
Go Monika go.

Monika's camel has one hump
Monika's camel has one hump
Monika's camel has one hump
Boom, boom, boom (move hips side to side with each boom)
Go Monika go.

Monika's camel has no humps
Monika's camel has no humps
Monika's camel has no humps
"OOOOOOOOOOOOOPS" Monika's a horse!

Teddy Bear, Teddy Bear, Touch the Ground

Teddy bear, teddy bear, jump up and down
Teddy bear, teddy bear, don't make a sound.
Teddy bear, teddy bear, turn all around,
Teddy bear, teddy bear, touch the ground

Teddy bear, teddy bear, touch the sky,
Teddy bear, teddy bear, look up high.

Teddy Bear, Teddy Bear, Touch Your Shoe

Teddy bear, teddy bear, touch your shoe,
Teddy bear, teddy bear, say echew.

Teddy bear teddy bear, touch your nose,
Teddy bear, teddy bear, touch your toes.

Teddy bear, teddy bear, stand tall,
Teddy bear, teddy bear, up against the wall.

Teddy Bear, Teddy Bear Read A Book

Teddy bear, teddy bear, read a book,
Teddy bear, teddy bear, take a look.

Teddy bear, teddy bear, go up the stairs,
Teddy bear, teddy bear, please no tears.

Teddy bear, teddy bear, turn off the light.
Teddy bear, teddy bear, say good-night.

What Are You Wearing?

What are you wearing? What are you wearing today?
If you are wearing red, stand up.
If you are wearing red, stand up.
If you are wearing red, sit down.
If you are wearing red, sit down.

If you are wearing blue, clap your hands.
If you are wearing blue, clap your hands.
If you are wearing blue clap your hands two times.
If you are wearing blue clap your hands two times.

If you are wearing yellow, nod your head.
If you are wearing yellow, nod your head.
If you are wearing yellow, nod your head two times
If you are wearing yellow, nod your head two times.

Wibbily Wobbily Wu

Wibbuly, wobbuly wu,
A monkey sat on you,
Wibbuly, wobbuly wee,
A monkey sat on me,

Wibbuly wobbuly Wary (Mary)
A monkey sat on Mary.

Wibbuly Wobbuly wu,
A monkey sat on you.
Wibbuly Wobbuly wee,
A monkey sat on me.
Wibbuly Wobbuly Wames
A monkey sat on James.

Hello

Hello, hello, hello and how are you?
I'm fine, I'm fine and I hope that you are too.

Jambo, jambo, jambo watoto. (children in Swahili)
Jambo, jambo, jambo sana jambo (everybody in Swahili)

Hello Numbers

Hello one child
Hello two children
Hello three children
Hello four children
Hello five children
Hello six children
Hello seven children
Hello eight children
Hello nine children
Hello ten children

Jambo Watoto

Jambo moja watoto (1)
Jambo mbili watoto (2)
Jambo tatu   watoto (3)

Jambo nne   watoto (4)
Jambo tano   watoto (5)
Jambo sita   watoto (6)
Jambo saba   watoto (7)
Jambo nane   watoto (8)
Jambo tisa   watoto (9)
Jambo kumi   watoto (10)

I Am Looking for

Well, I am looking for_____(child's name)
_____child's name, child's name_____
Are you here today?

Child responds: Yes I am, Yes I am here today!

(Repeat until saying all children's names)

When We All Get Together

The more we get ourselves together, together, together,
The more we get ourselves together, together, together,
The happier we will be, because your friends are my friends
and my friends are your friends.
The more we get ourselves together, the happier we will be.

The more we get ourselves together, together, together,
The more we get ourselves together, together, together,
The happier we will be, because estes amigos are yo amigos
and yo amigos are estes amigos.

If You're Pretty and You Know It

If you're pretty and you know it, clap your hands.
If you're pretty and you know it, clap your hands.
If you're pretty and you know it,
Then your face is gonna' show it.
If you're pretty and you know it, clap your hands.

If you're handsome and you know it, stomp your feet.
If you're handsome and you know it, stomp your feet.
If you're handsome and you know it,
Then your face is gonna' show it.
If you're handsome and you know it, stomp your feet.

If you're proud and you know it, nod your head.
If you're proud and you know it, nod your head.
If you're proud and you know it,
Then your face is gonna' show it
If you're handsome and you know it, nod your head.

Nine in the Bed

Nine in the bed
And the oldest one said,
"Move over, move over."
And they moved over,
And one jumped out.
There were eight in the bed,
And the oldest one said,
"Move over, move over."
And one jumped out.
There were seven in the bed,
And the oldest one said,
"Move over, move over."
And one jumped out.
There were six in the bed,
And the oldest one said,
"Move over, move over."
And one jumped out.
There were five in the bed,
And the oldest one said,
"Move over, move over."
And one jumped out.
There were four in the bed,
And the oldest one said,
"Move over, move over."
And one jumped out.
There were three in the bed,
And the oldest one said,
"Move over, move over."
There were two in the bed,
And the oldest one said,
"Move over, move over."
There was one in the bed,
And the youngest one said,
"I'm not moving over and
I'm staying on the bed."

The Rose Bush

Here we go round the rose bush,
The rose bush,
The rose bush.
Here we go round the rose bush,
So early in the morning.

This is the way we brush our teeth,
Brush our teeth, so early in the morning.

Here we go round the rose bush,
The rose bush,

The rose bush,
Here we go round the rose bush,
So early in the morning.

This is the way we comb our hair,
Comb our hair
Comb our hair, so early in the morning.

Here we go round the rose bush,
The rose bush,
The rose bush,
Here we round the rose bush,
So early in the morning.

This is the way we eat our breakfast,
Eat our breakfast,
Eat our breakfast, so early in the morning.

Peanut, Peanut Butter and Jelly Sandwich

Peanut, peanut butter and jelly sandwich,
Peanut, peanut butter and jelly sandwich,

First you take the peanuts and you plunk em, plunk em,
First you take the peanuts and you plunk em, plunk em.

Peanut, peanut butter and jelly sandwich,
Peanut, peanut butter and jelly sandwich.

Then you take the strawberries and you squish em, squish em,
Then you take the strawberries and you squish em, squish em.

Peanut, peanut butter and jelly sandwich,
Peanut, peanut butter and jelly sandwich.

Then you take the bread and you spread jelly on it
Then you take the bread and you spread jelly on it.

Peanut, peanut butter and jelly sandwich,
Peanut, peanut butter and jelly sandwich.

Then you take the sandwich and yum, yum, yum.
Then you take the sandwich and yum, yum, yum.

Head and Shoulders Baby

Head and shoulders baby, 1-2-3
Head and shoulders baby, 1-2-3.

Knees and ankles baby, 1-2-3
Knees and ankles baby, 1-2-3.

Clap your hands baby, 1-2-3
Clap your hands baby, 1-2-3.

Shrug your shoulders baby, 1-2-3
Shrug your shoulders baby, 1-2-3.

Jump up and down baby, 1-2-3
Jump up and down baby, 1-2-3.

Turn around baby, 1-2-3.
Turn around baby, 1-2-3.
Jump and turn around baby, 1-2-3
Jump and turn around baby, 1-2-3.

There Was a Little Monkey

There was a little monkey,
Who lived in a cage,
He nodded to the people
He showed his tail,
He laughed at a fly,
He laughed at a knat,
He laughed at a bee,
He laughed at me,
He clapped for the fly,
He clapped for the knat,
He clapped for the bee
But he didn't clap for me.

The Wheels on the Bus

The wheels on the bus turn round and round,
Round, round, round.
The wheels on the bus turn round and round
All through the town.

The horn on the bus goes honk, honk, honk,
The horn on the bus goes honk, honk, honk,
The horn on the bus goes honk, honk, honk.

The wipers on the bus, go twitch, twitch, twitch,
The wipers on the bus, go twitch, twitch, twitch,
The wipers on the bus, go twitch, twitch, twitch.

The people on the bus go hello everybody, hello everybody, hello everybody.
The people on the bus go hello everybody, hello everybody, hello everybody.
The people on the bus go hello everybody, hello everybody, hello everybody.

The driver on the bus says, sit down please, sit down please, sit down please.
The driver on the bus says, sit down please, sit down please, sit down Please.
The driver on the bus says, sit down please, sit down please, sit down please.

The babies on the bus say, goo, goo, goo, goo, goo.
The babies on the bus say, goo, goo, goo, goo, goo.
The babies on the bus say, goo, goo, goo, goo.

The mothers on the bus say, here's your milk, here's your milk,
Here's your milk.

Who Took the Candy from the Candy Jar?

Everyone: Who took the candy from the candy jar?
Leader: Mary took the candy from the candy jar.
Mary: Who Me?
All: Yes, you!
Mary: Couldn't be.
All: Then who?
Mary: Jimmy

Everyone: Jimmy took the candy from the candy jar?
Jimmy: Who me?
All: Yes you!
Jimmy: Couldn't be.
All: Then who?

Repeat above until every child has had an opportunity to be the responder.

Bringing Home My Doll Baby

I'm bringing home my doll baby,
Oh, won't my mommy be so happy with me"
I'm bringing home my doll baby,
Oh my, I am so proud of me

Ten Little Friends

One little, two little, three little friends
Playing in the yard, playing in the mud,
Four little, five little, six little friends,
Playing in the park, playing with a thud,
Seven little, eight little, nine little friends,
Playing in the gym, playing on the court,
Ten little friends playing all together.

Springtime Morning Springing

This is the way the dog barks, dog barks, dog barks
This is the way the dog barks,
On a springy morning.

This is the way cat walks, cat walks, cat walks
This is the way the cat walks,
On a springy morning.

This is the way the blackbird flies, blackbird flies, blackbird flies
This is the way the blackbird flies,
On a springy morning.

This is the way the cow moos, cow moos, cow moos.
This is the way the cow moos,
On a springy morning.

This is the way the pig oinks, pig oinks, pig oinks.
This is the way the pig oinks
On a springy morning.

This is the way the children laugh and play, laugh and play, laugh and play,
This is the way the children laugh and play,
On a springy morning.

Did You Ever See a Bird?

Did you ever see a bird, a bird, a bird?
Did you ever see a bird,
Fly this way and that way
And this way and that way
Did you ever see a bird
Fly this way and that?
Did you ever see a bunny, a bunny, a bunny
Did you ever see a bunny,
Hop this way and that way
And this way and that way
Did you ever see a bunny,
Hop this way and that?

Did you ever see a bumblebee, a bumblebee, a bumblebee
Did you ever see a bumblebee,
Buss this way and that way
Did you ever see a bumblebee
Buzz this way and that?

Daddy Pounds with One Hammer

Daddy pounds with one hammer, one hammer, one hammer, then he pounds with two.
(Use two hands to pound)
Daddy pounds with two hammers, two hammers, two hammers, then he pounds with three.
(Use two hands and one foot to pound)
Daddy pounds with three hammers, three hammers, three hammers, then he pounds with four.
(Use two hands and two feet to pound)
Daddy pounds with four hammers, four hammers, four hammers, then he pounds with five.
(Use two hands, two feet and nod head to pound)
Daddy pounds with five hammers, five hammers, five hammers, then he pounds with six.
(Use two hands, two feet, nodding head and shrugging shoulder to pound)
Daddy pounds with six hammers, six hammers, six hammers, then he said, I am tired!
(Stop pounding)

Miss Mary Mack

Miss Mary Mack
Miss Mary Mack,
When are you coming back?
Miss Mary Mack, when are you coming back?
Please, please, come back Miss Mary Mack
Please, please come back Miss Mary Mack
(clap to the beat with a partner)

Miss Jamie Mack

Miss Jamie Mack
Miss Jamie Mack, Mack, Mack
Holding that sack, sack, sack
She carried it so long, long, long
She started singing a song, song, song.
Then she picked up the bank, bank, bank
And began to thank, thank, thank everyone
For the bun and frank, frank, frank!
Miss Jamie Mack, Mack, Mack
See you after a while, while, while!
See you later with a smile, smile, smile.

Banana Fana Badana

Hey banana fana badana
Fee, fi, foo, where you a standin'?
Hey lady, lady, belady,
Fee fi foo lady, lady!
Hey banana fana badana
Fee fi, foo, where you standin'?
He Sadie, Sadie, beSadie,
Fee fi foo Sadie!
(Keep adding children's names in the song)

If All the Little Raindrops

If all the little raindrops,
Were sunshine and lemon drops,
Oh what a great world this would be,
Filled with nothing but love and harmony!

If all the little raindrops,
Were strawberry and jelly gum drops,
Oh what a great world this would be,
Filled with nothing but love and dignity!

The Limbo Rock

Hey come on friends let's do the limbo rock,
Bow those bodies down as low as they can go,
Come on move them down from head to toe,
Do the limbo rock, limb rock, limbo rock!

Come on under the limbo stick, lower, lower, lower,
That's it, now let's do the limbo trick, trick, trick,
Come on move that body like your slick, slick, slick,
Do the limbo rock limbo rock, limbo rock!

Bumpity Bump

Hey, put those backs against each other,
Bumpity, bump, bumpity bump,
Do the bumpity bump, do the bumpity bump!
Hey put those hips side to side, with each other
Bumpity, bumpity, bump, bumpity, bump,
Do the bumpity bump, do the bumpity bump!
Hey put those feet against each other,
Bumpity bump, do the bumpity bump!

5 Little Ducks Went Out to Play

5 little ducks went over to play,
Over the yard and way away,
Uncle duck said, "Quack, quack, quack"
And four little ducks came wobbling back.

Four little ducks went over to play,
Over the yard and way away,
Uncle duck said, "Quack, quack, quack"
And three little ducks came wobbling back.

Three little ducks went over to play,
Over the yard and way away,
Uncle duck said, "Quack, quack, quack" and
Two little ducks came wobbling back.

Two little ducks went over to play,
Over the yard and way away,
Uncle duck said, "Quack, quack, quack"
And one little duck came wobbling back.

One little duck went over to play,
Over the yard and way away,
Auntie duck said, "Quack, quack, quack"
And five little ducks came wobbling back.

Moving Like Shapes

Move, move, move like a big elephant
Move, move, move like a big frog.
Move, move, move like a beach ball.
Move, move, move like a pretty butterfly.

Clap, Clap Your hands,

Clap, clap your hands, 1, 2, 3.
Clap, clap, clap your hands like me.

Stomp, stomp your feet, 1, 2, 3
Stomp, stomp your feet like me.

Jump, jump up and down, 1, 2, 3.
Jump, jump up and down like me.

Roll, roll, roll your hands,
Roll, roll, roll your hands, 1, 2, 3.
Roll, roll, roll your hands like me.

Ring Around the Posie
Ring around the posie,
A bucket full of tosie,
Ashes to ashes, they all
Fall, fall, fall, down.

Beat, Beat the Drum

Beat, beat, beat, fast.
Beat, beat, beat, slow.
Beat, beat, beat, hard.
Beat, beat, beat, soft.
Beat, beat, beat, big.
Beat, beat, beat, small.

Hip Hop Alphabet Activities

The following alphabet hip hop activities can be used to help children learn a variety of literacy activities. These activities will allow children to use their whole bodies while learning.

Hip Hop with A

A is for aaaaaaaaaaaaaaaaaaaaaaaaaaaaaaaa
A apple
A alligator
A Africa
A amigo
A applejacks
Jump like apple jacks!

Hip, hip, hop hooray!!!!

Hip Hop with B

B is for bbbbbbbbbbbbbbbbbbbbbbb
B bee
B bumblebee
B bed
B bug
B bird
B big
B bumpity bump
Bumpity bump with your partner!
Hip hip hop, hooray!!!

Hip Hop with C

C is for ccccccccccccccccccccccccccccc
C cat
C candy
C cup
C can
C cap
C clock
C cake
Do the cake walk with a jerk and a strut!
Hi hip, hop, hooray!

Hip Hop with D

D is for dddddddddddddddddddddd
D dog
D donkey
D deer
D diaper
D drink
D disk
Do a dance, with dip.
Dip to the right, then dip to the left!
Hip hip, hop hooray!

Hip Hop with E

E is for eeeeeeeeeeeeeeeeeeeeeeeeeeeeeee
E is for elephant
E is for eat
E is for eel
E is for enormous
E is everyone
E is for each
E is for eat, eat, eat, eat, eat, eat, eat, eat all of your food, eat, eat, eat!
Hip, hip, hop, hooray!

Hip Hop with F

F is for ffffffffffffffffffffffffffffffffffffffff
F is for fun
F is for fan
F is for finger
F is for fat
F is for fabulous
F is for fantastic
Close your eyes, move your toes, move your hands, move your legs, move your shoulders. See if you can feel the beat, fantastic beat!!!!!!
Hip, hip, hop, hooray!

Hip Hop with G

G is for gggggggggggggggggggggggggggggggggggg
G is for gorilla
G is for go
G is for game
G is for giraffe
G is for gum
G is for glow
Give yourself a pat on the knees. Pat a friend's hand. Pat your head. Pat your feet.
Hip, hip, hop hooray!

Hip Hop with H

H is for hhhhhhhhhhhhhhhhhhhhhhhhhhhhhhhhh
H is for horse
H is for happy
H is for home
H is for honey
H is for help
H is for ham

Let's do the hambone! Hambone, hambone, forty cents a pound, not gonna eat my hambone, till the sun goes down. Put my hambone in the pot, not gonna eat it till the soup gets hot. Hambone, hambone, where you been, around the world and back again. (Slap hands criss cross your knees)
Hip, hip, hop hooray!

Hip Hop with I

I is for iiiiiiiiiiiiiiiiiiiiiiiiiiiiiiiiiiiiii
I is for ice cream
I is for ice
I is for igloo
I is for imagination
I is for icicle
I is for itsy- make your body parts go itsy bitsy, tiny, tiny, down to the floor!
Hip hip, hop hooray!

Hip Hop with J

J is for jjjjjjjjjjjjjjjjjjjjjjjjjjjjjjjj
J jelly
J jam
J jail
J juggler
J jingle
J jeans
J is for jumping jacks- Can you do jumping jacks? Jump, jump, jump!
Hip, hip, hop, hooray!!!!!!!!!!

Hip Hop with K

K is for kkkkkkkkkkkkkkkkkkkkkkkkkkkkkkk
K king
K kid
K kite
K ketchup
K kitten
K is for kick- Can you kick, kick, kick, kick, without touching a soul?
Go on, kick!
Hip, hip, hop, hooray!

Hip Hop with L

L is for lllllllllllllllllllllllllllllll
L light
L lamb
L limb
L list
L little
L lighthouse
L is for lifting- lift those arms up- high, higher, higher, now down, down, down- again---
Hip hip hop, hooray!

Hip Hop with M

M is for mmmmmmmmmmmmmmmm
M money
M monkey
M missile
M mirror
M month
M is for march
March, march, march, march, forward, then backward, forward, then backward.
Hip hip hop hooray!!!!

Hip Hop with N

N is for nnnnnnnnnnnnnnnnnnnnnnnnn
N is for nose
N is for noise
N is for number
N is for note
N is for name
N is for notebook
N is for no, no, no, no, shake your head to the beat of no, no, no!

Hip Hop with O

O is for ooooooooooooooooooooooooo
O is for octopus
O is for October

O is for octagon
O is for owl
O is for oatmeal
O is for operator
O is for open, open, open, open, open your arms wide, open them wide and open them real wide!
Hip, hip, hop, hooray!

Hip Hop with P

P is for pppppppppppppppppppppppppp
P is for puppy
P is for pig
P is for pen
P is for pencil
P is for penguin
Walk, and use your whole body to move like a penguin, just like a penguin!
Hip, hip, hop, hooray!

Hip Hop with Q

Q is for qqqqqqqqqqqqqqqqqqqqqqqqqq
Q is for quail
Q is for queen
Q is for quit
Q quietly tip toe, quietly tip toe, shhhhhhhhhhhhhhhhh, don't make a sound-----now touch the ground!!!!!!!!!!
Hip, hip, hop, hooray!

Hip Hop with R

R is for rrrrrrrrrrrrrrrrrrrrrrrrrrrrrrrrrrrrr
R is for rug
R is for ring
R is for rag
R is for race car
R is for roller blade
R is for rat
R is for run, run, run, run in place, run, run, run in place!
Hip, hip, hop, hooray!

Hip Hop with S

S is for sssssssssssssssssssssssssssssssssssss
S is for sunshine
S is for skunk
S is for stars
S is for steak
S is for studio
S is for ship
S is for stomp, stomp, stomp, stomp, stomp!
Hip, hip, hop, hooray!

Hip Hop with T

T is for tttttttttttttttttttttttttttttttt
T is for thumb
T is for toys
T is for tub
T is for towel
T is for tower
T is for tiptoe, tiptoe, tiptoe, tiptoe, tiptoe!
Hip, hip, hop, hooray!

Hip Hop with U

U is for uuuuuuuuuuuuuuuuuuuuuuuuuu
U is for umbrella
U is for unicorn
U is for underground
U is for up
Put your hands, up, one foot up, then the other foot
Up, jump, up, and then down!
Hip, hip, hop, hooray!

Hip Hop with V

V is for vvvvvvvvvvvvvvvvvvvvvvvvvvvv
V is for vase
V is for vitamin
V is for visitor
V is for Vermon
V is for Venice
V is for vice president
Visit, visit, visit, with a friend, visit, visit, with a friend!
Hip, hip, hop Hooray!!!!!!!!!!

Hip Hop with W

W is for wwwwwwwwwwwwwwwwwww
W is for water
W is for watermelon
W is for wings
W is for wagon
W is for woman
W is for white
W is for walk, walk, walk, walk, walk, and walk, walk!
Hip, hip, hop hooray!

Hip Hop with X

X is for xxxxxxxxxxxxxxxxxxxxxxxxxxxxxx
X is for x-ray
X is for xylophone

X is for xtra
X is for xxxxxx- criss cross, criss, cross, criss cross your legs, criss cross your hands, criss cross your fingers!!!!!!!!!!
Hip, hip, hop, hooray!

Hip Hop with Y

Y is for yyyyyyyyyyyyyyyyyyyyyyyyyyyyyyyyyy
Y is for yacht
Y is for yak
Y is for yard
Y is for yawn
Y is for yes
Y is for yarn
Y is for yawn, yawn, yawn, yawn, yawn, yawn, yawn!
Hip hip hop, hooray!!!!!!!!!!!!!!!!!!

Hip Hop with Z

Z is for zzzzzzzzzzzzzzzzzzzzzzzzzzzzzzzz
Z is fr zebra
Z is for zoom
Z is for zipper
Z is for zip
Z is for zap
Zip, zip, zip, zip, zip, zip, zip with your fingers! Zip, zip, zip, zip, zip, zip, zip, with your fingers!!!!!!!

Hip Hop Resources

Sakina's Kids Hip-Hop Class You Tube
Clean Hip-Hop Music
Children's Dance Song
Kid's Songs
Good Hip-hop Songs for Kids
How to Find Clean Hip Hop Music for Kids

17Rap Songs for Kids- SheKnows
http://www.sheknows.com/entertainment/articles105113/the-best-rap-songs-for=kids Jan 20, 2017

Brain Breaks-Children's Dance Song- Hip Hop Slow-Kid's Songs
https://www.youtube.com/watch?v=2oRh2yPDzpg Feb 14, 2014

Sakina's Kids Hip-hop Class: "Work" Music Video-YouTube
Https://www.youtube.com/watch?v=netGlffridQ
Feb 15, 2013

Good Hip-hop songs for kids: a list.- Slate
http://www.slate.com/articles/arts/family/2011/11/good_hip_hops_songs_for_kids_a list_html
Dec 20, 2011

Clean Hip-Hop Music- Common Sense Media
https://www.commonsensemedia.org/lists/clean-hip-hop-music

The Dance Buzz: How To Find Clean Hip Hop Music for Kids
http://thedancebuzz.blogspot.com/2012/04/how-to-find-clean-hip-hop-music

Rap Clean Enough for Kids: Top 10 Kid-Friendly Artists and Albums
https://www.parentmap.com/article/kid-friendly-hip-op April 16, 2012

Hip-Hop Songs
https://www.quora.com/Which-hip-hop-songs-can-go-into-4-radio-friendly-playlist-for-my-kids

Hip Hop Dance Songs on Pinterest/Hip hop
https://www.pinterest.com/explore/hip-hop-dance-songs/

Hip Hop Fast
https://www.pinterest.com/pin/118149190199377753/

Hip Hop Dance Moves for Kids: Hip Hop Dance- You Tube
https://www.youtube.com/watch?v=mG717Dx4C8Q
Aug 21, 2013

Hip Hop Dance Moves for Kids: Tutorial Jump Song- You Tube
https://www.youtube.com/watch?v=RjiyHYg4YQU
Aug 7, 2010

Flocabulary- Educational Hip-Hop
https://www.flocabulary.com

Hip Hop Body Rock- The Learning Groove
http://www.thelearninggroov.com/hip-hop-body-rock

Hip Hop/Rap Music Lyrics/SongLyrics.com
http://.www.songlyrics.com/hip-hop-rap-lyrics.php

Appendix A

Motivation to Share

Motivated to Share and Care Messages of Inspiration- A Collection By Robert Smith, Director of the University of Northern Iowa Center for Urban Education (UNI_CUE), Waterloo, Iowa

This is a series of daily inspirational encouragement messages designed to provide hope and support! They may be used in a variety of ways with people of all backgrounds and ages!

"When you stand up to speak on behalf of your own people, you are classified as a Communist, as race hater, as anything but good." ~ Muhammad Ali, The Greatest, 1973

"Black people have got to learn the white man's language if we're going to communicate with him." ~ Malcolm X, Malcolm X Speaks, 1965

"We black men have a hard enough time in our struggle for justice, and already have enough enemies as it is, to make the drastic mistake of attacking each other and adding more weight to an already unbearable load." Malcolm X, speech given in Los Angeles, California, 25 March 1960

A minority group has "arrived" when it has the right to produce some fools and scoundrels without the whole group paying for it. ~ Carl T. Rowan

"If you can't focus, you can't finish. If you can't finish, you will fail." ~ Matt Bishop, The 8 Pillars of Career and Business Success

"Simply put, Habits can be the very basis of your success or the only reason for your downfall." ~ Kenneth J Hutchins, 10 Powerful Habits of Successful People

Thought for the day ~ Successful people do what unsuccessful people aren't willing to do. Don't wish it were easier, wish you were better. ~ Jeff Olson

Thought for the day ~ You will never change your life until you change something you do daily . . . the secret of your success is found in your daily routine. ~ John C. Maxwell

"With confidence comes the ability to trust your own judgment every time!" ~ Cheryl Maloney, Simple Steps for Real Life

"Yet even as the world change, there are things which remain timeless. Good manners and right conduct is one of them." ~ Claire Stranberg, Raising Kids With Good Manners

Thought for the day ~ "If you were to write your life motto, what would it say? Look out for number one? Or look out for the needs of others?" ~ David Jeremiah, Helping Others

The real purpose of our existence is not to make a living, but to make a life; a worthy, well-rounded, useful life. ~RS

Thought for the day ~ "God has been profoundly real to me in recent years. In the midst of outer dangers. I have felt an inner calm. In the midst of lonely days and dreary nights I have heard an inner voice saying, "Lo, I will be with you." ~Martin Luther King, Strength to Love, 1963

Thought for the day ~ The only thing that stops anyone from knowing their self-respect is that they continue to look at others for consent to feel equal, happy and worthy. ~ Sean Parker, Self-Esteem

Thought for the day ~ Merely asking yourself who you really are won't cut it.: You are going to be defined by the actions that you take each and every day. ~ Gracia Hunter, How to motivate yourself in DARK times.

Thought for the day ~ The fountain of happiness must spring up in the mind, and he who seeks happiness by changing anything but his own disposition, will only multiply their sadness. ~ Brad Hanson, Brad Pieces of Wisdom

Thought for the day ~ Your mental attitude will determine your success in life. If your outlook on life is a positive one, you will find life will be easier. Everything comes down to your own attitude. And, only you are the one who decides what type of attitude you have, it is your choice!" ~ Catherine Pulsifer

Thought for the day ~ Your attitudes and the choices you make today will be your life tomorrow, build it wisely. ~ Unknown

Thought for the day ~ "Once our attitude and mindset towards God changes, we can go from ingratitude to gratitude." ~ Lilliet Garrison, Getting Unstuck

Thought for the day ~ "Nobody can impose your beliefs on you. It's always you who in the last instance can permit a belief to be true for you or not!" ~ Marc Reklau, 30 Days - Change your habits, Change your life

Thought for the day ~ Change is a fundamental feature of life, whether is difficult to face, whether positive or negative, change is inevitable. ~ Rebecca Jane, Mindfulness My Way

Thought for the day ~ To get happier, try gratitude, giving back, savoring, encouraging your optimism, and celebrating progress. ~ Jonathan Harnum, Practice Like This

Thought for the day ~ Successful people are famous for their brilliant time management skills. ~ Felix Oberman, The Ultimate guide to Declutter Your Life and Organize your Mind

Thought for the day ~ "We will need to build constructive beliefs, behaviour patterns, thought patterns, habits, values and principles to override the deconstructive ones." ~ Barry Naude, The Essential Skills for Success

Thought for the day ~ "Our success is measured by personal beliefs, not by anybody else's standards or beliefs." ~ Henry Marsh, the Breakthrough Factor

Thought for the day ~ The greatest charity is to help a person change from being a receiver to being a giver. ~ John Marks Templeton

Giving friendship is more rewarding than giving luxuries. ~ John Marks Templeton

Thought for the day ~ A man can fail many times but he isn't a failure until he begins to blame others. ~ John Burroughs

Thought for the day ~ There is no short cut to achievement. Life requires thorough preparation. Veneer isn't worth anything. - George Washington Carver

Thought for the day ~ "Quality questions create a quality life. Successful people ask better questions, and as a result, they get better answers." ~ Anthony Robbins

Thought for the day ~ Worry is a rocking chair that gives you something to do, but never gets you anywhere. ~ Erma Bombeck

Healthy minds tend to cause healthy bodies and vice versa. ~ John Marks Templeton

Thought for the day ~ The more you practice stepping into other peoples' shoes, the more you'll experience the results and benefits. ~ *Wendy Hearn*

Thought for the day ~ Character is the moral strength to do the right thing even when it costs more than you want to pay. ~ Michael Josephson

Thought for the day ~ Cut out any negative people, they will never smooth your path towards a great life. ~ Edmund Ronen, Unlock Your Inner Achiever

Thought for the day ~ In order to keep yourself motivated, therefore, focus is a key point that I cannot stress too greatly. ~ Theo Gold, Motivation

Thought for the day ~ You don't have to be a "person of influence" to be influential. In fact, the most influential people in my life are probably not even aware of the things they've taught me. ~ Scott Adams

Thought for the day ~ Being happy can be hard work sometimes. It is like maintaining a nice home – you've got to hang on to your treasures and throw out the garbage. ~ Andrew Matthews

Thought for the day ~ Ability is what you're capable of doing . . . Motivation determines what you do . . . Attitude determines how well you do it. ~ Lou Holtz

Thought for the day ~ Right is right even if no one is doing it. Wrong is wrong even if everyone is doing it. ~ St. Augustine

Thought for the day ~ Your life is your time. If you want to plan your life, then plan your time. ~ Andrian Teodoro, The Power of Positive Life

Thought for the day ~ Enjoy the journey, enjoy every moment, and quit worrying about winning and losing. ~ Matt Blondi

Thought for the day ~ Life will never be without surprises and challenges. ~ Rajneesh Chaturvedi, Taming Mind

Thought for the day ~ Be responsible for the energy you bring. ~ Jill Bolte Taylor

Thought for the day ~ Many of the most successful people have spoken about the importance gratitude has had on their lives. ~ Claire Shannon, Gratitude: Feel Grateful Today and Every Day

Thought for the day ~ "Knowledge is not power. The implementation of knowledge is power." ~ Larry Winget, People are Idiots and I Can Prove It

Thought for the day ~ Great minds have purposes; others have wishes. ~ Washington Irving

Thought for the day ~ Wisdom can be defined as the ability to anticipate the consequences of your choices in advance of making them. ~ Jenny Rogers, Manager As Coach: The New Way To Get Results

Thought for the day ~ What other people think of you is none of your business. ~ Regina Brett

Thought for the day ~ Negative thinking patterns will prevent you from doing many of the things that you need to do in order to build the extreme confidence that is required to live the life of your dreams. ~ Beau Norton, How to Be Confident and Destroy Low Self-Esteem: The Ultimate Guide for Turning Your Life Around

Thought for the day ~ Every day is a good day to examine our prime-time priorities. ~ William Arthur Ward

Thought for the day ~ All beliefs and belief systems boil down to having faith in something we would like to believe to be the truth. ~ Neville Berkowitz, How To Live in The Now

Thought for the day ~ You cannot change your past by thinking about it; you cannot change your future by simply thinking about it. ~ Joshua Pope; Why Are You Looking At This?

Thought for the day ~ Most times, we are afraid of things that may never happen. Often we project into the future. ~ Clodagh Swanson, Time To Shine

Thought for the day ~ A great way to ensure that you always see the positive side of life is by feeding your mind with the right things. ~ Nick Bell, Organize Yourself Starting Today!

Thought for the day ~ Try to do unto others as you would have them do to you, and do not be discouraged if they fail sometimes. It is much better that they should fail than you should. ~ Unknown

Thought for the day ~ "Being able to effectively communicate your thoughts, needs, desires, and worries is incredibly important in any relationship - including your work relationship." Louise R. Allen, Confidence

Thought for the day ~ I believe that our circumstances can change based on what words we read, hear, and speak. ~ Kathy Collins, 200 Motivational and inspirational Quotes

Thought for the day ~ "The best thing about a gratitude list is that it can change your mood and bring you back to focus on the positive things in life." D.D. Tai, Mind: How To Pleasure Your Mind Everyday

Thought for the day ~ People who are constantly negative have a tendency of rubbing off that negativity to others. It's not just annoying, it is unhealthy. Surround yourself with positive people and positive attitudes. ~ Louise R. Allen, Confidence

Thought for the day ~ As much as we want to, we all need to understand you truly cannot change other people. ~ Catherine Pulsifer

"Everyone thinks of changing the world, but no one thinks of changing himself." ~ Leo Tolstoy

Thought for the day ~ Kindness and compassion lead to forgiveness. - Tina Samples; Messed Up Men of the Bible

Thought for the day ~ You've heard that it's wise to learn from experience, but it is wiser to learn from the experience of others. ~ Rick Warren

Thought for the day ~ Helping others, without expecting anything in return is what true self-worth is all about. - Gavin Bird, Self Esteem: Change your life in one day!

Thought for the day ~ Life is too short to wake up in the morning with regrets. So love the people who treat you right, forget about the ones who don't and believe that everything happens for a reason.

If you get a chance, take it. If it changes your life, let it. Nobody said that it'd be easy, they just promised it would be worth it.~ Harvey MacKay

Thought for the day ~ "Many people in today's society waste a lot of their time on social media and entertainment to stimulate themselves but spend little to no time at all trying to improve themselves or their life situation." ~ Noel N, Daily Planner

Thought for the day ~ "You should note that the ability to think positively plays a very central role in our state of well-being as well as our quality of life." ~ Angel Greene, Self Help: Golden Nuggets for High Performers for Next Level Success

Thought for the day ~ "By looking for the good in others and praising it, we are doing ourselves a service too, as we tend to experience in our lives what we are giving our energy and attention to." ~ Don McArt, The Mental Makeover

Thought for the day ~ "It doesn't matter how many good ideas you come up with in your life time, if you're unable to focus on any one of them for a certain length of time you'll never see it come to fruition." Alex Altman, Time is Money

Thought for the day ~ "In Life We Can Have Results or Reasons." ~ Harald Anderson

Are You Part of the Solution?

Have you noticed how much easier and more fulfilling it is when we work together to accomplish a task?

Do you recall working with a group on a dreaded project, only to conclude with a positive experience and outcome?

Was there a time of crisis when you and others put aside any differences and worked together to help others in need?

There is strength in unity. When we gather together to tackle a problem with the desire to create an effective outcome, we may often find unexpected success.

An old man at the point of death summoned his sons around him to give them some parting advice. He requested a bundle of sticks and said to his eldest son, "Break it."

The son strained and strained, but in spite of all his efforts was unable to break the bundle. The other sons also tried, but none of them was successful.

"Untie the bundle," said the father, "and each of you take a stick." When they had done so, he said to them, "Now, break," and each stick was easily broken.

And . . . "A house divided against itself, cannot stand."

One of the United States' most beloved and revered presidents, Abraham Lincoln, made this point in a speech that he gave in Springfield, Illinois on 16 June 1858 when he was campaigning to become an Illinois Republican senator. At that time the country was divided in its belief as to whether slavery should be abolished.

Although the challenges that we encounter in our lives today may be trivial by comparison, we may find our workplace and communities divided when we pull against each other. There is strength when we draw together at work or at home. When we are facing challenges, we will find greater rewards if we work together to achieve our goals.

The idea presented by Lincoln in 1858 remains true even today. "We shall not fail — if we stand firm, we shall not fail. Wise counsels may accelerate or mistakes delay it, but, sooner or later, the victory is sure to come."

At home or work, look for ways to unite to resolve issues and solve problems. It may involve compromise, negotiation or a willingness to give up personal agendas for the good of the organization, family or community, but the success that can flow from these actions can often be more positively impactful than we could ever have imagined.

Affirmation for the Week

"I strive to be part of a solution instead of part of the problem, by uniting with others to bring about a better outcome."

Thought for the day ~ "God hand never slips. He never makes a mistake. His every move is for our own good and for our ultimate good." ~ Billy Graham

"The true test in life does not occur when all is going well. The true test takes place when we are faced with challenges." ~ Catherine Pulsifer

Thoughts for the day ~ "Attitude and ability are complementary to each other for success in life." ~ M.K. Soni

"Don't take life too serious. You'll never escape it alive anyway." ~ Elbert Hubbard

"I believe that there will ultimately be clash between the oppressed and those who do the oppressing. I believe that there will be a clash between those who want freedom, justice and equality for everyone and those who want to continue the system of exploitation. I believe that there will be that kind of clash, but I don't think it will be based on the color of the skin . . . ~Malcolm X

"Unless a sense of service and duty is instilled, our upward mobility will only be measured by cars and styling." ~ Niara Sudarkasa, in "Niara Sudarkasa: Educator for the 1990s," Essence, May 1989

"We should never make any apologies for doing what our times and circumstances compel us to do. The first emancipation was the burden of the white man, and it remained only a proclamation. But the second emancipation is the burden of the Black man, and that is why it must be made a reality." ~ Damon J. Keith, c.

"[I]f the great battle of human right against poverty, against disease, against color prejudice is to be won, it must be won not in our day, but in the day of our children's children." ~ W.E.B. Du Bois, "The Children's Number," Crisis, 1912

"[P]oor or whatever your circumstance, you are capable of being the best of people and that best, as a human, does not come from the outside in, it comes from the inside out." ~ Lucille Clifton, "A Simple Language," in Evans, ed., Black Women Writers, 1984

Thought for the day ~ Human relations are built on feelings, not on reason or knowledge. And feelings is not an exact science; like all spiritual qualities, it has the vagueness of greatness about it.

Thought for the day ~ "Goals make life worth living. They encourage us to improve our talents and stretch and challenge our intellectual and physical abilities." ~ William C. Oakes, Christlike Leadership: Leadership that Starts with an Attitude

Success is not final, failure is not fatal: It is the courage to continue that counts. ~ Winston Churchill

"The task ahead of us is never as great as the power behind us." ~ Ralph Emerson

Life isn't about waiting for the storm to pass...

We must learn to dance in the rain . . . ~ Vivian Greene

Live honestly, love generously, care deeply, and speak kindly...

And leave the rest to GOD!! ~ Ronald Regan

"But they that wait upon the Lord shall renew their strength; they shall mount up with wings as eagles; they shall run, and not be weary; and they shall walk, and not faint." Isaiah 40:31

Thoughts for the day ~ Always be nice to people on the way up; because you'll meet the same people on the way down.

~ Never regret, If it's good it's wonderful. If it's bad, it's experience. ~ Victoria Holt

~ Every morning in Africa a lion wakes up and realizes it must out run the slowest gazelle or it will starve. Every morning in Africa a gazelle wakes up and realizes it must out run the fastest lion or it will die. It doesn't matter if you are a lion or a gazelle, when the sun comes up you better be running".

Coming to Your Senses, Acknowledging Slavery

Imagine if Visa or Mastercard sent me the following letter: "Dear Mr. Soaries, We're pleased to send you a brand-new credit card. It's still going to carry platinum privileges, but we're changing the name from Platinum to Slave. We know you'll enjoy using your new Slave Card. The best card you can have. Slave."

You get my point. Financial institutions don't send us "slave cards"; they send out gold or platinum cards. They would never use the term slave in any reference, and we would be understandably offended if they did. Instead we proudly whip out our gold card and hand it over to the cashier as if we're extra special instead of especially enslaved.

The first step for getting out of slavery must be identifying the reality of our condition. We must acknowledge that the truth of Proverbs applies to us: "The borrower is servant to the lender" (22:7). The word translated as "servant" can also be accurately rendered as "slave."

"You are either part of the solution or part of the problem." ~ Eldridge Cleaver, c. 1968

"Never let blackness be your problem but somebody else's problem." ~ Adam Clayton Powell, Jr., speech

"Yes, prayer is powerful and miracles come from it every day. But if we fail to pray, we make it nearly impossible to be who God wants us to be." ~ J.W. Boggs

Thoughts for the day ~ "Every aspect of life has rules, and money is no exception. Come to grips with those rules and you can become very, very rich." ~ Andrea Plos, Sources of Wealth

There's no way to know how many people your life will influence. You don't know who is watching, listening, or learning from you." ~ Charles Stanley, Influence

Thought for the day ~ "No one is too unimportant to be ignored. No one is so significant that others don't matter. ~ Deborah Norville

Thoughts for the day ~ "When we become comfortable, do you know what happens around us? Absolutely nothing. Each day becomes just like the one before. We do what we have always done, therefore we get what we have always gotten." ~ Kip Davis, A Comfortable Situation

CHALLENGE - Effort and courage are not enough without purpose and direction ~ John F. Kennedy

"When you pray be careful of how you respond to what you get. I read somewhere that if you pray for rain . . . don't complain about the mud!" ~ Hyacinth Mottley, Words of Wisdom - Words of Faith

"I learned that it's not just talking to God, but listening to Him as well." - Kimberley Payne, Feed Your Spirit

"That man is the richest whose pleasures are the cheapest." - Henry David Thoreau

Every man's way is right in his own eyes, but the Lord weights the hearts. ~ Proverbs 21: Verse 2

Thought for the day ~ "It is a proven fact that what you see and hear constantly over time enters your heart, and what enters your heart enters your life, and will eventually determine the quality of your life." - Jide Adeniba, You Can Have It If You Really Want it

Thought for the day ~ The difference between us is how we use our days. SUCCESSFUL people understand these words and live each day knowing they will never have it again. They do what needs to be done, whether they like it or not. They have FOCUS, and know what it is they want to ACCOMPLISH. And, most importantly, they take ACTION and do it.

Work joyfully and peacefully, knowing that right thoughts and right efforts will inevitably bring about right results. ~ James Allen

"Of my two "handicaps," being female put many more obstacles in my path than being Black." - Shirley Chisholm, Unbought and Unbossed, 1970

"His control of the young Black man is more despotic than that of the southern plantation owner over Blacks in the South: for him, the weapons of control are economic, social, and political." - Addison Gayle, Jr., in Chapman, New Black Voices, 1972

"God has given each normal person a capacity to achieve some end. True, some are endowed with more talent than others, but God has left none of us talentless." - Martin Luther King, Jr., "Facing the Challenge of a New Age," speech given in Montgomery, Alabama, 19 December 1956

People may think you're a fool. Open your mouth and they'll know it.

"Never allow yourself to be cut off from the people. Predators use the separation tactic with great success. If you're going to do something radical, go to the masses...That is your....protection." - VUSUMZI MAKE, in Angelou, The Heart of a Woman, 1981

"It is time for the Negro middle class to rise up from its stool of indifference, to retreat from its flight into unreality, and to bring its heart, its mind, and its checkbook to the aid of the less fortunate." - Martin Luther King, Jr., c. 1966

"A man who views the world the same at fifty as he did at twenty has wasted thirty years of his life." Muhammad Ali

"Hating people because of their color is wrong. And it doesn't matter which color does the hating. It's just wrong." Muhammad Ali

"We have one life...it will soon be past...what we do for god...is all that will last." - Muhammad Ali

"Friendship is the hardest thing in the world to explain. It's not something you learn in school. But if you haven't learned the meaning of friendship, you really haven't learned anything." - Muhammad Ali

"I'm not combative. I just don't like being pushed around.....the press is {not} used to seeing Black men who stand up for their rights. That's because they don't know that many Black men. But Black people don't call me combative. They call me strong, which let's me know I'm on the right track." - Harold Washington, in "Mayor Washington Eulogized as Symbol of Hope for Blacks," Jet, 14 December 1987

Thoughts for the day ~ "A lot of people seeking new beginnings have never finished with the past." - Byron Pulsifer

"Life is not discovery of fate; it is continuous creation of future, through choices of thoughts, feelings and actions in the present." - Sanjay Sahay

"I want Dr. King to know that I didn't come to Selma to make his job difficult. I really did come thinking I could make it easier. If the white people realize what the alternative is, perhaps they will be more willing to hear Dr. King."----in a conversation with Mrs. Coretta Scott King. ~ Malcolm X.

"I believe in the brotherhood of man, all men, but I don't believe in brotherhood with anybody who doesn't want brotherhood with me. I believe in treating people right, but I'm not going to waste my time trying to treat somebody right who doesn't know how to return the treatment." - Malcolm X, SPEECH, DEC 12, 1964, New York City

"If violence is wrong in America, violence is wrong abroad. If it is wrong to be violent defending black women and black children and black babies and black men, then it is wrong for America to draft us, and make us violent abroad in defense of her. And if it is right for America to draft us, and teach us how to be violent in defense of her, then is right for you and me to do whatever is necessary to defend our own people right here in this country." - Malcolm X, speech, Nov. 1963, New York City

"When a person places the proper value on freedom, there is nothing under the sun that he will not do to acquire that freedom. Whenever you hear a man saying he wants freedom, but in the next breath he is going to tell you what he won't do to get it, or what he doesn't believe in doing in order to get it, he doesn't believe in freedom. A man who believes in freedom will do anything under the sun to acquire.....or preserve his freedom." —Malcolm X

"You don't have to be a man to fight for freedom. All you have to do is to be an intelligent human being." — Malcolm X

Thoughts for the day ~ "Each day is a very good day simply because God made it." - James Jason Positive Thinking

"Inspiration and motivation may come from others, but true inspiration comes from within." - Catherine Pulsifer.

Thoughts for the day ~ "Choose being kind over being right and you'll be right every time." - Richard Carson

"I have decided to stick with love. Hate is too great a burden to bear." - Martin Luther King, JR.

Thoughts for the day ~ "Problems cannot be solved at the same level of awareness that created them." - Albert Einstein

"The first step toward change is acceptance. Once you accept yourself, you open the door to change." - Will Garcia

Thoughts for the day – "Don't bother just to be better than your contemporaries or predecessors. Try to be better than yourself." ~ William Faulkner

"Change: A bend in the road is not the end of the road.....Unless you fail to make the turn." ~ Helen Keller

Thoughts for the day ~ "A great attitude does much more than turn on the lights in our worlds; it seems to magically connect us to all sorts of serendipitous opportunities that were somehow absent before the change." - Earl Nightingale

"Prepare while others are daydreaming." - William Arthur Ward

Thoughts for the day ~ "Surviving is important. Thriving is elegant." - Maya Angelou

"Never tell people how to do things. Tell them what to do and they will surprise you with their ingenuity." - General George S. Patton

Thoughts for the day ~ "Those moments when you woke up inspired or had a "light bulb" come on - that is your intuition." - Michael Henson, Morning Routine

"If you know what you want to achieve in life, then you are more inspired to change for the better." - Josh David, People Skills Guide

Thoughts for the day ~ "Real generosity is doing something nice for someone who will never find out." - Frank A. Clark

"We could never learn to be brave and patient if there were only joy in the world." - Helen Keller

Thoughts for the day ~ "I remember a former pastor once explaining the difference between wisdom and knowledge; he said that wisdom is the ability to apply what you know. - Nicole C. Calhoun, Victory's Road: A Graceful Drive Through Life's Obstacles

"Expect and prepare for criticism, discouragement, and sabotage from others. Laugh them off, avoid them, and take counter-measures as needed. - Mike Buffington, Hacking Laziness Thoughts for the day ~ "There's much you can't change, but there's something important you can change: you." - Rick Warren

"You lose nothing when fighting for a cause . . . in my mind - the losers are those who don't have a cause they care about." - Muhammad Ali

Thoughts for the day ~ "Life is not accountable to us. We are accountable to life." - Denis Waitley

"It is not length of life, but depth of life." - Ralph Waldo Emerson

Thoughts for the day ~ "A race of people is like an individual man; until it uses its own talent, takes pride in its own history, expresses its own culture, affirms its own selfhood, it can never fulfill itself." - Malcolm X

". . . . I always had a deep affection for Malcolm and felt that he had a great ability to put his finger on the existence and the root of the problems. He was an eloquent spokesman for his point of view and no one can honestly doubt that Malcolm had great concern for the problems we face as a race." - Dr. Martin Luther King, JR. in a telegram to Betty Shabazz after the murder of Malcolm X

Thoughts for the day ~ "You must choose whether you want to be in control or if you want to let life, circumstances or others control you." Theo Gold, Confidence: Become Unstoppable!

Thoughts for the day ~ "Before you make a life changing decision, think on it for 24 hours." Patricia Akins, Things They Don't Teach You in High School: But You Need To Know!

"If you can't change your fate, change your attitude." - Amy Tan

Thoughts for the day ~ "Service is the rent we pay for being. It is the very purpose of life and not something you do in your spare time." - Marion Wright Edelman

"Some people feel the rain. Others just get wet." - Bob Marley

Thoughts for the day ~ "A non-doer is very often a critic-that is, someone who sits back and watches doers, and then waxes philosophically about how the doers are doing. It's easy to be a critic, but being a doer requires effort, risk, and change." - Dr. Wayne W. Dyer

Thoughts for the day ~ "It is wise to direct your anger towards problems - not people; to focus your energies on answers - not excuses." ~ William Arthur Ward

"Change your meanings you alter your destiny. Life does not give us what we want. Life gives us whatever we expect." - Harald Anderson

Thoughts for the day ~ When I think of any of my successes, I am thankful to God from whom all blessings flow, and to my family and friends who enrich my life.

Thoughts for the day ~ "There is a great work/home life balance that you need to achieve. If you let your home life eat into your work life, you lose motivation quickly and if work life imposes too much on your family time, then your family time becomes less satisfactory." - Dana Taylor, Time Management

"What you need to understand when you choose specific friends and family members to help you with your depression is that they have lives too." - Joanna Jackson, Self Help

Thought for the day ~ "It bears repeating that wants are not needs. You might need a car but you do not need a Maserati. We all get this confused much of the time. Wisdom lies in Knowing the difference." - Frank Daley, How to Find Yourself

Thought for the day ~ "Practical wisdom is only to be learned in the school of experience. Precepts and instruction are useful so far as they go, but, without the discipline of real life, they remain of the nature of theory only." - Samuel Smiles

"If you're not ready to die for it, put the word 'freedom out your vocabulary." —Malcolm X

"I am not a racist. I am against every form of racism and segregation, every form of discrimination. I believe in human beings, and that all human beings should be respected as such, regardless of their color." —Malcolm X

"Dr. King wants the same thing I want. FREEDOM." —Malcolm X

"I for one believe that if you give people a thorough understanding of what confronts them and the basic causes that produce it, they'll create their own program, and when the people create a program, you get action." —Malcolm X

"We didn't land on Plymouth Rock, Plymouth Rock landed on us." — Malcolm X

Thoughts for the day ~ "Oftentimes, we aren't thankful for something until it's gone. Don't take your health for granted." - Marita Kinney

Thoughts for the day ~ "I have no special talent. I am only passionately curious." - Albert Einstein

"Bring everything up to the surface. Accept your humanity, your animality. Whatsoever is there, accept it without any condemnation. Acceptance is transformation, because through acceptance awareness becomes possible." - Osho

Thoughts for the day ~ "Our character is not defined in the good times, but in the hard times." - Paul Brodie

The smallest of actions is always better than the boldest of intentions.

Thoughts for the day ~ "I'm always thinking about creating. My future starts when I wake up every morning. . . . Every day I find something creative to do with my life." - Miles Davis

To be wronged is nothing unless you continue to remember it.

Thoughts for the day ~ "When everything seems to be going against you, remember that the airplane takes off against the wind, not with it." - Henry Ford

The basic building block of good communications is the feeling that every human being is unique and of value.

Thoughts for the day ~ "History give{s} eloquent testimony to the fact that conflicts are never resolved without trustful give and take on both sides." - Martin Luther King, Jr, "A Time to Break Silence," speech given at Riverside Church, New York City, 4 April 1967

"Humor may not be laughter, it may not even be a smile; it is a point of view, an attitude toward experience." - Howard Thurman, Meditations of the Heart, 1953

Thoughts for the day ~ "Most of us spend too much time on what is urgent and not enough time on what is important." - Stephen R. Covey

"Good things happen when you get your priorities straight." - Scott Caan

Thoughts for the day ~ "History give{s} eloquent testimony to the fact that conflicts are never resolved without trustful give and take on both sides." - MARTIN LUTHER KING, JR, "A Time to Break Silence," speech given at Riverside Church, New York City, 4 April 1967

"Humor may not be laughter, it may not even be a smile; it is a point of view, an attitude toward experience." - Howard Thurman, Meditations of the Heart, 1953

Thoughts for the day ~ "I don't believe an accident of birth makes people sisters or brother's. It makes them siblings, gives them mutuality of parentage. Sisterhood and Brotherhood is a condition people have to work at." - Maya Angelou

"The man who can make hard things easy is the educator." - Ralph Waldo Emerson

Thoughts for the day ~ "It is only the narrow people who live for themselves, who never read good books, who do not travel, who never open up their souls to permit them to come into contact with other souls---with the great world outside." - Booker T. Washington, Speeches of Booker T. Washington, 1932

"Nothing pains some people more than having to think." - Martin Luther King, Jr., Strength to Love, 1963

Thoughts for the day ~ Always be yourself. A recipe for disaster is trying to be a different person from who you are. Believe in yourself. . . . Be you!

"In Life We Can Have Results or Reasons." - Harald Anderson

Thoughts for the day ~ "Understanding is knowing what to do; wisdom is knowing what to do next; virtue is actually doing it." - Tristan Gylberd

"He that never changes his opinions, never corrects his mistakes, will never be wiser on the morrow than he is today." Tryon Edwards

Thoughts for the day ~ "The doorstep to the temple of wisdom is a knowledge of our own ignorance." - Benjamin Franklin

"Wise men talk because they have something to say; fools, because they have to say something." Plato

Thoughts for the day - We learn wisdom from failure...much more than from success; we often discover what we will do, by finding out what we will not do; and probably he who never made a mistake never made a discovery.

No matter how big your house is, how recent your car is, or how big your bank account is. Our graves will always be the same size. Stay humble.

Today's Daily Inspiration

People make mistakes, but seldom on purpose. Lord, may my patience with others grow and may I replace my frowns with smiles.

Random Daily Inspiration

Do not let yourself be judged by others or ruled by approval or disapproval. Lord, may I always trust in myself and You and live each day accordingly.

Extra Dose
Today is an opportunity to love, to work and to play. Lord, may I recognize the opportunities that come today and participate in them as much as I can.

"Anything in life that we don't accept will simply make trouble for us until we make peace with it."- Unknown

Today's Daily Inspiration
Are you too busy wishing away your day to get what you really want? Lord, help me set goals and find the means to achieve what is important to me.

Random Daily Inspiration
To pray constantly does not mean saying prayers constantly. To pray is to simply live in the awareness of Christ's presence and His love. Lord, all of my day is a prayer because I am with You and You are with me.

Extra Dose
Psalm 100:4
"Enter into his gates with thanksgiving, *and* into his courts with praise: be thankful unto him, *and* bless his name."

Today's Daily Inspiration
No one has the power to take your happiness or keep you from being happy and at peace unless you allow it. Lord, help me remember that I am sustained and supported by Your love for me who wants only for my safety and goodness.

Random Daily Inspiration
Take less for granted and you will become very busy enjoying all that you have. Lord, thank you for my blessings and for all those that I am able to share them with.

Extra Dose
Have mercy

Matt. 5:7 Blessed are the merciful: for they shall obtain mercy.

We all make mistakes. We all error. There are things we struggle with and there are even times when we just do the fool and fall short. This does not necessarily make us a bad person or even a sinner. As long as we can acknowledge our errors as errors, and ask God to forgive us, we can be reinstated back to the place where we were before the sin. We all sin and fall short. Anyone that pretends to never sin is a liar and they deceive themselves. There are situations, struggles, issues, etc. that we are all trying to grow past.

What's my point? Don't condemn people for errors! <u>When you wipe your hands of people that make mistakes, you only cause yourself to be condemned when you make mistakes. You cannot pass severe judgments on people without those same judgments coming back on you. So, don't deny others the mercy that you will need.</u>

Now, we should call sin sin, and we should not turn our heads the other way when we see our brothers and sisters in error, but we should be merciful towards them and try to help them back to their rightful place in God. If they don't hear you, that's another story. But if they will hear, acknowledge their error and repent, then we should be willing to help them move past it and give them direction for total deliverance and future avoidance. The mercy you give is the same mercy you shall have! **IN JESUS NAME AMEN!!**

Today's Daily Inspiration

Many of life's hassles are mere tests of our strength. Lord, help me remember that patience can often diffuse a situation quicker than a snap response.

Random Daily Inspiration

Give yourself more exercise than jumping to conclusions. Lord, grant me sincerity and wisdom in my daily life.

Today's Daily Inspiration

Talent is the ability to do easily that which others find difficult. Lord, help me to recognize and value the abilities that I have been given and use them gratefully.

Random Daily Inspiration

We are powerless to change our past, but we can change how we look at it. Lord, help me to realize that my past has made me a stronger person and show me that these experiences have taught me valuable life lessons.

Extra Dose –Bishop Rudolph W. McKissick, Jr

Stay in touch with your limitations so that you stay in touch with God who has no limits.

Extra, Extra Read All about It!

Don't Let the Past Get You Down

"But the Lord says, Do not cling to events of the past or dwell on what happened long ago. Watch for the new thing I am going to do. It is happening already---you can see it now! I will make a road through the wilderness and give you streams of water there."

- Isaiah 43:18-19 (TEV)

The Wilderness is a place that has no roads, or highways. One can easily become confused and lost there. However, the Lord promises to take care of us even in our wilderness experiences, and to bring us out. He tells us to look for the "new thing" that he is already doing for us. Therefore, let go of the past events, release the mistakes of yesterday and overcome your failures. Keep your eyes focused on the Lord; it is he who will provide the refreshing waters for your desert experience.

Don't let the past get you down. Ralph Waldo Emerson said, "Our greatest glory is not in never failing, but in rising up every time we fail." The Lord will help you through your desert experiences - just keep your eyes on him.

"We break the power of the past by living for the future."
- Dr. John Sim (Vanguard University of Southern Calif.)

"but this one thing I do, forgetting those things which are behind, and reaching forth unto those things which are before, I press toward the mark for the prize of the high calling of God in Christ Jesus."

- Philippians 3:13-14 (KJV)

Today's Daily Inspiration

In everything imitate God and you will come to know Him better and better. Lord, I ask Your help to come close to You in my thoughts and bring Your love to this earth.

Random Daily Inspiration

Keep yourself young in spirit always by thinking new thoughts and getting rid of old habits. Lord, may my spirit never become frail and my abilities never become barren.

Extra Daily Inspiration

Do not leave for another day a task which God would have you do today. Lord, give me the determination to not procrastinate and the joy to do my work well.

Today's Daily Inspiration

One of life's greatest rewards is not what we get, but what we become. Lord, teach me as I am able to learn and give me the courage to be all that I can.

> **A change in environment**
>
> Have you ever noticed that before God gives the promise He first gives out instructions? You get blessed when you know how to be obedient and faithfully and follow what God has instructed. Leave all of the people who want to stay settled. You will never take possession if you have people in your space who are scared to take risks. As long as you surround yourself with people who will settle for what is comfortable, you will not make it to the place God has assigned you to be in. If you have people around you who push you to stay settled in the comfortable, then leave. Some people in your space can't see it and will speak against, because they like where they are and want you to stay there with them. As you begin to change your environment, know some people who have been with you are not assigned to go with you to the next chapter of your life. Don't make the mistake of making someone permanent who was intended to be transitional. There are some people who are assigned to go with you for only part of the journey, and not the whole journey, and you need to know when their time is up. You need to say to them, don't try to hold me back just because you can't go with me. I would rather be alone with God than be with a bunch of people who are willing to settle. Lord, help me to do an inventory of my environment, and as I enter my new chapter, help me leave "last chapter people" behind who do not belong with me in my next chapter.

Random Daily Inspiration
There is no personal problem that you cannot solve. Lord, Your presence within me is all power. You are my help in every need.

Extra Dose
That you are alive is confirmation that God still has things for you to do. Lord, I ask for wisdom and gentleness as I do Your work on earth.

Today's Daily Inspiration
Prayer helps us see that God is not the cause of unpleasant happenings, but the healing of them. Lord, I trust in You for the right outcomes in all situations.

Random Daily Inspiration
Joy does not depend on your circumstances, but rather on your triumph over your circumstances. Lord, my joy comes from within where Your spirit fills my soul and You bless me with Your strength.

Extra Dose
When you lose your temper, you lose. Lord, help me to be patient with those around me, but most of all, help me be patient with myself. IN JESUS NAME AMEN!!

Today's Daily Inspiration
When you feel down, look up. Lord, at all times and in the midst of all that is happening, You are there comforting, healing, and bringing peace to my life.

Random Daily Inspiration
Take every opportunity to give praise not criticism. Lord, may I be an encouragement to those I am with today.

Extra Dose
What we endure in this life is nothing compared to the glory that God has in store for us in heaven. Lord, take every moment of my life as a prayer to praise and glorify Your holy name.

Today's Daily Inspiration
Today do what you can and expect no more of yourself. Lord, I will feel joy in my accomplishments today and gratitude for the things I have to do tomorrow.

Random Daily Inspiration
God has given each of us many talents and abilities. To use them reflects our commitment to Him. Lord, help me find new ways to use the talents that You've given me.

Extra Dose
It is you, not where you are or what you have, that makes the difference. Lord, may I always blossom where I am planted.

Today's Daily Inspiration
Each morning gives us one more chance to pray, one more chance to help another and one more chance to make this a better world. Lord, thank you for working in and through everything.

Random Daily Inspiration
Choose to be worthy to yourself and never confuse self-worth with behavior. Lord, help me to be less critical of my past and see that this moment right now is all that I can do anything about.

Extra Dose
Get rid of the excuses for not doing those things that make you happy. Lord, Your peace within me calms my spirit and opens my heart to recognize the joy of this day.

Today's Daily Inspiration
There is no better time than right now to do what we have been putting off. Lord, grant me motivation and focus that I may live so as to have no regrets about what I should have done.

Random Daily Inspiration
There is a time for everything. Take time to pray, to sing, to laugh, to work and to touch the hearts of others. Lord, help me be aware that today will never return so that I will not misuse my time or waste it unwisely.

Extra Dose
God promises His forgiveness to those who repent. Lord, I am sorry for all that I have done wrong this day and all the days of my life.

Matthew 5:23-24 New King James Version (NKJV)
Therefore if you bring your gift to the altar, and there remember that your brother has something against you, leave your gift there before the altar, and go your way. First be reconciled to your brother, and then come and offer your gift.

Today's Daily Inspiration
When you follow God's way, your life will flourish according to His great plan for you. Lord, guide me and make me aware of the ways You are working in my life.

Random Daily Inspiration
Often times that which we find difficult is that which teaches. Lord, may I always be able to see the good that comes from even my trials.

Extra Dose
Waste no time on situations that aren't worth your precious time. Lord, may I recognize pettiness for what it is and move on so that my imagination doesn't take over and give pettiness more value than it deserves.

Today's Daily Inspiration

To receive the wonderful healing power of love, wish others well even when things aren't going so well for you. Lord, I rejoice in You always because You are blessing me daily no matter what my circumstances may be.

Random Daily Inspiration

Enthusiasm will be yours if you love God, love people, and love life. Lord, the nearer I follow Your way, the happier I become!

Extra Dose

As a mother sets aside gifts for her children long before they need them, so, too, has God prepared for our needs long before we call out to Him. Lord, I give thanks and place my trust in Your loving arms.

Today's Daily Inspiration

Closeness with family makes us one in heart and mind. Lord, help me to fill our home with love and make it our safe haven from the troubles of the world.

Random Daily Inspiration

Jesus said, "Whatever you ask in prayer, believe that you have received it, and it will be yours.". Lord, I pray, I believe, and I thank you even before it is fulfilled.

Extra Dose

Time passes too quickly so waste none of it on anger, self-pity or the irritations of life. Lord, may my choices remove stress and free me to enjoy the goodness of today.

Today's Daily Inspiration

Speak to God openly and honestly from your heart and then do not allow yourself to worry. Lord, You are my protection and my provider when I put my trust in you.

Random Daily Inspiration

See opportunity in your difficulties, not difficulty in your opportunities. Lord, I will focus on the goodness today brings to me and look for the many reasons I have to feel joy.

Extra Dose

Most often a gentle approach is the best resolution to a conflict. Lord, I have been given today to improve myself and make life better for others. Help me walk in the way that You lead me.

Today's Daily Inspiration

Know that you make a difference, so choose to make your contribution one of goodness. Lord, help me to touch my world in a positive manner.

Random Daily Inspiration

Forget the useless and unhealthy things of your past that clutter your mind so that you can live a life that is alive and vibrant. Lord, help me to discard all that clouds my day so that I am able to live the life that You intend me to live.

Extra Dose
Keep your feet firmly planted in your faith and your eyes raised to the heavens. Lord, You are my strength, my encouragement and my source of all that is good.

Today's Daily Inspiration
It is not in the good times, but rather in the times of stress and misfortune, that our faith is tested. Lord, remove my doubts as they creep in and help me turn my times of turmoil into times of spiritual growth.

Random Daily Inspiration
If you would be ashamed to sign your name to your conversation, don't say it. Lord, my words can have far reaching effects. May the effect always be good.

Extra Dose
There is no moment like right now. Lord, help me start one thing today that I have been putting off.

Today's Daily Inspiration
Home is a place where we can have a bit of heaven on earth. Lord, bless our home and help make it a place of love and kindness.

Random Daily Inspiration
Great things happen when you believe and pray. Lord, grant me an amazing faith in life and the strength to meet its challenges.

Extra Dose
Our words are powerful tools and can influence even when we are not aware. Lord, help me to speak with kindness and sensitivity and to be a positive source of encouragement and support to others.

Today's Daily Inspiration
The more of God's love that you share, the more you receive. Lord, help me to be compassionate when someone needs an ear and encouraging when someone needs a little support.

Random Daily Inspiration
Learn to forgive. You can never be happy with anger or bitterness in your heart. Lord, bless me with the ability to forgive those who have offended me.

Extra Dose
Let life's lessons grow into wisdom so that you may be the light for someone else's darkness. Lord, help me put to good use that which today brings so that I am better prepared for tomorrow.

Today's Daily Inspiration
Sometimes we search for God in the wrong places. To help someone in need is the quickest way to touch His hand. Lord, in my ordinary day in my ordinary ways may I come to know and understand You more.

Random Daily Inspiration

Everything we need to deal with life's problems lies within us. Our trials are tests to see if we can discover the solution. Lord, I call out Your name when I face my difficulties and together we will overcome them.

Extra Dose

If the strong won't protect the weak, who will? Lord, grant me the courage to stand up for what I believe and the wisdom to be an encouragement to others.

Today's Daily Inspiration

We all need time for ourselves and time to be with our friends in order to be joyful. Lord help me to balance my day and renew my spirit.

Random Daily Inspiration

Don't overlook any of the talents God has chosen to give to you. Each one has the power to bring you more joy as you put it to good use. Lord open my eyes to all my abilities so none go to waste.

Extra Dose

<u>Prayer: Lord thank you for the laws of sowing and reaping. When I look at my life right now and see things I'm dissatisfied with, I realize that for the most part I am reaping what I've sown. Please help me be patient. It's my goal to be steadfast immovable always abounding in the work of the Lord. Begin to sow differently eventually I will reap differently. AMEN</u>

Today's Daily Inspiration

Add excitement to the day by meeting everything as though it is your very first time. Lord, give me the ability to change the ordinary into something special, to do more than just slide through the moments of the day and take time to notice that my life really is terrific most of the time.

Random Daily Inspiration

It is not making a mistake, but repeating it that is cause for concern. Lord, may I use my mistakes to guide me to better choices.

Extra Dose

Peace is one of our greatest needs because it provides for the strength we need in times of turmoil. Lord, I turn to You because You are my source of peace.

Today's Daily Inspiration

Much can be said by the look on your face. Lord, may I be quick to smile and display an attitude of graciousness and peace so that I am able to put those around me at ease and bring out the best in them.

Random Daily Inspiration

Great things happen when you believe and pray. Lord, grant me an amazing faith in life and the strength to meet its challenges.

Extra Dose

Allow the power of God to work within you because He is able to accomplish far more than we can dream. Lord, Your spirit empowers me. May I do Your Will and always give glory to You.

Today's Daily Inspiration

Every decision that you make opens the door to many new opportunities and experiences. Lord, help me make the most of my opportunities because it is through them that I am able to grow.

Random Daily Inspiration

We are not always what we ought to be or want to be, but through God's love we are not what we would be without Him. Lord, thank you for raising me to heights in this world that alone I could not reach and for giving me eternal life in the next.

Extra Dose

Shine a little brighter today because someone needs your light. Lord, may I reflect You like sun hitting a mirror.

Today's Daily Inspiration

Often times the happiness you seek is already near at hand. Lord help me to appreciate what I already have because You never stop blessing me even when I don't notice.

Random Daily Inspiration

Jesus promises to give us rest when we are weary. Lord I am tired and in need of rest. Thank You for Your promise!

Extra Dose

Prayer: Lord, I desire to love You with all my soul. That's why I am choosing even now to fill my mind with thoughts of Your character. To discipline my will to choose the path of obedience. To fill my heart with Your promises so that my emotions will stay in check, resting securely in Your love. Lord, I acknowledge that I have looked to others to fill that place in my heart that You alone can fill. And because of that emptiness inside that desperate need to feel loved I have been unable to love others in the way You have commanded. I ask You to flood my heart with an awareness of Your love for me today. Heal those insecure places in my heart that cause me to be self-protective self-seeking and self-consumed. IN JESUS NAME AMEN!!

Today's Daily Inspiration

If you count your blessings and answered prayers, there is less time for grumbling and complaining. Lord, may I always appreciate the wonders of my life and celebrate Your presence in it.

Random Daily Inspiration

If your family is a mess, you are not a success. Lord, bless me with the wisdom and strength to bring unity and peace to my family.

Today's Daily Inspiration

To be rich is to have friends, good health, and the energy to experience the many things that life offers. Lord I rejoice in the true and most meaningful riches of my life.

Random Daily Inspiration

Use the power of positive images in your mind to bring about good experiences. Lord I will let my faith in You nourish my thoughts so that I can develop a healthy and joyful reality.

Extra Dose

Prayer: LORD I come to you on this day I desire to find rest even in the midst of my busy life. Renew my mind, will, and emotions today. Let me walk in paths of righteousness, consciously determining to do what is right, rather what is convenient or commonplace. Lord I also acknowledge that hard times will come my way that is an inevitable fact of life. Help me not overreact or panic or give away to fear. I will have enemies. Not everyone will like me. But even in the midst of my enemies you prepare a table before me. I thank You that goodness and love follow me wherever I go THANK YOU FATHER, IN JESUS NAME.......AMEN

Today's Daily Inspiration

Prayer turns the attention from ourselves to God and helps us see His hand working in our lives. Lord You give me reasons for a daily commitment to achieving a full and energetic life.

Random Daily Inspiration

It is a bigger mistake to fear making a mistake than to actually make one. Lord, give me the confidence to live a full life and the ability to try again if I stumble.

Extra Dose

Beauty = your inner self, the unfading beauty of a gentle spirit, which is of great worth in God's sight.

Today's Daily Inspiration

Sometimes we search for God in the wrong places. To help someone in need is the quickest way to touch His hand. Lord, in my ordinary ways may I come to know and understand You more.

Random Daily Inspiration

No gift is so precious as love. Gracefully trust God and give Him your love. Lord I give You my heart.

Extra Dose

Everyday make time for Christ.
God creates --> Jesus saves --> Holy Spirit sustains !!

Today's Daily Inspiration

Choose the direction of your day and then make a point of enjoying your choices. Lord, help me to do what I can when I can, but also, help me to know when doing nothing is the better choice.

Random Daily Inspiration

In life it is those that persevere that will succeed. Lord, every day is a fresh beginning. With You, I will come closer to my goals each day if only I don't give up and quit.

Extra Dose

Isaiah 54:17 "No weapon formed against thee shall prosper; and ever tongue that shall rise against thee in judgment thou shall condemn. This is the heritage of the servants of the LORD, and their righteousness is of me, saith the LORD."

Today's Daily Inspiration

Emotions can be dealt with by motion. Lord, when I feel controlled by feelings and complaints, help to get me up and get me moving to change my disposition even if it's something simple like stretching or organizing something or starting something I've been putting off.

Random Daily Inspiration

Know that you can do even if things are not always easy. Lord, in You I have the support of an unlimited power source and can accomplish great things because You strengthen me.

Extra Dose

You will have an easier time keeping your thoughts positive if you look for good in every situation. Lord, help me change my focus and develop an awareness that situations often have more good in them than bad.

Today's Daily Inspiration

Study who you are and follow your heart because it will often lead you to miracles. Lord, in knowing who I am, I will become better able to know and serve You.

Random Daily Inspiration

Welcome God into every part of your life. He is always with you, ready to help, waiting to bless you with miracles and able to enrich your every moment. Lord, I call out your name often in praise, in thanksgiving and in every need.

Extra Dose

By being less judgmental of others, you will eliminate much frustration. Lord, I pray for the peace that comes from understanding and compassion.

Today's Daily Inspiration

Trouble comes to everyone, but feeling miserable is no reason to make others miserable. Lord, may I never destroy another's happiness.

Random Daily Inspiration

Love is the greatest good in life. It draws us to that which is good. Lord, may my mind and heart be guided by Your love.

Today's Daily Inspiration

Be wise enough to thank God for not giving you some of the things you've asked for and gracious enough to gratefully enjoy what He gave you in its place. Lord, You know better than I what is right and best for me.

Random Daily Inspiration

Have the courage to forgive. Lord, may I bring myself to a place of peace by never holding a grudge.

Extra Dose

Today's Daily Inspiration

Some can find fault in everything, but it takes a good and loving heart to find goodness, especially when it is less than obvious. Lord, bless me with gentleness and patience and the determination not to complain.

Random Daily Inspiration

We are powerless to change our past, but we can change how we look at it. Lord, help me to realize that my past has made me a stronger person and show me that these experiences have taught me valuable life lessons.

Extra Dose

All the good things in life don't mean much if we fail to enjoy them. Lord, may I pause to notice my blessings and be joyful.

Today's Daily Inspiration

Courage is not the lack of fear, but the ability to go on in spite of it. Lord, may I be strong in my abilities and courageous in my beliefs.

Random Daily Inspiration

Ultimate security does not come from relying on things or people, but from relying on God. Lord, I place my trust in You. Bless me and keep me in Your loving care.

Extra Dose

Prayer turns the attention from ourselves to God and helps us see His hand working in our lives. Lord, You give me reasons for a daily commitment to achieving a full and energetic life.

Today's Daily Inspiration

When you feel the need to tell someone how bad your day has been, tell them how good it's been instead. Lord, help me to highlight the parts of my day that will bring me to a peaceful and joyful place.

Random Daily Inspiration

Faith grows by speaking daily with God. Lord, You teach me Your promises when times are good so that I will be able to trust in You when times are hard.

Extra Dose

Each time you have a kind thought, say a kind word or do a kind deed you are living your love. Lord, as I see the world through loving eyes, I experience heaven on earth.

Today's Daily Inspiration

There are always better things to come than that which we have left behind. Lord, I look with excitement toward the unexpected joys of today.

Random Daily Inspiration

Be a little kinder and gentler today, for this will show your real strength. Lord, may I become more patient and have the courage to live my life according to the example You set forth.

Extra Dose

Do that which is right and learn to do it for the right reason. Lord, give us strength as we stand up to temptation and spiritual power as we resist the pressures and stresses that bear down on us.

Random Daily Inspiration

God values us so much that He gave us all that He has; His Son Jesus. Show that you value Him, too, by putting Him first in all aspects of your life. Lord, when I put You first in my life, order and peace follow.

Today's Daily Inspiration

One of the best parts of receiving blessings is enjoying them. Lord, may I take time to recognize my blessings and appreciate their wonder.

Random Daily Inspiration

There is no real happiness without God and no peace when we separate ourselves from Him. Lord, You said, "Peace I leave with you, My peace I give to you". I give you my troubled heart.

Extra Dose

Praise accomplishes great things. Lord, let me be your instrument in touching lives and changing hearts.

Today's Daily Inspiration

There is no good enough reason to ever feel we are a failure. No matter how hard we fall, God is there to restore our spirit and forgive our past. Lord, help me to understand that it is this moment that counts, not the last one and with each new moment, I have a new beginning.

Random Daily Inspiration

Avoid using the words 'If only...' and 'I should have...'. These can destroy your peace of mind and even your health. Lord, help me to stop punishing myself for past mistakes and live in the peace of the present.

Extra Dose

When we give in to fears and worries they will take charge of our lives. Lord, I place my trust in You so that I may experience every opportunity and not miss in life that which is meant for me

Today's Daily Inspiration

Think often of your friends and seldom of your enemies and you will surround yourself with good thoughts, leaving little or no room for darkness. Lord, help me search for goodness so that it is goodness that I find.

Random Daily Inspiration

Make a habit of setting aside time for prayer and meditation. Your rewards will be great. Lord, thank you for the peace, humility, joy and self-worth with which you bless me.

Extra Dose

When you get too comfortable God stirs things up. The mother eagle teaches her little ones to fly by making their nest so uncomfortable that they're forced out of it. Next they are pushed off a cliff edge. Can you imagine their thoughts: 'It's my mother doing this?' Who and where you are at this moment in time has been divinely appointed. God in His wisdom knows that you need the challenge of certain situations to mature and stretch you. The job you dread going to every day is developing your skills, endurance and sense of responsibility. Those people who rub you the wrong way are actually making you more like Jesus!
Paul says God "understands. . . and knows what is best for us at all times" (Ephesians 1:8). So instead of asking Him to change things, thank Him for the experience and the lessons you're learning. And if you can't figure out what those lessons are, ask Him. James says, "If. . . you need wisdom. . . ask God" (James 1:5). When you do, you'll discover – it's all part of His plan!

Today's Daily Inspiration

"If your soul is troubled. If you are anxious and worried. Know that the Lord knows and there is never a time that you cannot depend on him. Pease GOD let me see the wonders of this moment and face tomorrow with hope and joy."

Random Daily Inspiration

"Say little, love much, give of your heart and judge no one. This is how to walk the spiritual path. Lord, help me to aspire to all that is pure and good so that I may be your disciple."

Extra Dose

"How much you respond to love and goodness is how much you will increase love and goodness on earth. Lord, free me from the bondage of my bitterness and selfishness so that I will always be a reflection of You."

Today's Daily Inspiration

It takes far less effort to concentrate on one thought at a time and usually eliminates the confusion we often create for ourselves. Lord, I pray for clarity of thought and the wisdom that it brings.

Random Daily Inspiration

If your family is a mess, you are not a success. Lord, bless me with the wisdom and strength to bring unity and peace to my family.

Extra Dose

God is calling us to experience peace, satisfaction and joy as we have never experienced. Lord, I will follow You as You lift me to new levels of living.

Today's Daily Inspiration

Courage is not the lack of fear, but the ability to go on in spite of it. Lord, may I be strong in my abilities and courageous in my beliefs.

Random Daily Inspiration

Do not be afraid to ask everything of God. He is always present and always loving us. Lord, I trust in You and ask for Your help in all that I do and need and want. I also ask for Your help in accepting Your answers when they are different than I would want or expect.

Extra Dose

In a day when almost everything goes right, don't ruin it by focusing on the one thing that didn't. Lord, help me to allow the good in my life to prevail.

Today's Daily Inspiration

When you meet God in prayer, everything becomes new. Lord, may I be humbly joyful in my faith.

Random Daily Inspiration

We will live life fully only when we become aware of own inner power, which is our connection with God. Lord, the more I rely on You the more I am able to accomplish.

Extra Dose

Dear Lord, renew my determination to live a life that honors you, even when its difficult. I lift my emotions to you and desire to bring them under the Lord. I want to be ruled by your truth, love, and grace not by my feelings. God you know all about my enemies those people who oppose me and try to drag me down. I leave them in your hands. I'm not going to think about them, or give them one more moment of my mental time or emotional energy. IN JESUS NAME AMEN!!

Today's Daily Inspiration

Each day offers many situations for accomplishment, joy, change and personal growth. Lord, grant me the ability to recognize these moments and the energy to benefit from these daily opportunities.

Random Daily Inspiration

We can be serious about our work without being serious about ourselves. Lord, help me to enjoy the person that I am.

Extra Dose

The smallest kindness is worth more than the greatest intention. Lord, help me not to overlook the opportunities that I have to enrich the lives of others or think I am too busy to reach out with a word or even a smile.

Extra, Extra Dose

> **The LORD gives strength to his people; the LORD blesses his people with peace. Psalm 29:11**

> **Worry is a thin stream of fear that trickles through the mind, which, if encouraged, will cut a channel so wide that all other thoughts will be drained out. –Author Unknown**

> **A Time to Act: Focus not on your fears but your strengths.**

> **A Time to Pray: Heavenly Father, we thank You for the comfort you give us, when we come to You.**

Today's Daily Inspiration

Our goodness is one of God's many gifts to us. Lord, may I humbly appreciate my good qualities and give thanks to You through my actions.

Random Daily Inspiration

We call on God in our big problems, but often forget to call on Him in our ordinary moments, yet He is always there and always loving us. Lord, every time I seek Your help, You draw me closer to You.

Extra Dose

Look beyond a person's faults so that you can see the real person. Lord, may I learn to focus on the goodness that is in each person and love them because all are your children.

Today's Daily Inspiration

Today do what you can and expect no more of yourself. Lord, I will feel joy in my accomplishments today and gratitude for the things I have to do tomorrow.

Random Daily Inspiration

When we have to justify our actions, it may be that our actions are not just. Lord, Your will is goodness. May I always have the strength and courage to choose Your way so that I can simplify my life and enjoy the peace of Your presence.

Extra Dose

How easy it is to blame God for circumstances that don't go as we want. Lord, grant me wisdom and understanding to know that You are Love and, as a loving God, You only want the best for me.
Remember no matter what you are going through, count it all joy.

Today's Daily Inspiration
Stand tall and smile often and it will be very difficult to be unhappy. Lord, may my disposition reflect the joy and peace that is Your Will.

Random Daily Inspiration
Small acts of kindness make lasting memories. Lord, help me to remember that it is a privilege to pause for those moment in which I can really make a difference.

Extra Dose
Start the day with prayer and a commitment to conquer any difficulties that happen and a firmer commitment to not let them conquer you. Lord, bless me with all that I need to make the best of every situation.

Today's Daily Inspiration
When we want things around us to change, the best place to start in within ourselves. Lord, grant that my frustrations can be a motivation to better myself and my environment.

Random Daily Inspiration
Begin each day with the certainty that today is the best day of your life and watch what happens. Lord, I celebrate my life and give thanks for everything because for everything there is a reason.

Extra Dose
Pray even when your heart has no words rather than to pray words with no heart. Lord, You faithfully answer all prayers. I will trust in Your answers and never take Your love for granted.

> **The ultimate measure of a man is not where he stands in moments of comfort and convenience, but where he stands at times of challenge and controversy. – Dr. Martin Luther King, JR.**

Today's Daily Inspiration
We have many doors, but it is our choice which one to open. Lord, bless me with the wisdom to make the best of my daily life.

Random Daily Inspiration
No situation is too difficult if God is with you. Lord, we are a perfect team. You provide the tools and I provide the labor.

Extra Dose
One of the best parts of receiving blessings is enjoying them. Lord, may I take time to recognize my blessings and appreciate their wonder.
"The grass may seem greener on the other side, but the water bill is higher!"

Today's Daily Inspiration
We have been given a treasure of talents which should be accepted with responsibility and gratitude. Lord may my gifts flourish in great faith and charity so that they may also benefit others.

Random Daily Inspiration
Pray even when your heart has no words rather than to pray words with no heart. Lord You faithfully answer all prayers. I will trust in Your answers and never take Your love for granted.

Extra Dose
Any hardships you face in this world are nothing compared to the glory that will be revealed to you.

Today's Daily Inspiration
"Regret is a waste of time. Be grateful for all of your past. It is life's lesson. Lord, teach me so that I may live today completely."

Random Daily Inspiration
"Little irritations can ruin the day. Lord, keep me from worrying about small things and focus on the ceaseless wonders of Your Earth."

Extra Dose
"Peaceful minds are not confused or afraid. Lord, shrink my troubles to their real size and give me all that I will need to handle what comes my way". . . **IN JESUS NAME AMEN!!**

Today's Daily Inspiration
Fill your time with that which is important to you and you will feel accomplished. Lord, help me to know my priorities and to be focused enough to avoid distraction.

Random Daily Inspiration
Love one another as God loves You. Lord, may I treat others in such a manner so as to bring praise and glory to Your holy name.

Extra Dose
Faith is what lifts me to the level of possibility and opens the door to God's promises. Lord, continue to strengthen my belief and bless me with unyielding faith.

Today's Daily Inspiration
If you are stressed, you are probably making things more important than they really are. Lord, I pray for clarity of thought and calmness of spirit because I know that when my heart grows weary, You send me peace.

Random Daily Inspiration
Today picture yourself as the happiest person that you know and watch how contagious this enthusiasm for life is. Lord, may I bring out the best in those with whom I share today so they can in turn bring out more of my best.

Extra Dose
Grow and learn from every situation no matter how insignificant because to stand still is really going backwards. Lord, may my spirit always remain young and vibrant and my enthusiasm for each new day remain alive.

Today's Daily Inspiration
It is far better to feel fulfilled than to feel important because you have taken on too much. Lord, help me eliminate the unnecessary demands in my life which only cause stress.

Random Daily Inspiration

It's very possible that our problems may not be as big as they seem and could sometimes actually be a blessing. Lord, I place my trust in You to see me through my trials and help me to become a stronger and wiser person because of them.

Extra Dose

Forget what you have done for others and remember what they have done for you. Lord, a gift is given freely with no expectation. May I become a true giver from my heart, soul and my spirit! IN JESUS NAME AMEN!!

Today's Daily Inspiration

Look beyond people's behaviors and have compassion for what may be causing their insensitivities. Lord, I will not take everything personal because I don't know the weight of my neighbor's cross.

Random Daily Inspiration

God's plans for you are beyond your imagination. Lord, may I not limit myself to my past experiences, but be willing to accept new opportunities and challenges into my life.

Extra Dose

We have the ability to influence those around us and therefore it is necessary to think of ourselves as the center of peace so that we may bring calm to those who need it. Lord, may I bring Your peace to everyone I am with today.

Today's Daily Inspiration

Instead of overreacting, try under reacting because this response shows wisdom, patience and peace. Lord, help me respond to situations in a manner that allows me to solve problems rather than create more.

Random Daily Inspiration

If you live in the light of God, He will bless the work of your hands and you will see your efforts flourish. Lord, I am your servant. I do my daily work for You and I am filled with peace.

Extra Dose

Take today and make it beautiful. Lord, my life is no accident and neither is how I live it. Help me to fill it with smiles.

Today's Daily Inspiration

Expect more of yourself than you do of others and you will save yourself much stress and disappointment. Lord, help me to see how capable that I am.

Random Daily Inspiration

There is always something to thank God for. Lord, may my attitude of gratitude last a lifetime.

Extra Dose

Today's Daily Inspiration

Too much of a good thing can actually diminish the joy and make it a burden. Lord, help me avoid excess and keep my life simpler and freer.

Random Daily Inspiration

We are never alone and even when we turn away from God He promised not to abandon us. He knows that at such times we need Him more than ever. Call out His name. He is there. Lord, how wonderful to know that You are always watching over me.

Extra Dose

We are not here to live a life of worry, guilt, or fear. Lord, may I reacquaint myself with the true meaning of living in the Lord.

Today's Daily Inspiration

Avoid becoming defensive and possibly causing conflict by taking a moment to think before you respond. Lord, help me to believe in myself strongly so that I am able to turn down invitations that make me feel bad.

Random Daily Inspiration

Make a habit of setting aside time for prayer and meditation. Your rewards will be great. Lord, thank you for the peace, humility, joy and self-worth with which you bless me.

Extra Dose

Don't allow the difficult people around you to get you down. Lord, may I not make other people's problems my own and take on things that I can't do anything about anyway.

Today's Daily Inspiration

The best way to guide your own behavior is to make a commitment to always be a good example. Lord, may I be a reflection of Your love.

Random Daily Inspiration

Love who you are, for who you are, God loves. Lord, help me to never abuse myself with self-pity or excess, emotionally or physically, so that I may live my life to the fullest according to Your Will.

Extra Dose

Through the power of God within me, I am stronger than any of my circumstances. Lord, I seek, I knock and I ask and You are always there and ready to give me the miracles that I need!!

Today's Daily Inspiration

Strengthen your character by knowing which things in life are nonnegotiable to you. Lord, I pray for the strength to say no when saying yes would go against that in which I believe.

Random Daily Inspiration

We are the only ones who can change how we think or how we act. Lord, help me make positive decisions so that life doesn't just happen to me.

Extra Dose

Prayer is a great source of joy and the best protection from depression. When we talk, Lord, You help me see solutions for a better day.

Today's Daily Inspiration

"You cannot give what you don't have. Lord, I ask You for the wisdom and strength that I need to continue being for those that count on me. Give me my daily bread as I perform my daily work."

Random Daily Inspiration

"My soul is troubled. I am anxious and I worry. Lord, there is never a time that I cannot depend on You. Let me see the wonders of this moment and face tomorrow with hope and joy."

Extra Daily Inspiration

Today's Daily Inspiration

"There are times that each of us will be under great pressures and disappointments. Is it that we will be called upon to do an important piece of work? Is this God's way of getting us ready so that we will not break down under the stress of the work?"

Random Daily Inspiration

"Today do not give in to the material difficulties and troubles of this world. Turn to God with your heart and your soul and your mind because with Christ in you, these problems will not control you, but can be dealt with in a masterful way."

Extra Daily Inspiration

"The power that comes when the heart is focused upon God can reverse negative to positive and darkness to light. Listen to the voice of your inner spirit and do that which you know is right."

Today's Daily Inspiration

"Success is never permanent and failure is never fatal. Lord, give me the power to handle both with courage and know that each tempers the other to build strength and harmony in my life."

Random Daily Inspiration

"The moments that are really lived are the moments that things are done in the spirit of God's love. Today, Lord, I will focus on Your love and do Your will. When I stumble let me never forget that You are right next to me and will help me up."

Extra Daily Inspiration

"To reach Heaven, we must sail. Sometimes we sail with the wind and sometimes against the wind, but we must sail, not drift or be anchored. Lord, Thy Will be done so that I will stay on course all the days of my life."

Sometimes it is better to remove things from your "to do" list rather than adding to it. Lord, give me the courage to say no to the things that cause me to feel overwhelmed.

Random Daily Inspiration

Believe that God made you a good person and let that person come out. Lord, help me to remove my disbelief in who I am and who I can become and let me realize how truly loving and kind I am.

Extra Dose

Laughter is a great way to reduce stress and prevent taking ourselves too seriously. Lord, bless me with a healthy sense of humor.

Today's Daily Inspiration

Even the most difficult of trials is God's way of preparing us for something else. Lord, may I view my challenges as an opportunity to grow rather than as an opportunity to fail.

Random Daily Inspiration

Do what is right and good in the eyes of the Lord and receive the fullness of His blessings. Lord, I thank You for the gifts that I have received and ask forgiveness for all that I have done wrong.

Today's Daily Inspiration

Seek God's guidance, but know that the responsibility to act on it is yours. Lord, may I not be lazy because I have prayed and expect You to do everything for me.

Random Daily Inspiration

Worry about nothing, pray for everything, and thank God for His answers. Lord, I ask You to handle my problems with me and care for my needs.

Extra Dose

Be a little kinder and gentler today, for this will show your real strength. Lord, may I become more patient and have the courage to live my life according to the example You set forth. IN JESUS NAME AMEN!!

Today's Daily Inspiration

It is laughter that helps us cope with the upsets and chaos of everyday living. Lord, lighten my spirit so that I will not take myself so seriously and be able to find more moments to laugh.

Random Daily Inspiration

Jesus said, "Whatever you ask in prayer, believe that you have received it, and it will be yours." Lord, I pray, I believe, and I thank you even before it is fulfilled.

Extra Dose

One of life's greatest rewards is not what we get, but what we become. Lord, teach me as I am able to learn and give me the courage to be all that I can.

Today's Daily Inspiration

It is not as significant to have a good life, but rather to do good things with your life. Lord, I am grateful for the talents with which You have blessed me and I pray that they will not go unused.

Random Daily Inspiration

Do the ordinary things in your life well because they are your preparation for what is yet to come. Lord, You slowly teach all that I need to know. May I never be a complaining student.

Extra Dose

Don't think less of yourself than God thinks of you. He has created us with worth and value beyond our comprehension. Lord, help me to live daily knowing that I am very valuable and do make a difference.

Today's Daily Inspiration

Little acts of kindness throughout the day will make your life so much better and bring a little sunshine to others as well. Lord, may I make a habit of being gentle and loving with those around me.

Random Daily Inspiration

Practice speaking nicely of yourself to yourself. This will strengthen your confidence and become a guide in how to speak to others. Lord, may I look for the goodness in all people and forgive them their weaknesses.

Extra Dose

When we hand over what we can't handle to the One who can, miracles happen. Keep me free of stress, Lord, and in the best possible place to receive Your help.
IN JESUS NAME AMEN!!

Today's Daily Inspiration

Ask yourself if what you are spending your thoughts and energy on will matter in a week, a month, or a year. Lord, help me select my priorities wisely and use my time in ways that will make my life and those around me better and happier.

Today's Daily Inspiration

The phrase "Never Again" is too large a commitment and too easily discarded when we stumble. Lord, help me to work on being a better person today, so that in time, my good habits will require little or no effort.

Random Daily Inspiration

Take time to learn from the mistakes of others. We don't have time to make all of them ourselves. Lord, guide me onto paths that lead me to You.

Extra Dose

Rejoice. This is the day the Lord has made. Lord, my days pass so quickly. May I have a generous heart and the time to see the needs of those around me.

Today's Daily Inspiration

The best thing to let go of is your past. Lord, the goodness of my past is part of whom I am now, but the rest only serves to pull me away from You. Help me to keep my thoughts only on this moment.

Random Daily Inspiration

"The moments that are really lived are the moments that things are done in the spirit of God's love. Today, Lord, I will focus on Your love and do Your will. When I stumble let me never forget that You are right next to me and will help me up"

Extra Dose

Change first from the inside and the other things will follow. Lord, bless me the desire to become a better person and the firmness of will to succeed because I know that together we have the power to change my life.

Today's Daily Inspiration

Live with gratitude for all that you are and all that you have because often what looks good on the outside is not really what it seems. Lord, remind me to spend a few moments each day appreciating my life and becoming aware of how good it really is.

Random Daily Inspiration

To know someone doesn't mean to know every detail of that person's life. It means to feel affection, confidence and to believe in that person. Lord, may I really know You and have it reflect in how I treat others. Thought for the day ~ Wisdom is knowing how to properly handle the information and knowledge we have, especially when it comes to relationships." K.P. Yohannan, A Life of Balance
Thought for the day ~ "Since no single team member can ever have a monopoly on wisdom, cognitive diversity is almost always a source of strength." - Lance Thompson, Transcend from management to Leadership.

Today's Daily Inspiration

Do not run ahead of the Lord, but walk with Him, pray for His guidance and listen to His answers. Lord, let me put Your will first in my life.

Random Daily Inspiration

We are not always what we ought to be or want to be, but through God's love we are not what we would be without Him. Lord, thank you for raising me to heights in this world that alone I could not reach and for giving me eternal life in the next.

Extra Dose

Strengthen your character by knowing which things in life are nonnegotiable to you. Lord, I pray for the strength to say no when saying yes would go against that in which I believe.

Today's Daily Inspiration

Integrity is one of our most valuable assets. Lord, may I live responsibly and never have the need to make excuses for my behavior.

Random Daily Inspiration

Jesus came to us to serve not be served. Lord, help me to set aside my self-serving behaviors and model my life after You.

Extra Dose

"If the actions of another irritate you or you have been hurt or offended, do not attack. Do not compromise yourself. Remember clearly that the way of the Lord is the way of love and peace and gentleness."

> *Fires can't be made with dead embers, nor can enthusiasm be stirred by spiritless men. Enthusiasm in our daily work lightens effort and turns even labor into pleasant tasks. James A. Baldwin*

Today's Daily Inspiration

You will have an easier time keeping your thoughts positive if you look for good in every situation. Lord, help me change my focus and develop an awareness that situations often have more good in them than bad.

Random Daily Inspiration

When we give in to fears and worries they will take charge of our lives. Lord, I place my trust in You so that I may experience every opportunity and not miss in life that which is meant for me.

Today's Daily Inspiration

Forgive because we all need forgiving. Lord, may I let go of my hurts and find compassion for the burdens that others carry.

Random Daily Inspiration

God sends us His message, but we must be willing to receive it and then live it. Lord, when I yield to You, I become free and full of the richness of life.

Extra Dose

To become more efficient and happier, daily spend some quiet time with God and with yourself. Lord, what joy it is to know that You will listen.

Today's Daily Inspiration

Enjoy life while you've got the chance. Lord, may I view each day as a gift and a privilege.

Random Daily Inspiration

Do not run ahead of the Lord, but walk with Him, pray for His guidance and listen to His answers. Lord, let me put Your will first in my life.

Extra Dose

God gives abundantly to those who pass His gifts on to others. Lord, let Your blessings flow in to me and then out from me. I will neither be selfish nor let my gifts stagnate.

Today's Daily Inspiration

Spend less time trying to understand the behaviors of others and more time on the reasons you do things. Lord, help me to know myself better because then it will become possible to change the habits I don't like and improve on the ones I do.

Random Daily Inspiration

Never forget that home is Heaven and life on earth is only temporary. Lord, may I live with deep awareness of my spiritual nature and live a life of truth.

Extra Dose

Each day offers many situations for accomplishment, joy, change and personal growth. Lord, grant me the ability to recognize these moments and the energy to benefit from these daily opportunities.

Today's Daily Inspiration

"If we are confident in Christ, we will see success where others see failure and sunshine where others see darkness. Lord, help me to live each day to the fullest."

Random Daily Inspiration

"Today, Lord, help me to recognize and accept the love that comes to me, even if it isn't coming to me in the way I had expected it."

Extra Dose

"Lord, as I face whatever my challenge for today is, help me to remember that I am not alone and if it seems to overwhelm me let me not forget that it is then that You will carry me."

Today's Daily Inspiration

"Regret is a waste of time. Be grateful for all of your past. It is life's lesson. Lord, teach me so that I may live today completely."

Random Daily Inspiration

"Little irritations can ruin the day. Lord, keep me from worrying about small things and focus on the ceaseless wonders of Your Earth."

Extra Daily Inspiration

"Many temptations assault the soul. The next time one comes along that I cannot handle, Lord, give me something else to focus on."

Today's Daily Inspiration

Frequently remind yourself of that which is important in your life. Lord, help me to treasure my family and friends, recognize how valuable they are and tell them often how happy that I am because they are in my life.

Random Daily Inspiration

God did not talk about how much He loves us. He showed us by sending us His Son. Lord, may I learn to love selflessly and speak through my actions.

Extra Dose

It is easier to see another's faults than it is to see your own. Lord, help me sit in judgment of only myself and guide me in my attempts at overcoming my weaknesses. IN JESUS NAME AMEN!!!

Today's Daily Inspiration

Avoid the tendency to presuppose that things will turn out for the worse. Lord, help me keep an open mind so that I am able to see other solutions to my situations and then give me the determination to make a difference when I can.

Random Daily Inspiration

Make today the best day of your life. Lord, I have been greatly blessed not only by what I have, but by those burdens that I have been spared.

Extra Dose

You can never sincerely help others without also helping yourself. Lord, Your generosity touches every part of my life even when I least expect it. May I not let it go unnoticed and not give thanks.

Today's Daily Inspiration

We often don't realize how heavy the weight of worry is and how much energy it requires until we are able to let go of it. Lord, I place my trust in You to clear my thinking, help me resolve my concerns and bring me to a place of peace.

Random Daily Inspiration

God can calm your fears, bring rest to your worry and fix your broken heart if only you give Him all of the pieces. Lord, I ask You to fill me with Your peace as I turn my troubles over to You.

Extra Dose

Laughter is a speedy way to bring people together, build friendships and reduce stresses. Lord, help me participate in the many opportunities to feel the calming effect of laughter.

Today's Daily Inspiration

Keep your mind open to the possibility that things can turn out even better than expected. Lord, I trust in You and graciously accept all blessings that You send to me.

Random Daily Inspiration

Courage gives us the trust in God to follow our hearts no matter what obstacles seem to block our way. **Lord, I love You.**

Extra Dose

God will give you today, no more than you can handle today. It is when you choose to add yesterday's and tomorrow's troubles to it that it becomes too much to carry. Lord, help me remember that it is only right now that I can find all that I am looking for.

Today's Daily Inspiration

Make few promises and keep the ones you make. Lord, grant me the strength to keep my commitments, especially the ones that I make to myself.

Random Daily Inspiration

Every moment of anger uses up a moment of your happiness. Lord, help me to be patient, loving and kind at the times in which it is most difficult.

Extra Dose

Do not be held back by your fears. Lord, Your faith in me builds my confidence, Your gifts provide me with courage, and Your promises assure me that I will never face my fears alone. Together all is possible.

Today's Daily Inspiration

It's easy to give up, but no matter what the outcome is, if you do your best, you are always the winner. Lord, may I truly realize that it is the way I participate in life that counts for me.

Random Daily Inspiration

God will give you strength because He will give of Himself. Lord, thank You for the many gifts of which You always bless me.

Extra Dose

Right now is a good time to free yourself of the burden of that which needs to be done, but has been put off. Lord, little by little, help me remove my procrastinations so that I can fully live in the present.

Today's Daily Inspiration

Behave as though God is standing next to you because He is. Lord, we make a great team and together we are able to make a big difference.

Random Daily Inspiration

Pray together as a family and share each other's joys and burdens. Lord, he is not heavy. He's my brother/*sister*.

Extra Dose

<u>If you would be ashamed to sign your name to your conversation, don't say it. Lord, my words can have far reaching effects. May the effect always be good.</u>

Today's Daily Inspiration

Talking about how busy you are only adds stress to the stress you already feel. Lord, help me complete the tasks of my day and avoid taking on more than I can handle.

Random Daily Inspiration

If you exercise your mind, your spirit will never get old. Lord, give me the ability to rise above my worldly burdens and ability to always make things a little better.

Extra Dose

God knows what is best for you in all matters of your life. Rely on His wisdom. Lord, I place my trust in You because You answer every prayer.

Today's Daily Inspiration

Keep your mind open to the possibility that things can turn out even better than expected. Lord, I trust in You and graciously accept all blessings that You send to me.

Random Daily Inspiration

We are partially responsible for every wrong which we had the power to prevent. Lord, grant me the courage to not look the other way when I could make a difference.

Extra Dose

When we have to justify our actions, it may be that our actions are not just. Lord, Your will is goodness. May I always have the strength and courage to choose Your way so that I can simplify my life and enjoy the peace of Your presence.

Read All about It
Extra Extra Dose

Forget the hurts and unkindness's of all yesterday's so that today you will have room to be joyful and at peace. Lord, bless me with the ability to let go of that which causes me pain so that I may not miss the great joys that today will bring

Thoughts for the day ~ It takes a lot of courage to have an "attitude of gratitude" during the "dark" times. But once you have it, it empowers you.

If the grass is greener on the other side it's probably getting better care. Success is a matter of sticking to a set of common sense principles anyone can master.

Thoughts for the day ~ "Part of our responsibility as parents, as adults, is to set examples for children. But we have to like children in order to be really happy fulfilled adults." - Bobby McFerrin, 1988

Children are more influenced by sermons you act.. than by sermons you preach.

Thought for the day ~ Make today a great day . . . despite the mud that life brings.

Thought for the day ~ "One resolution I have made, and try always to keep, is this: To rise above the little things." - John Burroughs - Happy New Year

Thoughts for the day ~ "You cannot start the next chapter of your life if you keep re-reading the last one." - Michael McMillian

"The way to get started is to quit talking and begin doing." - Walt Disney

Today's Daily Inspiration

Patience with others brings peace to our own soul. Lord, help me to display patience even when I do not feel patient because everyone will benefit, but me most of all.

Random Daily Inspiration

Do not worry about tomorrow. Do you not have enough to be busy with today? Lord, help me use today wisely so that I have time for myself and others.

Extra Dose

Rely on the strength and understanding that you possess. Each of us has more of it in us that we can imagine possible. Lord, through faith in You I can face any difficulty and conquer it.

Today's Daily Inspiration

Frequently remind yourself of that which is important in your life. Lord, help me to treasure my family and friends, recognize how valuable they are and tell them often how happy that I am because they are in my life.

Random Daily Inspiration

Do not just ask God's help in the big things. It is the small things in your life that often make a big difference. Lord, as I go about the duties of my day, be with me, care for me and remove from my path unnecessary burdens.

Extra Dose

Call on God when you need a friend to make it through the day. Lord, may we share Your love and beauty so that our lives may not be lonely.

Today's Daily Inspiration

Whatever the problem, stressing over it will not solve it. Lord, I turn to You for solutions because I believe that You care for all of my needs. Bless me with the ability to remain level headed and calm as we work our way through my day.

Random Daily Inspiration

Have the strength to do what is right regardless of the consequences. Lord, show me Your way so that I may walk in Your truth.

Extra Dose

Strengthen your character by knowing which things in life are nonnegotiable to you. Lord, I pray for the strength to say no when saying yes would go against that in which I believe.

Random Daily Inspiration

Many people need you in many different ways. No one else can take your place. Lord, You blessed me with special abilities and need me to use them in this world. Thank you.

Extra Dose

If you are stressed, you are probably makings things more important than they really are. Lord, I pray for clarity of thought and calmness of spirit because I know that when my heart grows weary, You send me peace.

Thought for the day ~ "First, we are challenged to develop a world perspective. No individual can live alone, not nation can live alone, and anyone who feels that he can live alone is sleeping through a revolution. The world in which we live is geographically one. The challenge that we face today is to make it one in terms of brotherhood." - Martin Luther King Jr. . . . Remaining Awake Through a Great Revolution

"Those who are not looking for happiness are the most likely to find it, because those who are searching forget that the surest way to be happy is to seek happiness for others." - Martin Luther King Jr.

Thought for the day ~ "If you can't fly then run, if you can't run then walk, if can't walk then crawl, but whatever you do you have to keep moving forward." - Martin Luther King Jr. - Words of Encouragement

Thoughts for the day ~ "Absorb what is useful, Discard what is not, Add what is uniquely your own." - Bruce Lee

"Courage is knowing what not to fear." - Plato

Thoughts for the day ~ "The three great essentials to achieve anything worthwhile are, first, hard work; second, stick-to-itiveness; third, common sense." - Thomas Edison

"When you face discouragement, you can do one of two things, and the one you choose will color your perspective. You can look at others to place the blame, or you can look at yourself to discover your opportunities. The choice is yours." - John C. Maxwell, The Difference Maker, Making Your Attitude Your Greatest Asset

Thoughts for the day ~ "I discovered I always have choices and sometimes it's only a choice of attitude." - Judith M. Knowlton

"You have succeeded in life when all you really want is only what you really need." - Vernon Howard

Thoughts for the day ~ "How you think about a problem is more important than the problem itself — so always think positively." - Norman Vincent Peale

"I find that the harder I work, the more luck I seem to have." - Thomas Jefferson

Thoughts for the day – "I know that serving others has been a source of inspiration, a source of strength, a reinforcement of faith, and an illustration of my life's purpose." - Dr. Rachel Talton, Flourish: Have it All Without Losing Yourself

"The optimist lives on the peninsula of infinite possibilities; the pessimist is stranded on the island of perpetual indecision." - William Arthur Ward

Thoughts for the day ~ "I feel the more diverse the group, the greater the potential to discover alternative ways to do something that may lead to improvement." - Robert Stevenson

"Successful people have focus. They don't get easily distracted and they ignore things that are completely unnecessary." - Penelope Holmes

Thoughts for the day ~ When there is a hill to climb, don't think that waiting will make it smaller.

You can have RESULTS or EXCUSES not both

Thoughts for the day ~ "The turning point, I think, was when I really realized that you can do it yourself. That you have to believe in you because sometimes that's the only person that does believe in your success but you." - Tim Blixseth

Thoughts for the day ~ "I not only use all the brains that I have but all that I can borrow." - Woodrow Wilson

"Stop fretting about past decision. They have provided valuable wisdom. Go forward without fear or regret." Paul Martens, Unlocking Potential

Thoughts for the day ~ "Which way you choose to see your life in the future depends on your attitude today." Amy E. Dean

"God's wisdom leads us to live the best life possible. He promised to give us His wisdom when we look for it." - Heather Shore, God Uses Deeply Wounded People

Thoughts for the day ~ "What is your purpose for being here? (We all have one.) What can you contribute to the good of others? For when we seek and find that vision, God opens the path." - Roz Swartz Williams, The Mourning Chronicles

"There is no better than adversity. Every defeat, every heartbreak, every loss, contains its own seed, it's own lesson on how to improve your performance next time." - Malcolm X

Thoughts for the day ~ Not to know is bad; not to wish to know is worse.

Thoughts for the day ~ "We use prayer when we need something, but praying is also for giving thanks for all your blessing." - Catherine Pulsifer

"Yet prayer alone will not avail. Faith and works must always be associated." - John Harvey Kellogg, Plain Facts for Old and Young

Thoughts for the day ~ "Always remember that the future comes one day at a time." - Dean Acheson

"The pessimist complains about the wind; the optimist expects it to change; the realist adjusts the sails." - William Arthur Ward

Thoughts for the day ~ "Positive attitude is more of a philosophy that builds on the fact that having an optimistic disposition in any circumstance of life can help you in enhancing achievement and positive changes." - Dan Miller

Laugh and the world laughs with you; weep and you weep alone.

Thoughts for the day ~ "Often our eyes see "those who are". . . . But who are we? A simple reflection of those who are? I am reminded to look within my own soul for answers. For we are all given a spirit of wisdom. Today may I not only see those who are, but may I also see who I am." - Colleen Smith

"Practical wisdom is only to be learned in the school of experience. Precepts and instruction are useful so far as they go, but, without the discipline of real life, they remain of the nature of theory only." - Samuel Smiles

Thoughts for the day ~ "No one is born hating another person because of the color of his skin, or his background, or his religion. People must learn to hate, and if they can learn to hate, they can be taught to love, for love comes more naturally to the human heart than its opposite." - Nelson Mandela

"You can also be motivated by people that you admire and being in touch with positive people who share your desire to go forward in your life is a great idea." - Dane Taylor, Time Management

Thoughts for the day ~ "Rather than hoping for change, you first must be prepared to change." - Catherine Pulsifer

"Not only do I think that worrying about oversaturation and competition is an unhealthy "scarcity" mentality, but it's also a limiting belief that we put on ourselves that actually stops us from taking action." - Zakeer Hussain

Thoughts for the day ~ "Progress is impossible without change, and those who cannot change their minds cannot change anything." - George Bernard Shaw

When it rains, most birds head for shelter; the Eagle is the only bird that, in order to avoid the rain, starts flying above the cloud.

Thoughts for the day ~ "We all want more. That means change. But things never change for the better out of mere desire." - Christopher Babson, BOLD! Success System

"Some people feel they like they're supposed to wait for inspiration." - Strange Flow, the Extreme Motivation Book

Thoughts for the day ~ To effectively communicate, we must realize that we are all different in the way we perceive the world - use this understanding as a guide to our communication with others.

Nothing is so simple that it cannot be misunderstood.

Thoughts for the day ~ "Action may not always bring happiness; but there is no happiness without action." - Benjamin Disraeli

"Great minds discuss ideas; average minds discuss events; small minds discuss people." - Eleanor Roosevelt

Thoughts for the day ~ "One half of knowing what you want is knowing what you must give up before you get it." - Sidney Howard

"Beginnings are only difficult without any action." - Bryon Pulsifer

Thoughts for the day ~ "Genius is one percent inspiration and ninety-nine percent perspiration." - Thomas Edison

"Surround yourself with people who are going to motivate and inspire you." - Charles M. Marcus

Thoughts for the day ~ "Your words must match what you do. In so many words, you need to show sincerity with your words." - John Garret

"The best leaders are very often the best listeners. They have an open mind. They are not interested in having their own way but in finding the best way." - Wilfred Peterson

Thoughts for the day ~ Someone's opinion of you does not have to become your reality.

The genius of communication is the ability to be both totally honest and totally kind at the same time.

Thoughts for the day ~ Many of us are more capable than some of us....but none of us is as capable as all of us!!

Even when you choose your words well, if your tone of voice is hurried, hostile, or defensive, people may hear something very different from what you intended.

Thoughts for the day ~ "It is not the strongest or the most intelligent who will survive but those who can best manage change." - Charles Darwin

Thoughts for the day ~ "All I know is that when I pray, coincidences happen; and when I don't pray, they don't happen." - Dan Hayes

"There is not one time that prayer is required nor is there just one place. Prayer is something that you may engage in more than you think." Byron Pulsifer

Thoughts for the day ~ Communication sometimes is not what you first hear, listen not just to the words, but listen for the reason.

"Learning allows for more wisdom and knowledge. Additional knowledge about any situation increases the strength of an opinion." - Faye Horton

Thoughts for the day ~ "He who has a why to live can bear almost any how." - Friedrich Nietzsche

"Optimism is the faith that leads to achievement. Nothing can be done without hope or confidence." - Helen Keller

Thoughts for the day ~ "Do the best you can until you know better . . . Then when you know better, do better." - Maya Angelou

"Stop fretting about past decisions. They have provided valuable wisdom. Go forward without fear or regret. - Paul Martens, Unlocking Potential

Thoughts for the day ~ "We must not allow....any force to make us feel like we don't count. Maintain a sense of dignity and respect." - Martin Luther King

Realize that you can't please everyone. In fact, nobody can. Sometimes you need to just let some people go. Realizing this will relieve you from a lot of unnecessary burden so that you can focus on the people that you can positively interact with.

Thoughts for the day ~ Nothing you know is worth anything if you don't know how to be proud of yourself.

"(W)hat people think of me isn't any of my business." ~ Oprah Winfrey, in "An Intimate Talk with Oprah" Essence, August 1987

Thoughts for the day ~ "The greatest good you can do for another is not just to share your riches, but to reveal to him his own." - Benjamin Disraeli

The smallest of actions is always better than the boldest of intentions.

Thoughts for the day ~ "By patience and hard work, we brought order out of chaos, just as will be true of any problem if we stick to it with patience and wisdom and earnest effort." - Booker T. Washington, Up From Slavery, 1901

I try to do the right thing at the right time. They may just be little things, but usually they make the difference between winning and losing." Kareem Abdul Jabbar, in Star, May 1986

Thoughts for the day ~ "Most of us would find little time for looking after other people's faults if we gave strict attention to our own. Besides, seeing and knowing our own defects would make us more charitable concerning those of others." - Al Bryant....Words of Encouragement

"You can't hold a man down without staying down with him." - Booker T. Washington, c. 1900

Thoughts for the day ~ "It is our choices.....that show what we truly are, for more than our abilities." - J.K. Rowling

Don't think too much. You'll create a problem that wasn't even there in the first place.

Thoughts for the day ~ "Any situation that you find yourself in, is an outward reflection of your inner state of beingness." - Elmorya

"All truly wise thoughts have been thought already thousands of times; but to make them truly ours, we must think them over again honestly, till they take root in our personal experience." - Johann Wolfgang von Goethe

Thoughts for the day ~ "Make no judgments where you have no compassion." - Anne McCaffrey

"Great works are performed not by strength, but by perseverance." - Samuel Johnson

Thoughts for the day ~ "If a leader's actions don't back up his or her words, those who are trying to follow will first grow confused." - Bill Byrd

"Service is the rent we pay for being. It is the very purpose of life and not something you do in your spare time." - Marion Wright Edelman

Thoughts for the day ~ Beware of false knowledge; it is more dangerous than ignorance.

"I believe that there will ultimately be a clash between the oppressed and those that do the oppressing. I believe that there will be a clash between those who want freedom, justice and equality for everyone and those who want to continue the system of exploitation." - Malcolm X

Thoughts for the day ~ "The fundamental issue of life is the appeal of race to race, the appeal of clan to clan, the appeal of tribe to tribe, of observing the rule that self-preservation was the first law of nature." - Marcus Garvey, Philosophy and Opinions of Marcus Garvey, 1923

"In life you need either inspiration or desperation." - Anthony Robbins

Thoughts for the day ~ "Life isn't about finding yourself. Life is about creating yourself." - George Bernard Shaw

"However, remember an idea does no one any good unless it is seen through to the end." - Riley Stevens

Thoughts for the day ~ "Find out what people will submit to and you have found out the exact amount of injustice and wrong which will be imposed upon them." - Frederick Douglass, Life and Times of Frederick Douglass, 1892

"Why, of all the multitudinous groups of people in this country, [do] you have to single out the Negroes and give them this separate treatment? It can't be because of slavery in the past, because there are very few groups in this country that haven't had slavery some place back in the history of their group. It can't be color, because there are Negroes as white as drifted snow, with blue eyes, and they are just as segregated as the colored man. The only thing it can be is an inherent determination that the people who were formerly in slavery, regardless of anything else, shall be kept as near that state as possible." - Thurgood Marshall, Brown v. Board of Education

Thoughts for the day ~ "Let's not burn America down. Let's take her like she is and rebuild her. We must maintain and advocate and promote the philosophy of nonviolence." - Martin Luther King, Jr., in Jet, 4 April 1968

Nonviolence cannot be taught to a person who fears to die and has no power of resistance.

"Nonviolent resistance is not a method for cowards; it does resist." - Martin Luther King, Jr., Stride Toward Freedom, 1958

Thoughts for the day ~ "Stay committed to your decisions, but stay flexible in your approach." - Anthony Robbins

While one person hesitates because he feels inferior, the other is busy making mistakes and becoming superior." - Henry C. Link

Thoughts for the day ~ "Sometimes it just takes a new perspective on a situation to change how you feel and act about it." - Matthew Lewis Browne

"Most people fail in life because they major in minor things." - Anthony Robbins

Thoughts for the day ~ "Each of us can make a great difference in the lives of other people, particularly as we move along the Success Process ourselves growing in strength, gaining experience and knowledge." - Stedman Graham - Life

"Friendship is born at that moment when one person says to another, What! You too? I thought I was the only one." - C.S. Lewis- Friendship

Thoughts for the day ~ "You can't legislate integration, but you can certainly legislate desegregation. You can't legislate morality, but you regulate behavior. You can't make a man love me, but the law can restrain him from lynching me." - Martin Luther King, Jr., in U.S. News & World Report, 24 February 1964

"Women, in general, are not a part of the corruption of the past, so they can give a new kind of leadership, a new image for mankind." - Coretta King, in Walker, In Search of Our Mothers' Gardens, 1983

Thoughts for the day ~ "Man cannot discover new oceans unless he has the courage to lose sight of the shore." - Andre Gide

"If a man is not faithful to his own individuality, he cannot be loyal to anything." - Claude McKay, A Long Way From Home, 1937

Thoughts for the day ~ Look at the content of what people say to you for something POSITIVE that you can act upon to improve yourself. Don't just reject the whole messages.

"Compassion motivates us to address injustice; if we need to take action, we do it with compassion and wisdom, not anger or ignorance." Stephanie Gunning, Audacious Creativity

Thoughts for the day ~ "A proactive person is someone who tends to initiate change rather than reacting to events." - Jeffrey Morales, Leadership: 33 Lessons on How to Become A Proactive Leader

"It is difficult to say what is impossible, for the dream of yesterday is the hope of today and the reality of tomorrow." - Robert H. Goddard

Thoughts for the day ~ "Nothing truly valuable arises from ambition or from a mere sense of duty; it stems rather from love and devotion towards men and towards objective things." - Albert Einstein

"As we are liberated from our own fear, our presence automatically liberates others." - Marianne Williamson

Thoughts for the day ~ "Persistence is to the character of man as carbon is to steel." - Napoleon Hill

"Don't let other people erode your confidence. Successful people know that the greater their self-confidence, the greater their achievements." - Catherine Pulsifer

Thoughts for the day ~ Education was feared by slave owners because slaves might read of their national rights. - Black Chronicle, 1 June 1896

"Whether you like it or not the millions are here, and here they will remain. If you do not lift them up, they will pull you down....Education must not simply teach work---it must teach life." - W.E.B. Du BOIS, "The Talented Tenth," The Negro Problem, 1903

Thoughts for the day ~ "Even in the most successful life, there are always goals and objectives for the future. Therefore, the time to be happy is now - not in the future." - Eric J. Anderson - Happy

"Nurture your mind with great thoughts, for you will never go any higher than you think." - Benjamin Disraeli

Thoughts for the day ~ "Sometime we feel that if everything isn't perfect, we cannot be grateful for anything. We easily fall into all-or-nothing thinking. When we do, we miss the sunrise and the other forms of goodness that surround us." - Anne Wilson Schaef

"Great thoughts speak only to the thoughtful mind, but great actions speak to all mankind." - Theodore Roosevelt

Thoughts for the day ~ "The eyes sees only what the mind is prepared to comprehend. - Robertson Davies

It's not at all hard to understand a person; it's only hard to listen without bias." - Criss Jami

Thoughts for the day ~ "If your dream is to live a life full of happiness, bliss, and love, chances are what's holding you from that kind of life is either your pride or your fear." - Ken Black - Fear

"Confidence is one of the most desired attributes and when you manage to wear it in the way it is meant to, life will seem to be a lot happier for you." - Elijah Conner- Confidence

Thoughts for the day ~ "How do we nurture the soul? By revering our own life. By learning to love it all, not only the joys and the victories, but also the pain and the struggles." - Nathaniel Branden

"If this society fails, I fear that we will learn very shortly that racism is a sickness unto death." - Martin Luther King, Jr., in "Showdown for Violence," Look, 16 April 1968

Thoughts for the day ~ "Minds are like parachutes-- they only function when they are open." - Thomas Dewar

There is little difference in people, but that little difference makes a big difference. The little difference is attitude. The big difference is whether it is positive or negative.

Thoughts for the day ~ "When you consistently maintain a positive frame of mind, you'll become known as a problem-solver rather than a complainer. People avoid complainers. They seek out problem-solvers." - Joseph Sommerville, PhD, from The 5 Keys to Interpersonal Success

When a person finds themselves predisposed to complaining about how little they are regarded by others, let them reflect how little they have contributed to the happiness of others.

Thoughts for the day ~ "When we want to accomplish effective change in our life, we really need to know ourselves." Barry Naude, The Essential Skills for Success

"The good news is anything in the mind can be changed - the great news is we can do it ourselves!" - Stephanie Conkie, Happy Person, Happy Life

Thoughts for the day ~ "You could never experience true happiness if you are not grateful for what you already have." - Julia Broderick - Happiness

"You've heard that it's wise to learn from experience, but it is wiser to learn from the experience of others." - Rick Warren - Wisdom

Thoughts for the day ~ "Strong people don't need strong leaders." - Ella Baker, c. 1980

Don't be afraid of being outnumbered. Eagles fly alone. Pigeons flock together.

Thoughts for the day - When people are serving, life is no longer meaningless.

If you expect the world to be fair with you because you are fair, you're fooling yourself. That's like expecting the lion not to eat you because you didn't eat him.

Thoughts for the day ~ If you are not willing to learn, no one can help you. If you are determined to learn, no one can stop you.

Live so that when your children think of fairness, caring, and integrity they think of you.

Thoughts for the day ~ It is a dangerous thing to ask why someone else has been given more. It is humbling and indeed healthy to ask why you have been given so much.

"Everyone wants to live on top of the mountain, but all the happiness and growth occurs while you're climbing it." - Andy Rooney

Thoughts for the day ~ To blame is easy. To do it better is difficult.

Don't put yourself down; too many others will try to anyway.

Thoughts for the day – "What you do speaks so loud that I cannot hear what you say." - Ralph Waldo Emerson

"I can be changed by what happens to me, but I refuse to be reduced by it." - Maya Angelou

Thoughts for the day - Progress and growth are impossible if you always do things the way you've always done things.

We can become bitter or better as a result of our experience.

Thoughts for the day ~ "Everyday is not a good day, but there is good in every day."

"An invincible determination can accomplish almost anything and in this lies the great distinction between great men and little men." ~ Dr. Thomas Fuller - Determination

Thoughts for the day ~ No matter how you feel, get up, dress up and show up.

Keep your words soft and tender, tomorrow you may have to eat them.

Thoughts for the day ~ You can have results or excuses not both.

"It is wise to direct your anger towards problems - not people; to focus your energies on answers - not excuses." William Arthur Ward

Thoughts for the day ~ "Most people fail in life because they major in minor things." - Anthony Robbins

When you face discouragement you can do one of two things, and the one you choose will color your perspective. You can look at others to place the blame, or you can look at yourself to discover your opportunities.

Thoughts for the day ~ "The task of the excellent teacher is to stimulate 'apparently ordinary' people to unusual effort. The tough problem is not in identifying winners: it is in making winners out of ordinary people." - K. Patricia Cross

"Courage isn't something that is given to us overnight. It's a quality we cultivate regularly in the face of problems, hardships, disappointments, and loss." - Dr. B. Brown

Thoughts for the day ~ If the grass is greener on the other side it's probably getting better care. Success is a matter of sticking to a set of common sense principles anyone can master. - Unknown author

"Only those who will risk going too far can possibly find out how far they can go." - T.S. Eliot

Thoughts for the day ~ "The mind is not a vessel to be filled, but a fire to be ignited." - Plutarch

The future is a place you are creating, and the paths to it are not found, they are made. Follow your passion as long as you live and you will reach success.

Thoughts for the day ~ "If you can't sleep, then get up and do something instead of lying there worrying. It's the worry that gets you, not the lack of sleep." - Dale Carnegie

Miracles start to happen when you give as much energy to your dreams as you do your fears.

Thoughts for the day ~ "Each of us guards a gate of change that can only be unlocked from the inside." - Marilyn Ferguson

If you continue to talk about the drama that you don't want in your life, you will continue to attract it.

Thoughts for the day ~ "Never look back and regret, look back and smile at what you have learned." - Michelle C. Ustaszeski

"The only limit to our realization of tomorrow will be our doubts of today." - Franklin Delano Roosevelt

Thoughts for the day ~ "If you'll not settle for anything less than your best, you will be amazed at what you can accomplish in your lives." - Vince Lombardi

Thoughts for the day ~ "It is only the narrow people who live for themselves, who never read good books, who do not travel, who never open up their souls to permit them to come into contact with other souls----with great world outside." - Booker T. Washington, Speeches of Booker T. Washington, 1932

"Too many victories weaken you. The defeated can rise up stronger than the victor." Muhammad Ali, The Greatest, 1975

Thoughts for the day ~ "This applies to play as well as work. A day merely survived is no cause for celebration. You are not here to fritter away your precious hours when you have the ability to accomplish so much by making a slight change in your routine. No more busy work. No more hiding from success. Leave time, leave space, to grow. Now. Now! Not tomorrow!" - Og Mandino - Work

"You may plan to write a book someday, but you are living a book every day." - Wilfred Peterson - Book

Thoughts for the day ~ "Expect the best. Prepare for the worst. Capitalize on what comes." - Zig Ziglar

One moment of patience may ward off great disaster. One moment of impatience may ruin a whole life.

Thoughts for the day ~ "There was one or two things I had a right to, liberty or death. If I could not have one, I would have the other, for no man should take me alive. I should fight for my liberty as long as my strength lasted." - Harriet Tubman, in Bradford, Harriet, the Moses of Her People, 1869

Whoever works without knowledge works uselessly.

Thoughts for the day ~ "Don't get carried away with the stuff happening in your life or believe in instant gratification and sell yourself short, look for suitable ways to engage with what happens in your life." Scott Hinsborough, How To Increase Self Confidence

Ability is what you're capable of doing. Motivation determines what you do.. Attitude determines how well you do it.

Thoughts for the day ~ "Some people (including me) believe that a good day depends on the morning that you have, so why not start this journey by changing the first part of your day. You will be surprised to see what an impact can have on your life and how it can make you change not only the way you see the world, but also the way the world sees you." - Lucas Bailly - Believe

"If we can focus on making clear what parts of our day are within our control and what parts are not, we will not only be happier, we will have a distinct advantage over other people who fail to realize they are fighting an unwinnable battle." - Ryan Holiday, Stephen Hanselman - Failure

Thoughts for the day ~ "But out of all these gestures, the most indicative of being outgoing is the smile. Not only is it found as likeable by others, it also encourages them to start or continue interacting with you." - Mia Conrad - Communication

Thoughts for the day ~ "It was impossible for me to repeat the same old story month after month and keep up my interest in it. It was an old story to me, and to go through with it night after night was a task altogether too mechanical for my nature. I was now reading and thinking. New views of the subject were being presented to my mind." - Frederick Douglass, My Bondage and My Freedom, 1855

"The strong man is the man who can stand up for his rights and not hit back." - Martin Luther King, Jr., c. 1967

Thoughts for the day ~ "Do not wish to be anything but what you are, and try to be that perfectly." - St. Francis de Sales

"Success is the sum of small efforts, repeated day in and day out." - Robert J. Collier

Thoughts for the day ~ "Everyone who reads the health pages already knows there is a strong and definite link between stress and illness, so it follows that if you're not stressed - in other words, if you are happy and relaxed, you will be healthier." - Angel Greene - Health

"The legacy of heroes is the memory of a great name and the inheritance of a great example." - Benjamin Disraeli - Memory

Thoughts for the day ~ "But I still firmly believe that a little humor goes a long way in life. We need to not only be able to laugh at ourselves, but to take a deep breath when we get far too serious far too often." - Byron Pulsifer - Humor

"Every day is a new beginning. Treat it that way. . . . Stay away from what might have been, and look at what can be." - Marsha Petrie Sue - New Beginnings

Thoughts for the day ~ "I am more and more convinced that our happiness or our unhappiness depends far more on the way we meet the events of life than on the nature of those events themselves." - Wilhelm von Humboldt

The world cares very little about what a man or woman knows; it is what a man or woman is able to do that counts.

Thoughts for the day ~ "All life is interrelated. The agony of the poor impoverishes the rich; the betterment of the poor enriches the rich. We are inevitably our brother's keeper because we are our brother's brother. Whatever affects one directly affects all indirectly." - Martin Luther King, Jr., Where Do We Go From Here? 1968

"Encouragement to others is something everyone can give." Joel Osteen - Word of Encouragement

Thoughts for the day ~ "You know I learned a long time ago that you can't make it by yourself in this world. You need friends; you need somebody to pat you on the back; you need somebody to give you consolation in the darkest hours." - Martin Luther King Jr.

"Not only will we have to repent for the sins of bad people; but we also will have to repent for the appalling silence of good people." Martin Luther King Jr. -

Thoughts for the day ~ "Let it be thoroughly understood that our deceased brother did not embrace nonviolence out of fear or cowardice. Moral courage was his noblest virtue. - Benjamin Mays, eulogy of Martin Luther King, Jr. - Atlanta, Georgia 9 April 1968

"I have a dream that my four little children will one day live in a nation where they will not be judged by the color of their skin but by the content of their character." - Martin Luther King, Jr. - I Have A Dream

Thoughts for the day ~ "Thoughts lead on to purposes; purposes go forth in action; actions form habits; habits decide character; and character fixes our destiny." - Tyron Edwards - Destiny

"And don't forget in doing something for others that you have what you have because of others. Don't forget that. We are tied together in life and in the world. And you may think you got all you got by yourself." - Martin Luther King, Jr. - The Three Dimensions Of A Complete Life

Thoughts for the day ~ "All the energy, emotions, and hard work driving towards one goal you FULLY believe in - something you feel is entirely worth the efforts - then it becomes a reality." - Andrew Wright Sr. Confidence: Comfortable in My Shoes - Effort

Sometimes your joy is the source of your smile, but sometimes your smile can be the source of your joy." - Thich Nhat Hanh - Joy

Thoughts for the day ~ "In life what you sow is what you reap, don't expect to reap apple when you sow mango, and if you sow nothing you will reap nothing." Jide Adeniba, You Can Have it if You Really Want it

"Part of life is understanding that real change and progress comes with dedicated perseverance but also realizing that challenges, obstacles and roadblocks will appear from time to time." - Robert Rivers, Happiness is Possible

"The acceptable year of the Lord is any year when men decide to do right. The acceptable year of the Lord is any year when men will stop lying and cheating. The acceptable year of the Lord is that year when women will start using the telephone for constructive purposes and not to spread malicious gossip and false rumors on their neighbors. The acceptable year of the Lord is any year when men will stop throwing away the precious lives that God has given them in riotous living." - Martin Luther King, Jr. Guidelines for a Constructive Church

Thought for the day ~ "Before you make a life changing decision, think on it for 24 hours." - Patricia Akins, Things They Don't Teach You In High School: But You Need To Know! - Graduation

"Those moments when you woke up inspired or had a 'light bulb' come on - that is your intuition." - Michael Henson, Morning Routine - Wisdom

Today's Daily Inspiration

Others cannot make you angry or upset unless you give them this power. Lord, strengthen my ability to know that how I feel is my choice and help me respond in ways that make me a happier person.

Today's Daily Inspiration

The more frantic we feel on the inside, the more compulsive we try to organize the outside. Lord, help me bring peace and order to my inner spirit by letting go of the past, bring resolution to the issues that are pressing and making a commitment to enjoy my life right now.

Random Daily Inspiration

God is better to us than we deserve. Lord, thank you for the strength You give in my trials and especially thank you for the trials You have kept from my door.

Extra Dose

The moment of absolute certainty over decisions made never arrives, so make your decision and move on. Lord, grant me wisdom and confidence in making my choices and the ability to recognize when new decisions need to be made.

Random Daily Inspiration

With our blessings come responsibilities. Much is required of those to whom much has been given. Lord, may I use my blessings to be a blessing to others.

Extra Dose

God not only answers prayer, but He has all the answers to the prayers that we haven't bothered to ask. Lord, when you said "ask and you shall receive", may I keep in mind that no request is too small. "I'm Incredible. . . . . ..Find Your Incredible. . .. . ..Don't Waste No More Time"

Today's Daily Inspiration

When something bothers or upsets you, you can either complain about it or make peace with it. Lord, help me promptly deal with the distractions of my day and move on to the things that truly make my day a pleasure.

Random Daily Inspiration

Deal with the shortcomings of those around you as gently as you would your own. Lord, help me to treat others as I want to be treated.

Extra Dose

Imagine that you were paid for every kindness and charged for every unkindness. Would you be rich or poor? Lord, I often pray for material wealth. Let me not neglect my soul by now praying for the ability to build my spiritual wealth also.

Today's Daily Inspiration

Good is always coming to you. No matter what is happening in your life, you can bless it with prayer and be peaceful. Lord, You give me the courage to face any situation confidently and victoriously.

Random Daily Inspiration

It is good to know where you are, but better to know where you are going. Lord, may I use every day to grow closer to You.

Extra Dose

Enjoy God. Lord, I hand over all of my cares to You so that for this moment I am peacefully free.

Today's Daily Inspiration

If you are too easily offended and become upset too quickly, you are taking life far too seriously. Lord, help me avoid looking for things to complain about.

Random Daily Inspiration

Most of us never set our sights as high as Jesus intended we should. Lord, may the celebration of Your birth serve as a rebirth within me of my sense of commitment, consecration and purpose.

Today's Daily Inspiration

It is very humbling to realize that often what burdens us the most would be very missed if it were taken away. Lord, I will take the time to appreciate my life.

Random Daily Inspiration

God's generosity can never be exceeded and, in the most unlikely ways and places, we always receive more than we give. Lord, may I always be a giving person with my time, my love and my blessings.

Extra Dose

If you are waiting to be happy, you never will be. Lord, the only moment that I can count on and be in charge of is right now. Help me choose to be happy.

Extra Dose

Prayer may not always change a situation, but it will always change us. Lord, I accept Your answers to my prayers because I know that they will always be right and, in Your wisdom, best for me.

Today's Daily Inspiration

"No matter what faces me today, Lord, let me not spend my time pondering life, but rather living it. I have the opportunities of this day now. I may not get them again.

Random Daily Inspiration

"Lord, I ask You for new strength and new courage for this new day.

Extra Dose

"May my activities reflect Your love for me, my God. May I see Your blessings.

Today's Daily Inspiration

Imagine joy and you will find it. Lord, I thank You for the people that need me and love me, for the ability to hope and especially for the ability to love.

Today's Daily Inspiration

When someone makes you happy, let them know and you will both feel better. Lord, may Your love flow through me so that I can easily praise and encourage the goodness in others.

Extra Dose

God will never fail you or abandon you. Lord, I am sure that everything that happens is for the purpose of strengthening me and bringing me closer to You. I trust in You to continually bless me with all that I need to successfully handle my circumstances.

> "I can do all things through Christ who strengths me."
>
> Philippians 4:13

Today's Daily Inspiration

Each day guide your thoughts and actions so that you may set God's will above your own. Lord, may Your will be my will.

Random Daily Inspiration

It is better to try and fail than to fail because you are afraid to try. Lord, grant me the courage to live my life to the fullest.

Extra Dose

To be completely at peace, avoid hurting anyone for any reason. Lord, I will act with kindness and when others are hurtful to me, I will focus on Your presence within them to give me courage to respond gently.

Extra Dose

- Many more things go right in a day than go wrong, but you will never notice if that one trying moment becomes your focus. Lord, help me make a conscious effort to see the richness of my life and live with gratitude for all of its wonders.

Today's Daily Inspiration

"Today, Lord, keep my heart open to the needs of others. Let me see the wonders of faith in the most unlikely places."

Random Daily Inspiration

"Lord, today grant me enough courage and faith in You to overcome any adversity that comes my way."

Extra Dose

"Speak to God as you would your closest friend. Ask Him from your heart for what you want. And believe. Lord, let my faith in You never waiver."

Thoughts for the day ~ "Achieving a big goal is often similar to driving in a thick fog because when you move towards your goal, you don't need to know the entire way but you just need to know how take the next step." - Andrii Sedniev, The Achievement Factory: How to Fulfill Your Dreams and Make Life an Adventure

Thoughts for the day ~ "Many of the people who achieve the greatest successes, and who really feel fulfilled and satisfied with their lives, are those who have come from the most challenging circumstances or have faced the most adversity." - Grant Andrews, The Life of Your Dreams - Greatness

"Unless commitment is made, there are only promises and hopes; but no plans." - Peter F. Drucker - Commitment

Thoughts for the day ~ "I've learned that education, experience, and memories are three things that no one can take away from you." - H. Jackson Brown, Jr. - Memory

"People become really quite remarkable when they start thinking that they can do things. When they believe in themselves they have the first secret of success." - Norman Vincent Peale - New Beginnings

Thoughts for the day ~ "We must strive to live with purpose. When we live with purpose, we feel good inside." - Brenda Nathan, Gratitude Journal: A Daily Appreciation

"We who in engage in nonviolent direct action are not the creators of tension. We merely bring the surface the hidden tension that is already alive." - Martin Luther King, Jr. - Stress

"Like the ever-flowing waters of the river, life has its moments of drought and its moments of flood. Like the ever-changing cycle of the seasons, life has the soothing warmth of its summers and the piercing chill of its winters. And if one will hold on, he will discover that God walks with him and that God is able to lift you from the fatigue of despair to the buoyancy of hope, and transform dark and desolate valleys into sunlit paths of inner peace." - Rev. Martin Luther King., Eulogy for the Martyred Children - Life

"When you worry, you go over the same ground endlessly and come out the same place you started. Thinking makes progress from one place to another; worry remains static." - Harold B. Walker - Worry

"Let God into Your daily routine and help you solve your problems." - Ben Lance, Prayer: 81 Powerful Prayers for Connecting with God Everyday - Problem

Everybody Isn't gonna LOVE YOU . . . Most People Don't Even Love Themselves.

I can. I will. End of Story!

"You always do what you want to do. This is true with every act. You may say that you had to do something, or that you were forced to, but actually, whatever you do, you do by choice. Only you have the power to choose for yourself. - W. Clement Stone

"The secret of genius is to carry the spirit of the child into old age, which means never losing your enthusiasm." - Aldous Huxley

Today's Daily Inspiration

Complaining reinforces your own unhappiness. Lord, when I speak, help to say things that are worth listening to and reinforce a joyful spirit.

Random Daily Inspiration

Open your mind and empty your heart of fears so that you can know and experience God to the fullest. Lord, You are my peace, my assurance and the love that I hold on to.

Extra Dose

"For every beauty there is an eye somewhere to see it. For every truth there is an ear somewhere to hear it. For every love there is a heart somewhere to receive it."
—Ivan Panin

Today's Daily Inspiration

As you wake, remember that God is the first one waiting to talk with you. Good morning, Lord. Let's have a grand and wonderful day.

Random Daily Inspiration

We learn to trust in God through our trials and problems. Lord, let me use the suffering in my life as an opportunity to strengthen my faith.

"Something to think about & remember"

Psa. 77:11 I recall all you have done, O LORD; I remember your wonderful deeds of long ago. New Literal Translation

Has God ever let you down? Are you blaming God for a situation that you got yourself into? Well, let me assure you that God will never let you down. Even when we don't deserve it he comes through for us. So, what you must do in trying times is think back on all the times you thought there was no way out. You survived!! You even got so far out of it that you forgot it. Yep, you forgot it and now are feeling like there is no way out of this, right? Well, just remember God has always come through for you. Had he not, you would be somewhere busted, on the streets, without food or shelter, or in a cemetery! The mere fact that you are using email to read this says that, God has blessed you to provide for yourself and live better than many!!

People pay for what they do, and still more for what they have allowed themselves to become. And they pay for it very simply; by the lives they lead.

-James Baldwin

Extra Dose

Random Daily Inspiration
Be a patient person, but most of all, be patient with yourself. Lord may I be blessed with a calm spirit and diligence as I do my work today.

Extra Dose
Be a blessing to someone today with a smile, or hug, or gifts are whatever you can do but be a blessing!!! You never know that someone else is going through!

Random Daily Inspiration
Get and keep a good humored attitude toward life. This will bring you support rather than opposition. Lord, may I always be a peacemaker.

Extra Dose
> HAPPINESS KEEPS YOU SWEET
> TRIALS KEEP YOU STRONG
> AND SORROWS KEEP YOU HUMAN
> FAILURES KEEP YOU HUMBLE
> SUCCESS KEEPS YOU GLOWING
> BUT ONLY GOD KEEPS YOU GOING!

Today's Daily Inspiration
Don't worry about tomorrow because God is already taking care of it. Lord, help me set aside needless worry and anxiety so that I have time to do all that I need to do today.

Random Daily Inspiration
In your search for peace, look within. If you are looking elsewhere, you are looking in the wrong place. Lord, help me to open my heart to Your gift of peace and refuse to let anything in that disturbs it.

Extra Dose
Forgiveness frees the heart and moves us from the victim to the one who is in control of our lives. Lord, forgive us our trespasses as we forgive those who trespass against us.

Extra Dose
> *The Lord restored the fortunes of Job when he prayed for his friends, and the Lord increased all that Job had twofold.*
>
> *- Job 42:10 -*

If you are familiar with the story of Job, you will recall that Job's friends were not that friendly to him at all. In fact, when Job was at the worst of times, his friends judged, griped, criticized, accused and more. For Job, praying "for his friends" involved a lot more than asking God to bless those he loved and considered dear. It involved a significant amount of forgiveness, acceptance, humility and love. It also involved faith.

It wasn't until after Job showed grace and kindness to those who had brought him pain during his greatest moments of pain that God restored him. This is because Job had obeyed the law of love and asked God to give His goodness to others. When Job did that, God gave goodness to Job as well.

Learning to wait well with patience involves learning how to put into practice the regularity of living as a child of God. It means putting into practice those things we already know.

    Forgiving.
    Loving.
    Believing.

Working as unto the Lord, even if it's not your favorite place to work. Honoring the authority over you, even if you don't particularly like or respect that authority. Bearing with one another's burdens, even when you feel weighted down by your own.

Do what God has already said to do. Then watch Him usher you straight out of your detour and into your destiny.

Thoughts for the day ~ "Let us move on in these powerful days, these days of challenge to make America what it ought to be. We have an opportunity to make America a better nation." - Martin Luther King, Jr., " I Have Been to the Mountain top," speech given in Memphis, Tennessee, 3 April 1968

"Prejudice is like a hair across your cheek. You can't see it, you can't find it with your fingers, but you keep brushing at it because the feel of it is irritating." - Marian Anderson, c. 1966

Thoughts for the day ~ "You can choose courage or you can choose comfort, but you cannot choose both." - Brene Brown

You can be smart in one way, but there's a different type of smart that you need if you're going to be a great leader.

Thoughts for the day ~ "Perfection is not attainable, but if we chase perfection we can catch excellence." - Vince Lombardi

No matter how hard life gets.. remember to go to bed grateful that you have one.

Thoughts for the day ~ "The best way for us to perhaps influence others is to instead focus on ourselves by doing our best - then others will be influenced from our leadership by example." - Lisa Kardos, Optimize for Victory

"When you feel your purpose calling you, the most important thing you can do is move your feet and start moving in the direction of your calling." - Marilyn Atkinson; Rae Chois, The Art and Science of Coaching - Purpose

Random Daily Inspiration

The source of courage is having a deep sense of God's presence and hearing Him say, "I am with you always." Lord, You are my solution. You are with me always giving me all that I need.

Extra Dose

When you need to calm your emotions, stop and turn to God. Lord, I know that You are my help right now and will show me simple answers to what seems complicated and impossible.

Appendix B

Anti-Discrimination Position Statement

NAEYC's Anti-Discrimination Positon Statement - Revised July 2009

NAEYCs first commitment is to the rights and interests of all children. In that regard, NAEYC believes that individuals in the early childhood field should be hired, employed, promoted, and if necessary, terminated based solely on their competence and qualifications to perform their designated duties, and not on the basis of their gender, race, color, national origin, religious beliefs, age, marital status/family structure (including same sex unions or domestic partnerships), disability, sexual orientation, or any basis prohibited by law.

Anti-Discrimination Policy (1988; 1994)

At the March 1994 Governing Board meeting, the Board adopted the following Antidiscrimination Policy:

NAEYC's first commitment is to the rights and interests of all children. In that regard, NAEYC believes that individuals in the early childhood field should be hired, employed, promoted, and if necessary, terminated based solely on their competence and qualifications to perform their designated duties, and not on the basis of their gender, race, national origin, religious beliefs, age, marital status, disability, or sexual orientation.

Statement about Proposition 187 & NAEYC's Code of Ethical Conduct (1994)

The NAEYC Governing Board adopted the following resolution in response to Proposition 187 that was approved by California voters in the November 1994 elections:

NAEYC opposes any aspect of Proposition 187 that would require those who work with children and families to act in opposition to NAEYC's Code of Ethical Conduct. Similar initiatives—that would cause educators, doctors and nurses to deny services to children or to report undocumented individuals—are being considered in other states. NAEYC's Code of Ethical Conduct can serve as a helpful resource for debate about such proposals.

Where We STAND
naeyc

On Child Abuse Prevention

As the nation's largest organization of early childhood professionals and others dedicated to improving the quality of early childhood programs, the National Association for the Education of Young Children (NAEYC) is committed to safeguarding the well-being of all children. NAEYC recognizes that early childhood professionals and programs play an important role in preventing—not just reporting—child abuse and neglect.

NAEYC's position statements "Prevention of Child Abuse in Early Childhood Programs and the Responsibilities of Early Childhood Professionals to Prevent Child Abuse" (1996) and "Code of Ethical Conduct and Statement of Commitment" (2005) and other NAEYC publications clearly outline that early childhood programs and professionals should:

1. Adopt policies and practices that promote close partnerships with families.
2. Promote standards of excellence for early childhood programs.
3. Provide families a variety of supportive services.
4. Advocate for children, families, and teachers in community and society.
5. Collaborate with other professionals in the community.
6. Understand their legal and ethical obligation to recognize and report suspicions of abuse.

1. Adopt policies and practices that promote close partnerships with families. Close partnerships with families can reduce the potential for child abuse by family members. Early childhood programs can provide information and support to families regarding child development and effective strategies for responding to children's challenging behavior (NAEYC 1996; Olson & Hyson 2003). Communicating with families, especially about difficult topics, is crucial if educators are to provide support to families. This kind of communication is much easier when a supportive, reciprocal relationship already exists. Early childhood professionals should also:

- acknowledge and build upon family strengths and competencies;
- respect the dignity of each family and its culture, language, customs, and beliefs;
- help families understand and appreciate each child's progress within a developmental perspective;
- help family members enhance their parenting skills; and
- build support networks for families by providing opportunities for interaction with program staff, other families, community resources, and professional services (NAEYC 2005).

Scope of the Problem

- In 2007, almost 800,000 children were victims of *maltreatment*—various forms of abuse and neglect. Maltreatment causes stress that can disrupt early brain development.
- Children who have been abused are at higher risk for health problems as adults, including depression, eating disorders, alcoholism, and certain chronic diseases.
- Children of all races and ethnicities experience child abuse.
- Children of all ages experience abuse, but children under 4 are at greatest risk for severe injury and death from abuse.
- Most abuse happens within families, especially families in which there is a great deal of stress.

(CDC 2009)

---

2. Promote standards of excellence for early childhood programs. High-quality care and education helps to strengthen families and promote healthy social and emotional development, as well as preparing children for later school success. Programs should use developmentally appropriate practices and pursue NAEYC Accreditation, which requires a rigorous self-study process and an independent external assessment to determine whether high standards are met. Early childhood professionals should also inform the public about the need for and benefits of high-quality early childhood programs (NAEYC 1996).

3. **Provide a variety of supportive services to families.** In addition to knowing the signs of abuse and neglect, early childhood professionals should be able to recognize situations that may place children at risk. When working with families who are in those situations, professionals should provide appropriate information and referrals to community services and follow up to ensure that services have been provided (NAEYC 1996, 2005). Families' access to health care, housing, income support, and other social services may help protect children from abuse and neglect.

> **Families, Early Childhood Programs, and Child Abuse Prevention**
>
> Early childhood programs are in an excellent position to connect families of young children with supports that can prevent abuse and promote positive interactions. *Supporting Teachers, Strengthening Families,* an NAEYC child abuse prevention initiative, received generous support from 2002–2008 from the Doris Duke Charitable Foundation. Project resources may be downloaded at www.naeyc.org/ecp/trainings/stsf.
>
> Another initiative with a similar focus is the Center for the Study of Social Policy's *Strengthening Families Through Early Care and Education,* emphasizing how early childhood programs can build "protective factors" to prevent maltreatment, online at www.strengtheningfamilies.net/self_assessment.

4. **Advocate for children, families, and teachers in community and society.** Early childhood educators, as individuals and as a profession, should participate in the policy-making process by:

- advocating for well-designed, sufficiently funded, and effectively implemented public regulations, programs, and community support services that meet the individual needs of children and families and promote their well-being;
- cooperating with other individuals and groups in advocacy efforts; and
- opposing policies that impair child and family well-being (NAEYC 2005).

5. **Collaborate with other professionals in the community.** The early childhood community should work with other professionals concerned with the welfare of young children and families (NAEYC 2005). Collaboration with other agencies and disciplines promotes understanding of child development, supports and empowers families, and strengthens advocacy efforts (NAEYC 1996).

6. **Understand their legal and ethical obligation to recognize and report suspicions of abuse.** Early childhood professionals should:

- be familiar with the symptoms of child abuse and neglect, including physical, sexual, verbal, and emotional abuse;
- know and follow state laws and community procedures that protect children against abuse and neglect; and
- report suspected child abuse or neglect to the appropriate community agency and follow up to ensure that appropriate action has been taken. When appropriate, educators should inform parents or guardians that a referral has been made (NAEYC 2005).

References

CDC (Centers for Disease Control). 2009. *Understanding child maltreatment: Factsheet.* Online: www.cdc.gov/violenceprevention/pdf/CM-FactSheet-a.pdf.

NAEYC. 1996. *Prevention of child abuse in early childhood programs and the responsibilities of early childhood professionals to prevent child abuse.* Position statement. Online: www.naeyc.org/position-statements/prevention.

NAEYC. 2005. *Code of ethical conduct and statement of commitment.* Rev. ed. Washington, DC: Author. Online: www.naeyc.org/position-statements/ethical_conduct.

Olson, M., & M. Hyson. 2003. *Early childhood educators and child abuse prevention: Perspective, findings, actions.* Washington, DC: NAEYC. Online: www.naeyc.org/files/naeyc/file/ecprofessional/ECAandCAPReport.pdf

Early Childhood Inclusion: A Summary

Background

Today an ever-increasing number of infants and young children with and without disabilities play and learn together in a variety of places—homes, early childhood programs, and neighborhoods, to name a few. Promoting development and belonging for every child is a widely held value among early education and intervention professionals and throughout our society. Early childhood inclusion is the term used to reflect these values and societal views. However, the lack of a shared national definition has created some misunderstandings about inclusion. The DEC/NAEYC joint position statement offers a definition of inclusion. It also includes recommendations for how the joint position statement can be used to improve early childhood services for all children.

Definition of Early Childhood Inclusion

Early childhood inclusion embodies the values, policies, and practices that support the right of every infant and young child and his or her family, regardless of ability, to participate in a broad range of activities and contexts as full members of families, communities, and society. The desired results of inclusive experiences for children with and without disabilities and their families include a sense of belonging and membership, positive social relationships and friendships, and development and learning to reach their full potential. The defining features of inclusion that can be used to identify high quality early childhood programs and services are access, participation, and supports.

What is meant by Access, Participation, and Supports?

Access – means providing a wide range of activities and environments for every child by removing physical barriers and offering multiple ways to promote learning and development.
Participation – means using a range of instructional approaches to promote engagement in play and learning activities, and a sense of belonging for every child.
Supports – refer to broader aspects of the system such as professional development, incentives for inclusion, and opportunities for communication and collaboration among families and professionals to assure high quality inclusion.

Recommendations for Using this Position Statement to Improve Early Childhood Services

The following recommendations describe how the joint position statement can be used by families and professionals to shape practices and influence policies related to inclusion.

1. Create high expectations for every child, regardless of ability, to reach his or her full potential.
2. Develop a program philosophy on inclusion to ensure shared assumptions and beliefs about inclusion, and to identify quality inclusive practices.
3. Establish a system of services and supports that reflects the needs of children with varying types of disabilities and learning characteristics, with inclusion as the driving principle and foundation for all of these services and supports.
4. Revise program and professional standards to incorporate key dimensions of high quality inclusion.
5. Improve professional development across all sectors of the early childhood field by determining the following: who would benefit from professional development on inclusion; what practitioners

need to know and be able to do in inclusive settings; and what methods are needed to facilitate learning opportunities related to inclusion.
6. Revise federal and state accountability systems to reflect both the need to increase the number of children with disabilities enrolled in inclusive programs as well as to improve the quality and outcomes of inclusion.

Suggested Citation

DEC/NAEYC. (2009). *Early childhood inclusion: A summary.* Chapel Hill: The University of North Carolina, FPG Child Development Institute.

Summary Drawn from

DEC/NAEYC. (2009). *Early childhood inclusion: A joint position statement of the Division for Early Childhood (DEC) and the National Association for the Education of Young Children (NAEYC).* Chapel Hill: The University of North Carolina, FPG Child Development Institute.

Source

http://community.fpg.unc.edu/resources/articles/Early_Childhood_Inclusion_Summary

Where We STAND
naeyc and naecs/sde

On Early Learning Standards

Early learning standards define the desired outcomes and content of young children's education. Most states have developed such standards for children below kindergarten age.

The National Association for the Education of Young Children (NAEYC) and the National Association of Early Childhood Specialists in State Departments of Education (NAECS/SDE) believe that *early learning standards can be a valuable part of a comprehensive, high-quality system of services for young children.* But we caution that early learning standards support positive development and learning *only* if they:

- emphasize significant, developmentally appropriate content and outcomes;
- are developed and reviewed through informed, inclusive processes;
- are implemented and assessed in ways that support all young children's development; and
- are accompanied by strong supports for early childhood programs, professionals, and families.

Beyond Early Learning Standards: What Else Matters?

Early learning standards gain power only if they are connected to other essential ingredients of high-quality early childhood education. *Learn more about...*

- recommendations for early childhood curriculum, assessment, and program evaluation. See NAEYC and NAECS/SDE's 2003 position statement, online at www.naeyc.org/positionstatements/cape.
- teaching strategies and other elements of developmentally appropriate practice. See C. Copple & S. Bredekamp (eds.), *Developmentally Appropriate Practice in Early Childhood Programs Serving Children from Birth through Age 8*, 3d ed., Washington, DC: NAEYC, 2009. Access the position statement online at www.naeyc.org/positionstatements/dap.
- standards for early childhood programs and accreditation performance criteria, online at www.naeyc.org/academy/primary/standardsintro.
- standards for early childhood professional preparation programs as updated by NAEYC in 2009, online at www.naeyc.org/positionstatements/ppp.
- implementation of professional standards. See M. Hyson (ed.), *Preparing Early Childhood Professionals: NAEYC's Standards for Programs*, Washington, DC: NAEYC, 2003.

These four elements are described in detail in "Early Learning Standards: Creating the Conditions for Success," a joint position statement of NAEYC and NAECS/SDE (online at **www.naeyc.org/positionstatements/learning_standards**). They are discussed briefly below.

1. **Effective early learning standards emphasize significant, developmentally appropriate content and outcomes.**

- All areas of early development and learning (including cognitive, language, physical, social, and emotional) are emphasized in the standards.
- The content and desired outcomes are meaningful and important to children's current well-being and later learning.
- Early learning standards are not merely scaled-back versions of standards for older children. Instead, the standards are based on research about the processes, sequences, and long-term outcomes of early learning and development.
- Standards are linked to specific ages or developmental periods to ensure that the expectations are appropriate.
- Standards recognize and accommodate variations in children's cultures, languages, communities, and individual characteristics, abilities, and disabilities. This flexibility supports positive outcomes for *all* children.

2. **Effective early learning standards are developed and reviewed through informed, inclusive processes.**
   - Relevant, valid sources of expertise are called on to help develop and review the standards.
   - Multiple stakeholders are involved—community members, families, early childhood educators and special educators, and other professional groups.
   - Once the standards are developed, they are shared and discussed with all stakeholders.
   - Early learning standards are regularly reviewed and revised so they remain relevant and evidence-based.
3. **Effective early learning standards are implemented and assessed in ways that support all young children's development.**
   - Curriculum, classroom practices, and teaching strategies support the standards by connecting with young children's interests and abilities to promote positive development and learning.
   - Assessment instruments are clearly connected to important learning represented in the standards; are technically, developmentally, and culturally valid; and provide information that is comprehensive and useful.
   - Information gained from assessments must benefit children. Assessment and accountability systems should improve practices and services and should not be used to rank, sort, or penalize young children.
4. **Effective early learning standards require a foundation of support for early childhood programs, professionals, and families.**
   - Evidence-based program standards and adequate resources for high-quality programs create environments in which standards can be implemented effectively.
   - Significant expansion of professional development is essential to help early childhood teachers and administrators implement the standards.
   - Standards have the most positive effects if they are accompanied by respectful family communication and support.

Early Learning Standards in the States

The National Child Care Information Center (NCCIC) maintains an up-to-date record of the status of state early learning guidelines, with links to each state's website. Visit http://nccic.acf.hhs.gov/pubs/good-start/elgwebsites.html.

A survey of states' development and implementation of early learning standards (C. Scott-Little, J. Lesko, J. Martella, & P. Milburn, "Early Learning Standards: Results from a National Survey to Document Trends in State-Level Policies and Practices," *Early Childhood Research and Practice* 9(1), 2007, revealed that:
- almost every state had developed early learning standards for prekindergarten-age children;
- 14 states had completed infant/toddler standards as of June 2006, and 8 more were in the process of developing such standards;
- almost half of the states had some process to monitor programs' use of early learning standards; and
- compared with the results of earlier surveys, more states have provided guidance about how to use the standards with children who have disabilities or with culturally and linguistically diverse children.

Issues remain about the content of early learning standards, appropriate uses of the standards, and alignment with curriculum and K–12 learning standards. The paper, including the survey instrument, is online at http://ecrp.uiuc.edu/v9nl/little.html.

Responding to Linguistic and Cultural Diversity Recommendations for Effective Early Childhood Education

A position statement of the National Association for the Education of Young Children

Adopted November 1995

Linguistically and culturally diverse is an educational term used by the U.S. Department of Education to define children enrolled in educational programs who are either non-English-proficient (NEP) or limited-English-proficient (LEP). Educators use this phrase, linguistically and culturally diverse, to identify children from homes and communities where English is not the primary language of communication (Garciá 1991). For the purposes of this statement, the phrase will be used in a similar manner.

This document primarily describes linguistically and culturally diverse children who speak languages other than English. However, the recommendations of this position statement can also apply to children who, although they speak only English, are also linguistically and culturally diverse.

Introduction

The children and families served in early childhood programs reflect the ethnic, cultural, and linguistic diversity of the nation. The nation's children all deserve an early childhood education that is responsive to their families, communities, and racial, ethnic, and cultural backgrounds. For young children to develop and learn optimally, the early childhood professional must be prepared to meet their diverse developmental, cultural, linguistic, and educational needs. Early childhood educators face the challenge of how best to respond to these needs.

The acquisition of language is essential to children's cognitive and social development. Regardless of what language children speak, they still develop and learn. Educators recognize that linguistically and culturally diverse children come to early childhood programs with previously acquired knowledge and learning based upon the language used in their home. For young children, the language of the home is the language they have used since birth, the language they use to make and establish meaningful communicative relationships, and the language they use to begin to construct their knowledge and test their learning. The home language is tied to children's culture, and culture and language communicate traditions, values, and attitudes (Chang 1993). Parents should be encouraged to use and develop children's home language; early childhood educators should respect children's linguistic and cultural backgrounds and their diverse learning styles. In so doing, adults will enhance children's learning and development.

Just as children learn and develop at different rates, individual differences exist in how children whose home language is not English acquire English. For example, some children may experience a silent period (of six or more months) while they acquire English; other children may practice their knowledge by mixing or combining languages (for example, "Mi mamá me put on mi coat"); still other children may seem to have acquired English-language skills (appropriate accent, use of vernacular, vocabulary, and grammatical rules) but are not truly proficient; yet some children will quickly acquire English-language proficiency. Each child's way of learning a new language should be viewed as acceptable, logical, and part of the ongoing development and learning of any new language.

Defining the Problem

At younger and younger ages, children are negotiating difficult transitions between their home and educational settings, requiring an adaptation to two or more diverse sets of rules, values, expectations, and behaviors. Educational programs and families must *respect* and *reinforce* each other as they work together to achieve the greatest benefit for all children. For some young children, entering any new environment—including early childhood programs—can be intimidating. The lives of many young children today are further complicated by having to communicate and learn in a language that may be unfamiliar. In the past, children entering U.S. schools from families whose home language is not English were expected to immerse themselves in the mainstream of schools, primarily through the use of English (Soto 1991; Wong Fillmore 1991). Sometimes the negative attitudes conveyed or expressed toward certain languages lead children to "give up" their home language. Early childhood professionals must recognize the feeling of loneliness, fear, and abandonment children may feel when they are thrust into settings that isolate them from their home community and language. The loss of children's home language may result **in the disruption of family communication patterns, which may lead to the loss of intergenerational wisdom; damage to individual and community esteem; and children's potential nonmastery of their home language or English.**

NAEYC's Position

NAEYC's goal is to build support for equal access to high-quality educational programs that recognize and promote all aspects of children's development and learning, enabling all children to become competent, successful, and socially responsible adults. Children's educational experiences should afford them the opportunity to learn and to become effective, functioning members of society. Language development is essential for learning, and the development of children's home language does not interfere with their ability to learn English. Because knowing more than one language is a cognitive asset (Hakuta & García 1989), early education programs should encourage the development of children's home language while fostering the acquisition of English.

For the optimal development and learning of all children, educators must **accept** the legitimacy of children's home language, **respect** (hold in high regard) and **value** (esteem, appreciate) the home culture, and **promote** and **encourage** the active involvement and support of all families, including extended and nontraditional family units.

When early childhood educators acknowledge and respect children's home language and culture, ties between the family and programs are strengthened. This atmosphere provides increased opportunity for learning because young children feel supported, nurtured, and connected not only to their home communities and families but also to teachers and the educational setting.

The Challenges

The United States is a nation of great cultural diversity, and our diversity creates opportunities to learn and share both similar and different experiences. There are opportunities to learn about people from different backgrounds; the opportunity to foster a bilingual citizenry with skills necessary to succeed in a global economy; and opportunities to share one's own cherished heritage and traditions with others.

Historically, our nation has tended to regard differences, especially language differences, as cultural handicaps rather than cultural resources (Meier & Cazden 1982). "Although most Americans are reluctant to say it publicly, many are anxious about the changing racial and ethnic composition of the country" (Sharry 1994). As the early childhood profession transforms its thinking,

> The challenge for early childhood educators is to become more knowledgeable about how to relate to children and families whose linguistic or cultural background is different from their own.

Between 1979 and 1989 the number of children in the United States from culturally and linguistically diverse backgrounds increased considerably (NCES 1993), and, according to a report released by the Center for the Study of Social Policy (1992), that diversity is even more pronounced among children younger than age 6. Contrary to popular belief, many of these children are neither foreign born nor immigrants but were born in the United States (Waggoner 1993). Approximately 9.9 million of the estimated 45 million school-age children, more than one in five, live in households in which languages other than English are spoken (Waggoner 1994). In some communities, however, the number of children living in a family in which a language other than English is spoken is likely to be much larger. Head Start reports that the largest number of linguistically and culturally diverse children served through Head Start are Spanish speakers, with other language groups representing smaller but growing percentages (Head Start Bureau 1995).

> The challenge for teachers is to provide high-quality care and education for the increasing number of children who are likely to be linguistically and culturally diverse.

Families and communities are faced with increasingly complex responsibilities. Children used to be cared for by parents and family members who typically spoke the home language of their family, be it English or another language. With the increasing need of family members to work, even while children are very young, more and more children are placed in care and educational settings with adults who may not speak the child's home language or share their cultural background. Even so, children will spend an ever-increasing amount of their waking lives with these teachers. What happens in care will have a tremendous impact on the child's social, emotional, and cognitive development. These interactions will influence the child's values, view of the world, perspectives on family, and connections to community. This places a tremendous responsibility in the hands of the early childhood community.

Responding to linguistic and cultural diversity can be challenging. At times the challenges can be complicated further by the specific needs or issues of the child, the family, or the educational program. Solutions may not be evident. Individual circumstances can affect each situation differently. There are no easy answers, and often myths and misinformation may flourish. The challenges may even seem to be too numerous for any one teacher or provider to manage. Nonetheless, despite the complexity, it is the responsibility of all educators to assume the tasks and meet the challenges. Once a situation occurs, the early childhood educator should enter into a dialogue with colleagues, parents, and others in an effort to arrive at a negotiated agreement that will meet the best interest of the child. For example,

- A mother, father, and primary caregiver each have different cultural and linguistic backgrounds and do not speak English. Should the language of one of these persons be affirmed or respected above the others? How can the teacher affirm and respect the backgrounds of each of these individuals?
- The principal is concerned that all children learn English and, therefore, does not want any language other than English spoken in the early childhood setting. In the interest of the child, how should the educator respond?
- An educator questions whether a child will ever learn English if the home language is used as the primary language in the early childhood setting. How is this concern best addressed?

Solutions exist for each of these linguistic and cultural challenges, just as they do for the many other issues that early childhood educators confront within the early childhood setting. These challenges must be viewed as opportunities for the early childhood educator to reflect, question, and effectively respond to the needs of linguistically and culturally diverse children. Although appropriate responses to every linguistically and culturally diverse situation cannot be addressed through this document, early childhood educators should consider the following recommendations.

Recommendations for a Responsive Learning Environment

Early childhood educators should stop and reflect on the best ways to ensure appropriate educational and developmental experiences for all young children. The unique qualities and characteristics of each individual child must be acknowledged. Just as each child is different, methods and strategies to work with young children must vary.

The issue of home language and its importance to young children is also relevant for children who speak English but come from different cultural backgrounds, for example, speakers of English who have dialects, such as people from Appalachia or other regions having distinct patterns of speech, speakers of Black English, or second- and third-generation speakers of English who maintain the dominant accent of their heritage language. While this position statement basically responds to children who are from homes in which English is not the dominant language, the recommendations provided may be helpful when working with children who come from diverse cultural backgrounds, even when they only speak English. The overall goal for early childhood professionals, however, is to provide every child, including children who are linguistically and culturally diverse, with a responsive learning environment. The following recommendations help achieve this goal.

A. **Recommendations for working with children**

   Recognize that all children are cognitively, linguistically, and emotionally connected to the language and culture of their home.

   When program settings acknowledge and support children's home language and culture, ties between the family and school are strengthened. In a supportive atmosphere young children's home language is less likely to atrophy (Chang 1993), a situation that could threaten the children's important ties to family and community.

   Acknowledge that children can demonstrate their knowledge and capabilities in many ways.

   In response to linguistic and cultural diversity, the goal for early childhood educators should be to make the most of children's potential, strengthening and building upon the skills they bring when they enter programs. Education, as Cummins states, implies "drawing out children's potential and making them more than they were" (1989, vii). Educational programs and practices must recognize the strengths that children possess. Whatever language children speak, they should be able to demonstrate their capabilities and also feel the success of being appreciated and valued. Teachers must build upon children's diversity of gifts and skills and provide young children opportunities to exhibit these skills in early childhood programs.

   The learning environment must focus on the learner and allow opportunities for children to express themselves across the curriculum, including art, music, dramatization, and even block building. By using a nondeficit approach (tapping and recognizing children's strengths rather than focusing the child's home environment on skills yet unlearned) in their teaching, teachers should take the time to observe and engage children in a variety of learning activities. Children's strengths should be celebrated, and they should be given numerous ways to express their interests and talents. In doing this, teachers will provide children an opportunity to display their intellect and knowledge that may far exceed the boundaries of language.

   Understand that without comprehensible input, second-language learning can be difficult.

   It takes time to become linguistically proficient and competent in any language. Linguistically and culturally diverse children may be able to master basic communication skills; however, mastery of the more cognitively complex language skills needed for academic learning (Cummins 1989) is more dependent on the learning environment. Academic learning relies on significant amounts of information presented in decontextualized learning situations. Success in school becomes more and more difficult as children are required to learn, to be tested and evaluated based on ever-increasing amounts of information, consistently presented in a decontextualized manner. Children learn best when they are given a context in which to learn, and the knowledge that children acquire in "their first language can make second-language input much more comprehensible" (Krashen 1992, 37). Young children can gain knowledge more easily when they obtain quality instruction through their first language. Children can acquire the necessary language and cognitive skills required to succeed in school when given an appropriate learning environment, one that is tailored to meet their needs (NAEYC & NAECS/SDE 1991; Bredekamp & Rosegrant 1992).

Although verbal proficiency in a second language can be accomplished within two to three years, the skills necessary to achieve the higher level educational skills of understanding academic content through reading and writing may require four or more years (Cummins 1981; Collier 1989). Young children may seem to be fluent and at ease with English but may not be capable of understanding or expressing themselves as competently as their English-speaking peers. Although children seem to be speaking a second language with ease, *speaking* a language does not equate to being *proficient* in that language. Full proficiency in the first language, including complex uses of the language, contributes to the development of the second language. Children who do not become proficient in their second language after two or three years of regular use probably are not proficient in their first language either.

Young children may seem to be fluent and at ease speaking a second language, but they may not be fully capable of understanding or expressing themselves in the more complex aspects of language and may demonstrate weaknesses in language-learning skills, including vocabulary skills, auditory memory and discrimination skills, simple problem-solving tasks, and the ability to follow sequenced directions. Language difficulties such as these often can result in the linguistically and culturally diverse child being over referred to special education, classified as learning disabled, or perceived as developmentally delayed.

B. Recommendations for working with families

Actively involve parents and families in the early learning program and setting.

Parents and families should be actively involved in the learning and development of their children. Teachers should actively seek parental involvement and pursue establishing a partnership with children's families. When possible, teachers should visit the child's community (for example, shops, churches, and playgrounds); read and learn about the community through the use of books, pictures, observations, and conversations with community members; and visit the home and meet with other family members.

Parents and families should be invited to share, participate, and engage in activities with their children. Parent involvement can be accomplished in a number of ways, including asking parents to share stories, songs, drawings, and experiences of their linguistic and cultural background and asking parents to serve as monitors or field trip organizers. Families and parents should be invited to share activities that are developmentally appropriate and meaningful within their culture. These opportunities demonstrate to the parent what their child is learning; increase the knowledge, information, and understanding of all children regarding people of different cultures and linguistic backgrounds; and establish a meaningful relationship with the parent. The early childhood educator should ensure that parents are informed and engaged with their child in meaningful activities that promote linkages between the home and the early care setting.

Encourage and assist all parents in becoming knowledgeable about the cognitive value for children of knowing more than one language, and provide them with strategies to support, maintain, and preserve home-language learning.

In an early childhood setting and atmosphere in which home language is preserved, acknowledged, and respected, all parents can learn the value of home-language development and the strength it provides children as they add to their existing knowledge and understanding. Parents and teachers can learn how to become advocates regarding the long-term benefits that result from bilingualism.

Parents and teachers recognize the acquisition of English as an intellectual accomplishment, an opportunity for economic growth and development, and a means for achieving academic success. There are even times when parents may wish for the ability, or have been mistakenly encouraged, to speak to their children only in English, a language of which the parents themselves may not have command. The educator should understand the effects that speaking only in English can have upon the child, the family, and the child's learning. The teacher must be able to explain that speaking to the child only in English can often result in communications being significantly hindered and verbal interactions being limited and unnatural between the parent and the child. In using limited English, parents may communicate to children using simple phrases and commands (for example, "Sit down" or "Stop"); modeling grammatically incorrect phrases (for example, "We no go store"); or demonstrating other incorrect usages of language that are common when persons acquire a second language. From these limited and incorrect verbal interactions, the amount of language the child is hearing is reduced, and the child's vocabulary growth is restricted, contributing to an overall decrease in verbal expression. When parents do not master the second language yet use the second language to communicate with their child, there is an increased likelihood that the child will not hear complex ideas or abstract thoughts—important skills needed for cognitive and language development. The teacher must explain that language is developed through natural language interactions. These natural interactions occur within the day-to-day setting, through radio and television, when using public transportation, and in play with children whose dominant language is English. The parent and the teacher must work collaboratively to achieve the goal of children's learning English.

Through the home language and culture, families transmit to their children a sense of identity, an understanding of how to relate to other people, and a sense of belonging. When parents and children cannot communicate with one another, family and community destabilization can occur. Children who are proficient in their home language are able to maintain a connectedness to their histories, their stories, and the day-to-day events shared by parents, grandparents, and other family members who may speak only the home language. Without the ability to communicate, parents are not able to socialize their children, share beliefs and value systems, and directly influence, coach, and model with their children.

Recognize that parents and families must rely on caregivers and educators to honor and support their children in the cultural values and norms of the home.

Parents depend on high-quality early childhood programs to assist them with their children's development and learning. Early childhood programs should make provisions to communicate with families in their home language and to provide parent–teacher encounters that both welcome and accommodate families. Partnerships between the home and the early childhood setting must be developed to ensure that practices of the home and expectations of the program are complementary. Linguistic and cultural continuity between the home and the early childhood program supports children's social and emotional development. By working together, parents and teachers have the opportunity to influence the understanding of language and culture and to encourage multicultural learning and acceptance in a positive way.

C. **Recommendations for professional preparation**

Provide early childhood educators with professional preparation and development in the areas of culture, language, and diversity.

Efforts to understand the languages and cultural backgrounds of young children are essential in helping children to learn. Uncertainty can exist when educators are unsure of how to relate to children and families of linguistic and cultural backgrounds different from their own. Early childhood educators need to understand and appreciate their own cultural and linguistic backgrounds. Adults' cultural background affects how they interact with and/or teach young children. The educator's background influences how children are taught, reinforced, and disciplined. The child's background influences how the child constructs knowledge, responds to discipline and praise, and interacts in the early childhood setting.

Preservice and inservice training opportunities in early childhood education programs assist educators in overcoming some of the linguistic and cultural challenges they may face in working with young children. Training institutions and programs can consider providing specific courses in the following topic areas or include these issues in current courses: language acquisition; second-language learning; use of translators; working with diverse families; sociolinguistics; cross-cultural communication; issues pertaining to the politics of race, language, and culture; and community involvement.

Recruit and support early childhood educators who are trained in languages other than English.

Within the field of early childhood education, there is a need for knowledgeable, trained, competent, and sensitive multilingual/multicultural early childhood educators. Early childhood educators who speak more than one language and are culturally knowledgeable are an invaluable resource in the early childhood setting. In some instances the educator may speak multiple languages or may be able to communicate using various linguistic regionalisms or dialects spoken by the child or the family. The educator may have an understanding of sociocultural and economic issues relevant within the local linguistically and culturally diverse community and can help support the family in the use and development of the child's home language and in the acquisition of English. The early childhood teacher who is trained in linguistic and cultural diversity can be a much-needed resource for information about the community and can assist in the inservice cultural orientation and awareness training for the early childhood program. The bilingual educator also can be a strong advocate for family and community members.

Too often, however, bilingual early childhood professionals are called upon to provide numerous other services, some of which they may not be equipped to provide. For example, the bilingual professional, although a fluent speaker, may not have the vocabulary needed to effectively communicate with other adults or, in some instances, may be able to read and write only in English, not in the second language. In addition, bilingual teachers should not be expected to meet the needs of *all* linguistically and culturally diverse children and families in the program, especially those whose language they do not speak. Bilingual providers should not be asked to translate forms, particularly at a moment's notice, nor should they be required to stop their work in order to serve as interpreters. Bilingual teachers should not serve in roles, such as advising or counseling, in which they may lack professional training. These assignments may seem simple but often can be burdensome and must be viewed as added duties placed upon the bilingual teacher.

Preservice and inservice training programs are needed to support bilingual early childhood educators in furthering educators' knowledge and mastery of the language(s) other than English that they speak, and training should also credit content-based courses offered in languages other than English. Professional preparation instructors must urge all teachers to support multilingual/multicultural professionals in their role as advocates for linguistically and culturally diverse children. Early childhood professionals should be trained to work collaboratively with the bilingual early childhood teacher and should be informed of the vital role of the bilingual educator. Additionally, there is a need for continued research in the area of linguistic and cultural diversity of young children.

D. **Recommendations for programs and practice**
Recognize that children can and will acquire the use of English even when their home language is used and respected.

Children should build upon their current skills as they acquire new skills. While children maintain and build upon their home language skills and culture, children can organize and develop proficiency and knowledge in English. Bilingualism has been associated with higher levels of cognitive attainment (Hakuta & García 1989) and does not interfere with either language proficiency or cognitive development. Consistent learning opportunities to read, be read to, and see print messages should be given to linguistically and culturally diverse children. Literacy developed in the home language will transfer to the second language (Krashen 1992). Bilingualism should be viewed as an asset and an educational achievement.

Support and preserve home language usage.

If the early childhood teacher *speaks* the child's home language, then the teacher can comfortably use this language around the child, thereby providing the child with opportunities to hear and use the home language within the early childhood setting. Use of the language should be clearly evident throughout the learning environment (e.g., in meeting charts, tape recordings, the library corner). Educators should develop a parent information board, using a language and reading level appropriate for the parents. Teachers should involve parents and community members in the early childhood program. Parents and community members can assist children in hearing the home language from many different adults, in addition to the teacher who speaks the home language. Parents and community members can assist other parents who may be unable to read, or they can assist the teacher in communicating with families whose home language may not have a written form.

If the early childhood educator *does not speak* the language, he or she should make efforts to provide visible signs of the home language throughout the learning environment through books and other relevant reading material in the child's language and with a parent bulletin board (get a bilingual colleague to help review for accuracy of written messages). The teacher can learn a few selected words in the child's language, thus demonstrating a willingness to take risks similar to the risks asked of children as they learn a second language. This effort by the teacher also helps to validate and affirm the child's language and culture, further demonstrating the teacher's esteem and respect for the child's linguistic and cultural background. The teacher should model appropriate use of English and provide the child with opportunities to use newly acquired vocabulary and language. The teacher also must actively involve the parent and the community in the program.

If the teacher is *faced with many different languages* in the program or classroom, the suggestions listed above are still relevant. Often teachers feel overwhelmed if more than one language is spoken in the program; however, they should remember that the goal is for children to learn, and that learning is made easier when children can build on knowledge in their home language. The teacher should consider grouping together at specific times during the day children who speak the same or similar languages so that the children can construct knowledge with others who speak their home language. The early childhood educator should ensure that these children do not become socially isolated as efforts are made to optimize their learning. Care should be taken to continually create an environment that provides for high learning expectations.

Develop and provide alternative and creative strategies for young children's learning.

Early childhood educators are encouraged to rely on their creative skills in working with children to infuse cultural and linguistic diversity in their programs. They should provide children with multiple opportunities to learn and ways for them to demonstrate their learning, participate in program activities, and work interactively with other children.

To learn more about working with linguistically and culturally diverse children, early childhood educators should collaborate with each other and with colleagues from other professions. To guide the implementation of a developmentally, linguistically, and culturally appropriate program, collaborative parent and teacher workgroups should be developed. These committees should discuss activities and strategies that would be effective for use with linguistically and culturally diverse children. Such committees promote good practices for children and shared learning between teachers and parents.

Summary

Early childhood educators can best help linguistic and culturally diverse children and their families by acknowledging and responding to the importance of the child's home language and culture. Administrative support for bilingualism as a goal is necessary within the educational setting. Educational practices should focus on educating children toward the "school culture" while preserving and respecting the diversity of the home language and culture that each child brings to the early learning setting. Early childhood professionals and families must work together to achieve high-quality care and education for *all* children.

References

Bredekamp, S., & T. Rosegrant, eds. 1992. *Reaching potentials: Appropriate curriculum and assessment for young children.* Vol. 1. Washington, DC: NAEYC.

Center for the Study of Social Policy. 1992. *The challenge of change: What the 1990 census tells us about children.* Washington, DC: Author.

Chang, H. N. L. 1993. *Affirming children's roots: Cultural and linguistic diversity in early care and education.* San Francisco: California Tomorrow.

Collier, V. 1989. How long: A synthesis of research on academic achievement in second language. *TESOL Quarterly* 23: 509–31.

Cummins, J. 1981. The role of primary language development in promoting educational success for language minority students. In *Schooling and language minority students: A theoretical framework,* eds. M. Ortiz, D. Parker, & F. Tempes. Office of Bilingual Bicultural Education, California State Department of Education. Los Angeles: Evaluation, Dissemination, and Assessment Center, California State University.

Cummins, J. 1989. *Empowering minority students.* Sacramento: California Association for Bilingual Education. Garciá, E. 1991. *The education of linguistically and culturally diverse students: Effective instructional practices.* Santa Cruz: National Center for Research on Cultural Diversity and Second Language Learning, University of California.

Hakuta, K., & E. Garciá. 1989. Bilingualism and education. *American Psychologist* 44 (2): 374–79.

Head Start Bureau, Administration on Children, Youth, and Families, Department of Health and Human Services. 1995. *Program information report.* Washington, DC: Author.

Krashen, S. 1992. *Fundamentals of language education.* Torrance, CA: Laredo Publishing.

Meier, T.R., & C.B. Cazden. 1982. A focus on oral language and writing from a multicultural perspective. *Language Arts* 59: 504–12.

National Association for the Education of Young Children (NAEYC) and National Association of Early Childhood Specialists in State Departments of Education (NAECS/SDE). 1991. Guidelines for appropriate curriculum content and assessment in programs serving children ages 3 through 8. *Young Children* 46 (3): 21–38.

National Center for Education Statistics (NCES). 1993. *Language characteristics and schooling in the United States, a changing picture: 1979 and 1989.* NCES 93-699. Washington, DC: U.S. Department of Education, Office of Educational Research and Improvement.

Sharry, F. 1994. *The rise of nativism in the United States and how to respond to it.* Washington, DC: National Education Forum.

Soto, L.D. 1991. Understanding bilingual/bicultural children. *Young Children* 46 (2): 30–36.

Waggoner, D., ed. 1993. *Numbers and needs: Ethnic and linguistic minorities in the United States* 3 (6).

Waggoner, D. 1994. Language minority school age population now totals 9.9 million. *NABE News* 18 (1): 1, 24–26.

Wong Fillmore, L. 1991. When learning a second language means losing the first. *Early Childhood Research Quarterly* 6: 323–46.

Resources

Banks, J. 1993. Multicultural education for young children: Racial and ethnic attitudes and their modification. In *Handbook of research on the education of young children,* ed. B. Spodek, 236–51. New York: Macmillan.

Collier, V. 1989. How long: A synthesis of research on academic achievement in second language. *TESOL Quarterly* 23: 509–31.

Collier, V., & C. Twyford. 1988. The effect of age on acquisition of a second language for school. *National Clearinghouse for Bilingual Education* 2 (Winter): 1–12.

Derman-Sparks, L., & the A.B.C. Task Force. 1989. *Anti-bias curriculum: |Tools for empowering young children.* Washington, DC: NAEYC.

McLaughlin, B. 1992. *Myths and misconceptions about second language learning: What every teacher needs to unlearn.* Santa Cruz: National Center for Research on Cultural Diversity and Second Language Learning, University of California.

Neugebauer, B., ed. 1992. *Alike and different: Exploring our humanity with young children.* Redmond, WA: Exchange Press, 1987. Reprint, Washington, DC: NAEYC.

Ogbu, J.U. 1978. *Minority education and caste: The American system in cross cultural perspective.* New York: Academic.

Phillips, C.B. 1988. Nurturing diversity for today's children and tomorrow's leaders. *Young Children* 43 (2): 42–47.

Tharp, R.G. 1989. Psychocultural variables and constants: Effects on teaching and learning in schools. *American Psychologist* 44: 349–59.

Media Violence in Children's Lives

A position statement of the National Association for the Education of Young Children

Adopted April 1990

Reaffirmed July 1994

During the past decade, America has witnessed an alarming increase in the incidence of violence in the lives of children. On a daily basis, children in America are victims of violence, as witnesses to violent acts in their homes or communities, or as victims of abuse, neglect, or personal assault. The causes of violent behavior in society are complex and interrelated. Among the significant contributors are poverty, racism, unemployment, illegal drugs, inadequate or abusive parenting practices, and real-life adult models of violent problem-solving behavior. NAEYC, the nation's largest organization of early childhood professionals, is deeply concerned about the destructive effect of violent living conditions and experiences on many of our nation's children.

At the same time that there has been an increase in the number of reported violent acts directed at children, there has been an increase in the amount and severity of violent acts observed by children through the media, including television, movies, computer games, and videotapes, and an increase in the manufacture and distribution of weapon-like toys and other products directly linked to violent programming. NAEYC believes the trend toward increased depiction of violence in the media jeopardizes the healthy development of significant numbers of our nation's children.

In response, NAEYC's Governing Board appointed a panel of experts to guide the development of initiatives and resources to assist teachers and parents in confronting the issue of violence in the lives of children. This position statement addresses one aspect of the problem—media violence—and is the first in a series of projects the Association plans to address this important issue. We have chosen to address the issue of media violence first because, of all the sources and manifestations of violence in children's lives, it is perhaps the most easily corrected. The media industry ought to serve the public interest and ought to be subject to government regulation.

Position

NAEYC condemns violent television programming, movies, videotapes, computer games, and other forms of media directed to children. NAEYC believes that it is the responsibility of adults and of public policy to protect children from unnecessary and potentially harmful exposure to violence through the media and to protect children from television content and advertising practices that exploit their special vulnerability (Huston, Watkins, & Kunkel, 1989). NAEYC believes that television and other media have the potential to be very effective educational tools for children. Research demonstrates that television viewing is a highly complex, cognitive activity, during which children are actively involved in learning (Anderson & Collins, 1988). Therefore, NAEYC supports efforts to use media constructively to expand children's knowledge and promote the development of positive social values. NAEYC also supports measures that can be taken by responsible adults to limit children's exposure to violence through the media. Such efforts include but are not limited to:

- legislation requiring reinstatement of guidelines for children's television by the Federal Communication Commission, including requirements for videotapes and elimination of television programs linked to toys

- legislation limiting advertising on children's programming, and standards for toys to ensure that they are not only physically safe but also psychologically safe
- legislation enabling the development of voluntary television-industry standards to alleviate violence in programming, specifically exempting such efforts from anti-trust regulation
- promotion of more developmentally appropriate, educational programming that meets children's diverse needs for information, entertainment, aesthetic appreciation, positive role models, and knowledge about the world (Huston et al., 1989)
- development and dissemination of curriculum for teachers to improve children's critical viewing skills and to teach nonviolent strategies for resolving conflicts
- development of resources to assist parents in the constructive and educational use of media with their children

During early childhood, the foundation is laid for future social, emotional, cognitive, and physical development. During this formative period, young children are particularly vulnerable to negative influences. In most instances, children have no control over the environmental messages they receive. Up until age seven or eight, children have great difficulty distinguishing fantasy from reality, and their ability to comprehend nuances of behavior, motivation, or moral complexity is limited. This special vulnerability of children necessitates increased vigilance to protect them from potentially negative influences. Parents are ultimately responsible for monitoring their children's viewing habits; however, parents cannot be omniscient and omnipresent in their children's lives. Parents need assistance in protecting their children from unhealthy exposure to violence. Therefore, limits must be placed on the content of programming directed at children. Restricting violence in children's programming should not be considered censorship, any more than is protecting children form exposure to pornography (Carlsson-Paige & Levin, 1990). Likewise, industry standards to limit violence in children's programming should be developed as action taken in the public interest.

Rationale

This position statement is based on research examining the amount of violence present in the media as well as the effect of exposure to violent programming on children's development. Data clearly indicate that violence in the media has increased since 1980 and continues to increase. In addition, there is clear evidence to support the negative impact of viewing violence on children's development.

How Violent are the Media for Children?

The problem of violence in the media is not new but has become much worse since the Federal Communication Commission's decision to deregulate children's commercial television in 1982. For example, air time for war cartoons jumped from 1-1/2 hours per week in 1982 to 43 hours per week in 1986 (Carlsson-Paige & Levin, 1987; Tuscherer, 1988). Children's programs featured 18.6 violent acts per hour a decade ago and now have about 26.4 violent acts each hour (Gerbner, 1990). Adults need to recognize that the content of programming has changed, and as a result the potential for negative effects on children's development is greater. Next to family, television and other media may be the most important sources of information for children, rivaling the school as a principal factor influencing their development.

How do Violent Media Affect Children's Development?

Research consistently identifies three problems associated with heavy viewing of television violence: Children may become less sensitive to the pain and suffering of others; they may become more fearful of the world around them; and they may be more likely to behave in aggressive or harmful ways toward others (National Institute of Mental Health, 1982; Singer & Singer, 1984, 1986; Singer, Singer, &

Rapaczynski, 1984; Rule & Ferguson, 1986; Simon, 1989). Exposure to media violence leads children to see violence as a normal response to stress and as an acceptable means for resolving conflict.

Of great concern to early childhood educators is the negative effect of viewing violent programs on children's play. The importance of children's imaginative play to their cognitive and language development is well documented (Piaget, 1962, 1963; Johnson, Christie, & Yawkey, 1987). Research demonstrates that watching violent programs is related to less imaginative play and more imitative play in which the child simply mimics the aggressive acts observed on television (NIMH, 1982). In addition, many media productions that regularly that regularly depict violence also promote program-based toys, which encourage children to imitate and reproduce in their play the actual behaviors seen on television or in movies. In these situations. children's creative and imaginative play is undermined, thus robbing children of the benefits of play for their development (Carlsson-Paige & Levin, 1990). In their play, children imitate those characters reinforced for their aggressive behavior and rehearse the characters' scripts without creative or reflective thought. Children who repeatedly observe violent or aggressive problem-solving behavior in the media tend to rehearse what they see in their play and imitate those behaviors in real-life encounters (Huesmann, 1986; Rule & Ferguson, 1986; Eron & Huesmann, 1987). In short, children who are frequent viewers of media violence learn that aggression is a successful and acceptable way to achieve goals and solve problems; they are less likely to benefit from creative, imaginative play as the natural means to express feelings, overcome anger, and gain self-control.

Recommendations
What Should Policymakers and Broadcasters do?

NAEYC supports the reinstitution of FCC standards establishing limits on violent depictions during hours children are likely to watch television. Standards would also control the degree to which violence is depicted so as to be perceived by children as a normal and acceptable response to problems, as equated with power, as leading to reward or glorification of the perpetrator. An additional strategy would be to develop a parental guidance rating system for network and cable television, videotapes, and computer games similar to that established for movies.

NAEYC further supports the reestablishment of industry standards to limit children's exposure to violence. The self-regulating code of the National Association of Broadcasters (1980) was a responsible position of the television industry toward young children. As an immediate action, laws prohibiting the adoption of such voluntary standards as violations of anti-trust regulation should be repealed.

Industry standards should also limit advertising during children's programming in recognition of children's inability to distinguish the advertising from programming content and to prevent acts of aggression or violence being separated from consequences by intervening commercials. Studies show that children up to eight years of age are less likely to "learn the lesson" of a program when ads intervene between an anti-social act and its consequences.

Finally, broadcasting standards should prohibit product-based programming and feature-length programs whose primary purpose is to sell toys, especially when those toys facilitate imitation of violent or aggressive acts seen on television. Children are unable to evaluate the quality and play value of such products depicted on television. Program-based advertising creates in children an insatiable desire for these single-use toys; children start to believe that they can't play without the specific props seen on television (Carlsson-Paige & Levin, 1990).

What can Teachers do?

NAEYC believes that early childhood teachers have a responsibility to assist children in developing skills in nonviolent conflict resolution, to assist children to become critical viewers of all forms of media, and to encourage the constructive use of the media for instilling positive social values. Teachers need to be aware of what is currently being broadcast to children and to inform parents of the impact of violent media on children's development. Unfortunately, the effect of deregulation on the quality of children's television has made it necessary for teachers and parents to be more vigilant that they would have to be if the government and television industry acted more responsibly toward children.

Teachers can work with children when themes of television violence appear in their play to facilitate more appropriate problem solving and/or creative, imaginative play. Teachers should inform parents when negative or violent themes appear as a regular part of their children's play and support parents in their efforts to monitor children's viewing habits.

As professionals, early childhood educators should share their knowledge of child development and the effects of violent media viewing with legislators and sponsors of children's programming. It is the professional responsibility of early childhood educators to advocate for more developmentally and educationally appropriate programming for children. Teachers need to recognize that media are also a powerful teacher that can and should be used constructively with children. Contrary to popular belief, television viewing is not a passive activity; children are mentally active during television viewing (Anderson & Collins, 1988). The use of media as an educational tool should not be rejected because much of commercial television currently lacks educational value or promotes violence. Instead, early childhood professionals should advocate for policy that eliminates violence and improves the educational value of media, and should use media constructively in their work with children.

What can parents do?

The absence of government regulation of children's television has made parents' job more difficult, necessitating more parental monitoring of what children see on television. This unfortunate situation places additional, unnecessary pressure on parents. Even when industry standards are developed, NAEYC believes that parents are responsible for monitoring the quality and quantity of the media to which their children are exposed. Standards will make the job easier, however. In the meantime, parents can watch television and other media with their children and evaluate the shows together. Children do not interpret programs the same way adults do. Adults need to talk with children about what they observe through the media, to find out how children are interpreting what they see and to help clarify misinterpretations. Parents can designate an approved list of media options for their children and give children choices from among approved shows.

Parents need to be aware that much of what children watch on television is not specifically intended for children. It has been estimated that only 10% of children's viewing time is spent watching children's television; the other 90% is spent watching programs designed for adults (Van Dyck, 1983). Parents can assist children in finding alternatives to viewing adult television. In addition, parents can use videotapes of high quality children's programming and public television when commercial alternatives are not available.

As consumers, parents should recognize and use their influence with sponsors of children's programs. The primary purpose of commercial television is not to entertain or to educate but to sell products. Parents can communicate with advertisers on programs that are valuable, as well as sponsors of programs that are violent. Parents can also help their children become educated consumers and involve them in writing complaints to broadcasters and companies that use violent images in an attempt to sell toys and other products. As taxpayers, parents can encourage their legislators to adopt policies to protect children from media violence.

Conclusion

The prevalence of violence in American society is a complex social problem that will not be easily solved. Violence in the media is only one manifestation of the larger society's fascination with violence. However, media violence is not just a reflection of violent society, it is also a contributor. If our nation wishes to produce future generations of productive adults who reject violence as a means of problem solving, we must reassert the vital role of government in protecting its most vulnerable citizens and, together, work to make media part of the solution.

References

Anderson, D., & Collins, P. (1988). *The impact on children's education: Television's influence on cognitive development.* Washington, DC: U.S. Department of Education, Office of Educational Research and Improvement.

Carlsson-Paige, N., & Levin, D. (1987). *The war play dilemma: Balancing needs and values in the early childhood classroom.* New York: Teachers College Press, Columbia University.

Carlsson-Paige, N., & Levin, D. (1990). *Who's calling the shots? How to respond effectively to children's fascination with war play and war toys.* Santa Cruz, CA: New Society Publishers.

Eron, L., & Huesmann, L. (1987). Television as a source of maltreatment of children. *School Psychology Review, 16,* 195-202

Gerbner, G., & Signorielli, N. (1990). *Violence profile 1967 through 1988-89: Enduring trends.* Philadelphia: University of Pennsylvania, Annenberg School of Communication.

Huesmann, L. (1986). Psychological processes promoting the relation between exposure to media violence and aggressive behavior by the viewer. *Journal of Social Issues., 42,* 125-140.

Huston, A., Watkins, B., & Kunkel, D. (1989). Public policy and children's television. *American Psychologist, 44,* 424-433.

Johnson, J., Christie, J., & Yawkey, T. (1987). *Play and early childhood development.* Glenview, IL: Scott, Foresman.

National Association of Broadcasters. (1980). *The television code* (21st ed). New York: Author.

National Institute of Mental Health. (1982). *Television and behavior: Ten years of scientific progress for the eighties. Vol 1: Summary report.* Washington, DC: U.S. Government Printing Office.

Piaget, J. (1962). *Play, dreams, and imitation in children* (C. Gattegno & F.M. Hodgson, Trans.). New York: Norton. (Original work published 1951)

Piaget, J. (1963). *The origins of intelligence in children.* (M. Cook, Trans.). New York: Norton. (Original work published 1936)

Rule, B., & Ferguson, T. (1986). The effects of media violence on attitudes, emotions and cognition. *Journal of Social Issues, 42,* 29-50

Simon, P. (1989, August 21)). Coming soon: An act that should reduce television violence. *Newsday.*

Singer, D., & Singer, J. (1984). TV violence: What's all the fuss about? *Television & Children, 7*(2), 30-41.

Singer, J.L., & Singer, D.G. (1986). Family experiences and television viewing as predictors of children's imagination, restlessness, and aggression. *Journal of Social Issues, 42,* 107-124.

Singer, J., Singer, D., & Rapaczynski, W. (1984). *Journal of Communication, 34*(2), 73-89.

Tuscherer, P. (1988). *TV interactive toys: The new high tech threat to children.* Bend, OR: Pinnaroo Publishing.

Van Dyck, N.B. (1983). Families and television. *Television & Children, 6*(3), 3-11.

STILL Unacceptable Trends in Kindergarten Entry and Placement

A position statement developed by the National Association of Early Childhood Specialists in State Departments of Education

2000 Revision and Update

Endorsed by the National Association for the Education of Young Children March 2001

Introduction

The **National Association of Early Childhood Specialists in State Departments of Education (NAECS/SDE)** is a national organization of early childhood specialists who work in state education agencies. The goals of the organization are:

- to enhance the efforts of the State Departments of Education on behalf of young children;
- to strengthen communication and coordination among states;
- to influence and support policies and legislation that affect the education, health, and welfare of children and their families;
- to offer assistance and leadership in researching, analyzing, and recommending standards for quality early childhood and teacher preparation programs; and
- to promote communication and coordination between State Departments of Education and other agencies and professional organizations serving young children.

For several years, members of the association representing all sections of the country have observed with concern the persistence of practices which narrow the curriculum in kindergarten and primary education, constrict equal educational opportunity for some children, and curtail the exercise of professional responsibility of early childhood educators.

This position statement on entry and placement in kindergarten reflects those concerns. It is based upon current research as well as the experiences and expertise of **NAECS/SDE** members. **NAECS/SDE** offers this position paper in an effort to increase public awareness about educational policies and practices affecting young children. Our hope is that it will serve as a catalyst for change at local, state, and national levels.

Overview of Position Statement

For the last two decades the members of **NAECS/SDE** have continued to call attention to attitudes and practices which erode children's legal rights to enter public school and participate in a beneficial educational program. Dramatic changes in what children are expected to do upon entry and in kindergarten have resulted in well-intentioned interventions which are often inequitable, ineffective, and wasteful of limited public resources.

In 1987 the first edition of this position statement was published; it has been widely cited and continues to influence thinking. Unfortunately, the practices, which caused the members of the

Association to become alarmed in the 1980's, continue—this in spite of a preponderance of evidence of their lack of benefit and even of harm to children. This update of the 1987 document has been prepared in response to requests from the membership and the early childhood field.

Classroom teachers continue to report that they have little or no part in decisions, which determine curriculum and instructional methodology. Instead, those decisions are made by administrators who are influenced by public demand for more stringent educational standards and the increased availability of commercial, standardized tests.

Additional pressure on kindergarten programs sometimes comes from primary teachers, who themselves face requirements for more effective instruction and higher pupil achievement. They argue that the kindergarten program should do more. In addition, a growing number of states and localities have raised the age of kindergarten eligibility, providing further evidence of changed expectations for kindergarten education and kindergarten children.

A number of highly questionable practices have resulted from the trend to demand more of kindergarten children. These practices include:

1. inappropriate uses of screening and readiness tests;
2. discouragement or outright denial of entrance for eligible children;
3. the development of segregated transitional classes for children deemed unready for the next traditional level of school; and
4. an increasing use of retention.

Two predominant considerations underlie these practices. The first is a drive to achieve homogeneity in instructional groupings. Some educators believe that instruction will be easier and more effective if the variability within the class is reduced. There is, however, no compelling evidence that children learn more or better in homogenous groupings. In fact, most of them learn more efficiently and achieve more satisfactory social/emotional development in mixed-ability groups.

The second is a well-intentioned effort to protect children from inappropriately high demands on their intellectual and affective abilities. When parents are counseled to delay a child's entry or when children are placed in "developmental" or "readiness" classes to prepare for kindergarten or "transitional" classes to prepare for first grade, it is often because the school program is perceived to be too difficult for some children. In this view, children must be made ready for the demands of the program, in contrast to tailoring the program to the strengths and needs of the children.

Delaying children's entry into school and/or segregating them into extra-year classes actually labels children as failures at the outset of their school experience. These practices are simply subtle forms of retention. Not only is there a preponderance of evidence that there is no academic benefit from retention in its many forms, but there also appear to be threats to the social-emotional development of the child subjected to such practices. The educational community can no longer afford to ignore the consequences of policies and practices which: 1) assign the burden of responsibility to the child, rather than the program; 2) place the child at risk of failure, apathy toward school, and demoralization; and 3) fail to contribute to quality early childhood education.

Therefore, NAECS/SDE calls for policymakers, educators, and all concerned about young children to use the summary principles and discussions which follow to guide and inform decisions about kindergarten entry and placement:

Summary of Principles for Kindergarten Entry and Placement by the National Association of Early Childhood Specialists in State Departments of Education

1. **Kindergarten teachers and administrators guard the integrity of effective, developmentally appropriate programs for young children . . .**
   . . . they do not yield to pressure for acceleration of narrowly focused skill-based curricula or the enforcement of academic standards derived without regard for what is known about young children's development and learning.

2. **Children are enrolled in kindergarten based on their legal right to enter . . .**
   . . . families are not counseled or pressured to delay entrance of their children for a year by keeping them at home or enrolling them in other programs. Rather, families are strongly encouraged to enroll age-eligible children.

3. **Kindergarten teachers and administrators are informed about assessment strategies and techniques and are involved responsibly in their use . . .**
   . . . they do not defer assessment decisions solely to psychometricians and test publishers.

4. **Retention is rejected as a viable option for young children . . .**
   . . . it is not perpetuated on the basis of false assumptions as to its educational benefit.

5. **Tests used at kindergarten entrance are valid, reliable, and helpful in initial planning and information-sharing with parents . . .**
   . . . they are not used to create barriers to school entry or to sort children into what are perceived to be homogeneous groups.

6. **All children are welcomed—as they are—into heterogeneous kindergarten settings . . .**
   . . . they are not segregated into extra-year programs prior to or following regular kindergarten.

Discussion of Principle 1

Kindergarten teachers and administrators guard the integrity of effective, developmentally appropriate programs for young children . . .
. . . they do not yield to pressure for acceleration of narrowly focused skill-based curricula or the enforcement of academic standards derived without regard for what is known about young children's development and learning.

Most of the questionable entry and placement practices that have emerged in recent years have their genesis in concerns over children's capacities to cope with an increasingly inappropriate curriculum in the kindergarten. External pressures in recent decades have so changed the focus of the curriculum in kindergarten that it is often difficult to distinguish between curriculum and methodology in classrooms for young children and those of later elementary grades.

Several factors have interacted to bring about those changes. Research about the capabilities of young children has been misrepresented and misunderstood. A popular belief has developed that children are smarter now primarily because of exposure to television and because so many go to preschool. A rather large number of overzealous parents have also contributed to the problem by insisting that their children be "taught" more and by expecting these children to learn to read in kindergarten. This parental view of kindergarten has reinforced the notion that didactic methods of teaching (many of questionable value even for older elementary children) should be accepted practice in kindergarten.

Too often teachers are told, or they believe, that it is not enough to set the stage for learning by preparing a rich and varied environment and encouraging children to engage in activities which carry their development forward. In too many kindergartens, the core of rich creative experiences with real materials has now been replaced with abstract curriculum materials requiring pencil-and-paper responses. Often these are linked to tightly sequenced and often inappropriate grade-level lists of expected skill acquisition in each of the subject areas. Ironically, children who are ready to learn to read are more likely to advance as far as they are able in an active learning classroom.

(Bredekamp & Copple, 1997; Goodlad & Anderson, 1987; Hills, 1987a; IRA & NAEYC, 1998; Kagan et al, 1995; Katz, 1991; NAEYC & NAECS/SDE, 1991; Shore, 1998; Shipman, 1987; Snow et al, 1998)

Discussion of Principle 2

Children are enrolled in kindergarten based on their legal right to enter . . .

. . . families are not counseled or pressured to delay entrance of their children for a year by keeping them at home or enrolling them in other programs. Rather, families are strongly encouraged to enroll age-eligible children.

Serious negative consequences accompany the rising trend to discourage parents from enrolling their age-eligible children in kindergarten. The dilemma is that the very children being counseled out of school are the ones who, if provided a flexible appropriate kindergarten curriculum, could benefit the most. The "gift of time" that many parents have been persuaded to give children by delaying school entry can result instead in denying them opportunities for cognitive growth through social interaction with their age-mates. It also implies that children have failed at school even before they begin. By the end of the primary level, children whose kindergarten entry is delayed do not perform better than peers who enter on time. Further, children who enter late are disproportionately represented in referrals to special education. This means their access to special help is also delayed a year.

Public schools cannot ethically select some children who are eligible under the law and reject others. Children subjected to delayed entry disproportionately represent racial and linguistic minorities, low-income children, and males. Denial of entrance to school, blatant or subtle, increases the disparity between social classes and could be construed as a denial of a child's civil rights. It places the financial burden for alternative schooling on parents. This is an equity problem.

Curiously, states with quite different entry cutoff dates perceive the same problems. While there is some evidence that older children tend to do better initially, the differences due to age are small and disappear with time. The specific entry date is irrelevant and recent legislative action in several states to raise the entry age will not accomplish what is intended. The quality and appropriateness of the kindergarten curriculum should be the focus of the reform. Age is the only non-discriminatory entry criterion.

No matter where the kindergarten entry date is set, there will always be a younger group of children within a given classroom. It is both unfair and unreasonable to establish expectations for achievement on what the oldest children can do. Delaying entry has been shown to contribute to greater variation among children in the same class—in chronological age, size, motor ability, experiential backgrounds, and other learning characteristics.

Educators should be sensitive to and respectful of the wishes of some parents to postpone their children's initiation into the larger world of school. However, school personnel also have the responsibility to assure that parents do not make this decision based on anxiety over the suitability of the kindergarten program for their child. Educators have an important role to play in educating parents about the myths associated with perceived benefits of holding children out of school.

(Bellissimo et al, 1995; Bredekamp & Copple, 1997; Katz, 1991; Graue, 1993; Meisels, 1992; NAEYC, 1995; Shipman, 1987; Shepard & Smith, 1985; Shore, 1998; Smith & Shepard, 1987; Spitzer et al, 1995; West et al, 1993)

Discussion of Principle 3

Kindergarten teachers and administrators are informed about assessment strategies and techniques and are involved responsibly in their use . . .
. . . they do not defer assessment decisions solely to psychometricians and test publishers.

Assessment is a process of determining whether particular characteristics are present in an individual or a program and the amount or extent of them. Standardized tests are one form of measurement. Assessment can also be accomplished through teacher observation, checklists, rating scales, and questionnaires.

Because testing is so prevalent, many teachers are faced with challenges for which their training and experience have left them unprepared. Today's early childhood educators must be able to: 1) recommend appropriate measures to be used in the beginning of school years; 2) interpret and use the information which the measures produce; 3) communicate to other educators and parents what test information means about student progress; and 4) prevent and/or correct misuses of testing.

To fulfill these responsibilities requires that early childhood educators become informed about the functions of tests and measures, their properties, and the legitimate uses of test data. Tests, which fit one purpose adequately, may be totally unsuited to another. Most importantly, early educators must know about the various forms of assessment, which can supplement or replace test scores.

Further, as children enrolling in school represent more diverse language and culture, new assessment responsibilities are placed upon educators at every level. *"For the optimal development and learning of all children, educators must accept the legitimacy of children's home language, respect and value the home culture, and promote and encourage the active support of all families."* (**NAEYC,** 1995, p.2)

As tests have increased in popularity, instances of their abuse have increased. Abuses occur when:

- Assessment tools are used for purposes for which they were not designed (e.g., screening tests used to diagnose a child's development);
- Assessment tools do not meet acceptable levels of quality (e.g., no reliability or validity studies are available);
- An assessment tool is used as the sole basis for a decision about placing a child in a specific educational program;
- An assessment tool is used as the sole basis for a decision about placing a child in a specific educational program;
- An assessment tool or test determines curricular objectives;
- Test scores are used as a single measure of school and/or teacher effectiveness; and
- Teachers lack sufficient training and experience in the use of assessments.

(Bredekamp & Copple, 1997; Hills, 1987b; Meisels, 1987; NAEYC, 1987; NAEYC, 1995; NAEYC & NAECS/SDE, 1991; NEGP, 1998; Shepard, 1994; Shepard et al, 1998; Standards for Educational and Psychological Testing, 1985)

Discussion of Principle 4

Retention is rejected as a viable option for young children...
... it is not perpetuated on the basis of false assumptions as to its educational benefit.

Retention policies should be highly suspect given the lack of demonstrated effectiveness and prevalent bias against certain groups of children. The current methodology used in selecting students for retention makes it impossible to predict accurately who will benefit. Pro-retention policies as a strategy for establishing rigorous academic standards are likely to be self-defeating. Lowered expectations developed by parents and teachers actually decrease the probability that retained children will attain their potential.

Although research does not support the practice of grade retention, many educators and parents do. It is true that teachers see children they have retained making progress. It is also true they have no opportunity to see how well the children might have progressed had they been promoted.

The vast majority of control-group studies, which are structured to measure this comparison, come down clearly on the side of promotion. Students recommended for retention but advanced to the next level end up doing as well as or better academically than non-promoted peers. Children who have been retained demonstrate more social regression, display more behavior problems, suffer stress in connection with being retained, and more frequently leave high school without graduating.

The term "ending social promotion" creates a climate that supports an increase in the practice of retaining children. Most schools are not employing less costly strategies that are proven to support children's achievement, thus avoiding social promotion. These include:

- high quality preschool;
- improving the quality of child-care settings;
- full-time kindergarten;
- lowered class-size;
- tutoring outside of class time;
- summer programs;
- after-school programs; and
- multiage grouping.

Ending conditions, which prevent all children from maximum learning, must be a priority for us all.

(CPRE, 1990; Cosden et al, 1993; MBE, 1990; Goodlad & Anderson, 1987; May & Welch, 1984; Meisels, 1992; Norton, 1983; Plummer, et al., 1987; Shepard & Smith, 1986; Smith & Shepard, 1987; Shepard & Smith, 1989; Shepard & Smith, 1990; USDE, 1999)

Discussion of Principle 5

Tests used at kindergarten entrance are valid, reliable, and helpful in initial planning and information-sharing with parents...
... they are not used to create barriers to school entry or to sort children into what are perceived to be homogeneous groups.

Kindergarten testing is a common practice in today's public schools. Unfortunately, screening and readiness tests are being used interchangeably to determine the educational fate of many young children before they enter kindergarten. Developmental screening tests broadly and briefly tap developmental domains and are designed primarily to predict future school success—screening to find children who, after further assessment, appear to be good candidates for selective programs. As such, they must contain predictive validity as well as the accepted standards for all tests of reliability, validity, sensitivity, and specificity. Screening procedures should include vision, hearing, and health assessments.

Readiness tests, by definition and statistical design, do not predict outcomes and therefore cannot be substituted for such purposes. These tests assist teachers in making instructional decisions about individual children. Children who do poorly on readiness tests are likely to benefit the most from the kindergarten. The paradox is that if readiness tests are substituted for developmental screening measures, certain children are being channeled away from the regular classroom.

Testing children who have home languages other than English creates unique challenges. Care must be take to use instruments and processes, which clearly identify what the child knows, and is able to do both in English and in the home language. It is not appropriate to make assumptions about proficiency in the home language based on level of proficiency in English. Careful assessment may reveal that the child could benefit from additional home-language development.

A major problem with kindergarten tests is that relatively few meet acceptable standards of reliability and validity. Based on several widely used tests, the probability of a child being misplaced is fifty percent—the same odds as flipping a coin. The burden of proof is on educational and testing professions to justify the decisions they make in the selection or creation of screening instruments. Otherwise, educators are left speculating about what the results mean. Flawed results lead to flawed decisions, wasted tax dollars, and misdiagnosed children.

Even when credible, appropriate tests are selected, kindergarten screening and developmental assessment are still uncertain undertakings because:

- Normal behavior of young children is highly variable.
- Young children are unsophisticated in generalizing from one situation to another and are novices in testing behaviors.
- Young children may not be able to demonstrate what they know and can do clearly because of difficulties in reading, writing, responding, and in using pencils or other markers, or certain abstract symbols.
- Young children may not be able to demonstrate what they know and can do clearly because of differences in language and culture.
- Separation anxiety, the time of day the test is administered, and rapport with the examiner can all distort results, especially with young children.

Parents have a unique perspective about their child's development and learning history. For this reason, their knowledge about the behavior and attainments of their children is invaluable to teachers. Any full assessment of a child's progress must take the parent's information into account. Moreover, parents have a moral and legal right to be informed about the basis for educational decisions affecting their children.

Children entering school come from markedly different backgrounds. Assessment procedures must not penalize children at school entry for responses that have heretofore been appropriate for them or which they have not yet had a chance to develop. Screening and assessment does not substitute for an observant, competent, caring teacher and a responsive curriculum.

(Bredekamp & Copple, 1997; Hargett, 1998; Hills, 1987b; Meisels, 1987; NAEYC, 1987; NAEYC & NAECS/SDE, 1991; NEGP, 1998; Shepard, 1994; Shepard et al, 1998)

Discussion of Principle 6

All children are welcomed—as they are—into heterogeneous kindergarten settings . . .
. . . they are not segregated into extra-year programs prior to or following regular kindergarten.

The responsibility of the school is to accept children with the language, aptitudes, skills, and interests they bring. The function of the schools is to support the child's development and learning in all areas. The expectation is not that all children enter only with specific prerequisite skills.

The dramatic growth of extra-year programs represents an attempt by the educational system to cope with an escalating kindergarten curriculum and the varied backgrounds of entering children. However, these programs often increase the risk of failure for children who come to school with the educational odds against them. Selection and placement in "transitional," "developmental," or "readiness" classes often brand the children as failures in their own eyes and those of parents, peers, and teachers.

Children placed in segregated programs often encounter lowered expectations, have fewer positive peer role models for success and confidence, and lack access to regular curriculum. For all of these reasons, their future progress tends to be more limited and many of them continue in the slow track throughout their schooling.

"Regardless of what language children speak, they still develop and learn. Educators recognize that linguistically and culturally diverse children come to early childhood programs with previously acquired knowledge and learning based on the language used in their home. For young children the language of the home is the language they have used since birth, the language they use to make and establish meaningful communicative relationships, and the language they use to begin to construct their knowledge and test their learning." (**NAEYC**, 1995, p. 1)

Heterogeneous class groupings are more likely than are homogenous ones to encourage growth among children who come with home languages other than English or who are developing more slowly. Experiences within the regular classroom should be organized so that differences among children are valued rather than being viewed as a barrier to effective instruction. Flexible peer groupings, multiage and ungraded structures, and cooperative learning are some alternatives that can foster learning and self-esteem by valuing the gifts and talents of all children.

(Bredekamp & Copple, 1997; Goodlad & Anderson, 1987; Gredler, 1984; Katz et al, 1990; May & Welch, 1984; Meisels, 1992; Nye et al, 1994; Oakes, 1985; Robinson, 1990; Robinson & Wittebols, 1986; Shepard & Smith, 1990; Slavin, 1986)

A Call to Action

The primary consideration should be what is best for young children, not institutions, politicians, or professionals. Children do not benefit from retention or delayed entry or extra-year classes. The case has been made that children are placed in double jeopardy when they are denied, on highly questionable premises, the same educational opportunities as their peers.

Belief in the pure maturational viewpoint underlies many of the deleterious practices described in this paper. The adult belief that children unfold on an immutable timetable, however appealing, cannot be over-generalized to intellectual, social, linguistic, and emotional development. A responsive, success-oriented kindergarten curriculum and a well-trained teacher are bound to have a powerful effect on young children's learning. Children come to school as competent, naturally motivated learners. One of the school's critical responsibilities is to ensure that these characteristics are maintained and strengthened, not destroyed.

The issue is not whether to keep children with age-mates (Heterogeneous multiage grouping can stimulate and support children's development.) It is whether we can continue to uphold practices and program predicated on failure. Failure by any name does not foster success for any students.

What adjustments do schools need in order to make education more responsive to the needs of young children? Reducing class size, making the curriculum less abstract and therefore more related to children's conceptual development, insisting that only the most appropriately trained, competent, child-oriented teachers are placed in kindergarten programs, and assuring every child access to a high quality prekindergarten program are among better means to achieving the educational goal of success for all students.

Limited federal, state, and local resources are being used inappropriately as a result of well-intentioned but misdirected policies. However, simply to stop retention and extra-year classes will not assure success for all children. **NAECS/SDE** recommends that attention and resources be diverted from ineffective policies/and directed toward seeking long-term lasting cures for the ills of the kindergarten/primary curriculum.

A consensus is needed among the educational community and families that only those practices beneficial to young children will be permitted. We can have equitable, excellent, and economical public education for all of the nation's kindergarten children.

References

Andersen, S. (1993). The trouble with testing. American School Board Journal, 180(6), 24-26.

Bellisimo, Y, Sacks, C.H & Mergendoller, J.R. (1995). Changes over time in kindergarten holding out: Parent and school contexts. Early Childhood Research Quarterly, 10(2), 205-222.

Bredekamp, S. & Copple, C. (Eds.). (1997). Developmentally appropriate practice in early childhood programs. Rev. ed. Washington, DC: National Association for the Education of Young Children.

Center for Policy Research in Education, Rutgers University. (1990). Repeating grades in school: Current practice and research evidence. New Brunswick, NJ: Author.

Cosden, M., Zimmer, & Tuss, P. (1993). The impact of age, sex and ethnicity on kindergarten entry and retention decisions. Educational Evaluation and Policy Analysis, 15(2), 209-222.

Goodlad, J.I. & Anderson, H. (1987). The nongraded elementary school. New York, NY: Teachers College Press.

Graue, M.E. (1993). Ready for what?: Constructing meanings of readiness for kindergarten. Albany, NY: State University of New York.

Graue, M.E. & DiPerna, J. (2000). Redshirting and early retention: Who gets the "gift of time" and what are its outcomes? American Educational Research Journal. In Press.

Gredler, G.R. (October, 1984). Transition classes: A viable alternative for the at-risk child? Psychology in the Schools, 21, 463-470.

Hancock, C.R. (1994). Alternative assessment and second language study: What and why? ERIC Digest. Washington, DC: ERIC Clearinghouse on Languages and Linguistics.

Hargett, GR. (1998). Assessment in ESL and bilingual education: A hot topics paper. Portland, OR: Northwest Regional Educational Laboratory.

Hills, T.W. (September, 1987). Children in the fast lane: Implications for early childhood policy and practice. Early Childhood Research Quarterly, 2(3), 265-273.

Hills, T.W. (1987b). Screening for school entry. ERIC Digest. 18(4), 1-5.

Horm-Wingard, D.M., Winter, P.C., & Plofchan. (2000). Primary level assessment for IASA Title 1: A call for discussion. Prepared with the State Collaborative on Assessment and Student Standards Comprehensive Assessment Systems for IASA Title 1 Study Group on Early Childhood Assessment. Washington, DC: Council of Chief State School Officers.

International Reading Association and the National Association for the Education of Young Children. (1998). Learning to read and write: Developmentally appropriate practices for young children. Young Children, 53, 30-46.

Kagan, S.L., Moore, E. & Bredekamp, S. (Eds.). (1995). Reconsidering children's early development and learning: Toward common views and vocabulary. Goal 1 Technical Planning Group Report 95-03. Washington, DC: National Education Goals Panel.

Katz, L.G (1991). Readiness: Children and schools. ERIC Digest EDO-PS-91-4. Champaign-Urbana, IL: ERIC Clearinghouse on Elementary and Early Childhood Education.

Katz, L.G, Evangelou, D. & Hartman, J.A. (1990). The case for mixed-age grouping in early childhood education programs. Washington, DC: National Association for the Education of Young Children.

Massachusetts Board of Education. (1990). Structuring Schools for success: A focus on grade retention. MA: Author.

May, D.C. & Welch, E.L. (1984). The effects of developmental placement and early retention on children's later scores on standardized tests. Psychology in the Schools, 21, 381-385.

Meisels, S.J. (1992). Doing harm by doing good: Iatrogenic effects of early childhood enrollment and promotion policies. Early Childhood Research Quarterly. 7(2), 155-175.

Meisels, S.J. (January, 1987). Uses and abuses of developmental screening and school readiness testing. Young Children. 42(2), 4-6, 68-73.

National Association of Early Childhood Specialists in State Departments of Education. (1987). Unacceptable trends in kindergarten entry and placement. Author.

National Association for the Education of Young Children. (1995). NAEYC Position statement on school readiness. Young Children, 46(1).

National Association for the Education of Young Children. (1987). Position statement on standardized testing of young children 3 through 8 years of age. Washington, DC: NAEYC.

National Association for the Education of Young Children. (1995). Responding to linguistic and cultural diversity: Recommendations for effective early childhood education. Washington, DC: NAEYC.

National Association for the Education of Young Children & National Association of Early Childhood Specialists in State Departments of Education. (1991). Guidelines for appropriate curriculum content and assessment in programs serving children ages 3 through 8. Young Children, 46, 21-38.

Norton, S.M. (1983). It's time to get tough on student promotion – Or is it? Contemporary Education, 54(4), 283-286.

Nye, B.A., Boyd-Zaharias, J. & Fulton, B.D. (1994). The lasting benefits study: A continuing analysis of the effect of small class size in kindergarten through third grade on student achievement test scores in subsequent grade levels—seventh grade (1992-83), technical report. Nashville: Center of Excellence for Research in Basic Skills. Tennessee State University.

Oakes, J. (1985). Keeping track: How schools structure inequality. New Haven, CN: Yale University Press.

Plummer, D.L., Liniberger, M.H., & Graziano, W.G. (1987). The academic and social consequences of grade retention: A convergent analysis. Current Topics in Early Childhood Education, Vol. VI. Katz, Ed. Norwood, NJ: Ablex Publishing Corporation.

Robinson, G.E. (1990). Synthesis of research on class size. Educational Leadership, 47(7), 80-90.

Robinson, G. & Wittebols, J. (1986). Class size research: A related cluster analysis for decision-making. Educational Research Service, Arlington, VA.

Shepard, L.A. (1994). The challenges of assessing young children appropriately. Phi Delta Kappan. 76: 206-13.

Shepard, L.A., Kagan, S.L. & Wurtz, E. (Eds.). (1998). Principles and recommendations for early childhood assessments. Washington, DC: National Education Goals Panel.

Shepard, L.A. & Smith, M.L. (Eds.). (1989). Flunking grades: Research and policies on retention. London: Falmer Press.

Shepard, L.A. & Smith, M.L. (1990). Synthesis of research on grade retention. Educational Leadership, 47(8), 84-88.

Shepard, L.A. & Smith, M.L. (November, 1986). Synthesis of research on school readiness and kindergarten retention. Educational Leadership. 44(3), 78-86.

Shipman, V.C. (January, 1987). Basic abilities needed as a precondition for school. Paper presented for the Conference on the Assessment of Readiness sponsored by the Center for Education Studies in the Office of Educational Research and Improvement of the U.S. Department of Education. Washington, DC.

Shore, R. (1998). Ready schools. Washington, DC: National Education Goals Panel.

Slavin, R. (Ed.) (1986). Ability grouping and student achievement in elementary schools: A best-evidence synthesis. The Johns Hopkins University Center for Research on Elementary and Middle Schools, Report No. 1., Baltimore, MD: Johns Hopkins University.

Smith, M.L. & Shepard, L.A. (October, 1987). What doesn't work: Explaining policies of retention in the early grades. Phi Delta Kappan. 69(2), 129-134.

Snow, C.E. Perspectives on second-language development: Implications for bilingual education. Educational Researcher, 21(2), 16-19.

Snow, C.E., Burns, M.S. & Griffin, P. (Eds.). (1998). Preventing reading difficulties in young children. National Research Council. Washington, DC: National Academy Press.

Spitzer, S., Cupp, R. & Parke, R.D. (1995). School entrance age, social acceptance, and self-perceptions in kindergarten and 1st grade. Early Childhood Research Quarterly, 10(4), 433-450.

Standards for educational and psychological testing. (1985). Washington, DC: American Psychological Association, American Educational Research Association, and National Council on Measurement in Education.

US Department of Education. (1999). Taking Responsibility for Ending Social Promotion: A guide for educators and state and local leaders. Washington, DC: Author.

West, J., Hauskin, E.G. & Collins, M. (1993). Readiness for kindergarten: Parent and teacher beliefs. Washington, DC: National Center for Education Statistics.

CPSIA information can be obtained
at www.ICGtesting.com
Printed in the USA
LVHW01s0317150817
545019LV00002B/3/P

9 781524 924058